This work has been published with the aid of a grant from The Harry S. Truman Research Institute for the Advancement of Peace, The Hebrew University of Jerusalem.

Political Parties in the West Bank under the Jordanian Regime, 1949–1967

AMNON COHEN

Cornell University Press

ITHACA AND LONDON

ALSO BY AMNON COHEN

Palestine in the 18th Century

Population and Revenue in the Towns of Palestine in the Sixteenth Century [with Bernard Lewis]

Yehudey Yerushalayim ba-Me'a ha-Shesh Esre [The Jewish Community in Sixteenth-Century Jerusalem]

Peraqim be-Toledot Yerushalayim be-Reshit ha-Tequfa ha-Othmanit [Jerusalem in the Early Ottoman Period]

Translation first published 1982 by Cornell University Press.
Published in the United Kingdom by Cornell University Press Ltd.,
Ely House, 37 Dover Street, London WIX 4HQ.

Published in Hebrew under the title *Miflagot Bagada Hamaaravit Bitqufat Hashilton Hayardeni.*
Copyright © 1980 by The Magnes Press of the Hebrew University of Jerusalem.

International Standard Book Number 0-8014-1321-4
Library of Congress Catalog Card Number 80-25666
Printed in the United States of America
Librarians: Library of Congress cataloging information appears on the last page of the book.

Contents

Preface

When Israel took over the West Bank from Jordan after the Six-Day War in June 1967, it found no political parties functioning openly in the area. They had all been outlawed more than a decade before, under an order issued by King Husayn in April 1957. The ban had come in the wake of widespread political unrest throughout Jordan, including the West Bank, following the dismissal of the Sulayman al-Nabulsi government. The opposition parties had come out against the new government of Fakhri al-Khalidi and demanded that it be replaced by a cabinet representing all the main parties in Jordan—the National Socialists, the Baath, the Qawmiyun, and the so-called National Front (the Communists). The unrest in the early months of 1957 took the form of street demonstrations, some of which were violent. The authorities tried first to avoid any action that might exacerbate the situation, but the growing violence in the streets and the gathering political storm among the parties induced the government to take drastic measures, including the banning of all political parties at the end of April that year.

Although it appeared to be somewhat reluctant to take this draconian step, the Hashemite regime had made the necessary preparations some time in advance. At the beginning of January 1957, the Jordanian Security Services had ordered detailed lists to be drawn up of all political activists in Jordan, to make ready for their possible arrest.[1] The policy pursued in the early months of 1957 is reminiscent of developments in Jordan thirteen years later, in September 1970. Then, also, King Husayn let the opposition of the day, the PLO, increase unabated its attacks on the regime and gain self-confidence, then unexpectedly struck and suppressed it. In the same way, in 1957, Husayn had decided as early as January that he would outlaw the political parties, but chose to allow the situation to deteriorate to such a degree that the move would seem justified—that is, given the chaos threatening Jordan by April of

7

that year, it could be made to seem that Husayn had no choice but to issue his ban. Under the order, all party offices were closed down, their property was seized, and hundreds of party activists were arrested.

Although after 1957 there were no official parties in Jordan, the main parties simply went underground. Some parties did disappear completely, including the "Mufti's Party" (for want of a better name) and the Arab Constitutional Party (al-Hizb al-Dusturi al-Arabi). Of those that continued to function after the banning order, some, including the Syrian Nationalist Party (al-Hizb al-Qawmi al-Suri), the National Socialist Party (al-Hizb al-Watani al-Ishtiraki), the Moslem Brothers, the Liberation Party (Hizb al-Tahrir), and the Resurrection Party (al-Baath), had become increasingly less active by the time Israel entered the West Bank in 1967, and then ceased to function completely. Two of the underground parties continued to operate after Israel's occupation of the West Bank: the Arab Nationalists (al-Qawmiyun al-Arab), who later evolved into the Front for the Liberation of Palestine, and the Communists.

The Communists, the Qawmiyun, the Baath, the Moslem Brothers, and the Liberation Party were the most vital and significant of the parties operating in Jordan during the 1950–67 period, and their activities were carefully documented and analyzed in a research project conducted in Jerusalem between 1968 and 1975. This book presents the major findings of that research.

Parties, as a form of political organization in a given society or country, are a focal concern of the modern political analyst and political historian. Parties, as a means of organized expression of a societal world view or of certain selected notions of a society, are of equal interest to the student of political ideas and ideology and also, on occasion, to the philosopher. But in the contemporary Arab world, where party activity is somewhat limited and the tradition of local research and documentation is even rarer, the researcher in any of these disciplines is at a disadvantage, for many of the tools and much of the information needed for a clear picture of the society are lacking. In those Arab countries that reached political maturity relatively early (Egypt, for example), there has been some research into the major political parties, but it has been scant, and our ignorance is still great. About those Arab countries where political maturity came somewhat later, our ignorance is almost total.

In Jordan, few published political memoirs, whether written by a major political leader or by his opponents, can shed much light on party politics. The press in Jordan gives some picture of the outward workings of the major parties but provides little useful information about their structure, membership, or dogma. Fortunately for us, however, because the autocratic king would brook no opposition, political parties were a focal concern of the Jordanian Security Services, which kept a close watch on all known political activists. These authorities gathered valuable information about the major parties and deposited it in their archives. Thus much of the information that the parties had not committed to paper, or that was deliberately destroyed by the parties when they were outlawed, is available to the researcher in the security services' archives. The security authorities had, of course, little scholastic interest in this information and made no attempt to organize it. Also, much of the more detailed information is of little value to the researcher. Although the material is therefore difficult to work with, it does provide the researcher with a thorough and often intimate view of the inner machinations of the political parties at their various levels and among a wide range of population groups. The material, which encompasses all party activity in Jordan from 1949, was preserved intact in a room on the ground floor of the District Governor's Building in Jerusalem. After the Israeli occupation of the city, it was removed to the Israel State Archives, where it has been carefully organized and catalogued. The usual moratorium on sensitive state papers does not in this case pertain, and the entire archive was made immediately available to researchers. Also, political or security considerations have not led to the deliberate destruction of certain papers. Thus we have the unique opportunity of having direct access to a complete and comprehensive archive that provides a more detailed and authentic picture of the party activity in the West Bank than is usually available to the researcher of a similar subject in the Arab world.

The Jordanian Security Services' archives contain two principal categories of material. The first comprises the files compiled by the security authorities. These include the various reports submitted, arranged in chronological order and not usually classified by subject (one report might, for example, deal with several different parties). Most of these reports describe, on the basis of information provided by informers or extracted during the interrogation of party members, the activities and plans of the various parties, and often include detailed lists of members' names and addresses. These files have been numbered, in part by the Jordanian Security Services and in part by the staff at the Israel State Archives. I have cited in the footnotes the number of the file and the page of each document referred to. The second category comprises the various publications put out by the party—newspapers, booklets, pamphlets, and leaflets. These have not been numbered or catalogued, and in citing them I have noted the name and date of the item concerned.

Many of the leading party activists left the West Bank in 1967; those who remained were often very difficult to trace and, when found, were reluctant to talk. Accordingly, I decided not to attempt a comprehensive field survey, doubting that in the prevailing political atmosphere in the area such an exercise would be of much value. All the same, some former party activists did agree to speak to me on condition that I would not quote them by name. Their testimony served to corroborate the material I found in the security services' files and, on occasion, provided some valuable information not available from any other source at my disposal.

The Jordanian press served as a useful secondary source of information, and I made use of the collections at the National Library in Jerusalem and in the Israeli Foreign Ministry archives.

I first became aware of the Jordanian Security Services' archives in 1968. When I started working on the files dealing with the political parties (there is a wealth of other information contained in the archives, of immense value to the student of modern Jordan and the Palestinians), I found that most of them dealt with the 1950s and early 1960s. Those files dealing with the years immediately preceding the 1967 war tend to be rather skimpy and superficial, testifying to the sharp decline in party activity during those years. I did find, however, that the material filed during the 1950s and early 1960s was comprehensive and detailed. This made some form of teamwork essential. Accordingly, I assembled a group of researchers and together we painstakingly went through the archives, sifting the huge mass of material for information on a wide range of predetermined topics. The initial findings were published in 1972 by the Hebrew University's Institute for the Study of the Palestinian Arabs (later known as The Truman Institute). I cannot here acknowledge my debt to each member of the large team of investigators who participated in the project. I would, however, like to thank those of my students whose initial findings served as the basis for parts of this book: Gideon Braude (Al-Qawmiyun al-Arab), Ella Landau (Al-Qawmiyun al-Arab and The Liberation Party), and Rachel Simon (The Moslem Brothers and The Liberation Party). Though later revised, rewritten, and further elaborated in this book, their earlier versions served as an indispensable basis for this translation. Avraham Sela, who also participated in the project, later developed his work on the Baath Party into a master's thesis at the Hebrew University, and this may appear as a separate work. I owe a special debt of thanks to my assistant Amatzia Baram, who provided me with invaluable aid and advice in preparing the present text for publication. David Bernstein undertook the difficult task of translating the Hebrew manuscript, which he did in a most conscientious and masterful way; I thank him most sincerely. A word about the translation: the original transliteration of the Hebrew edition included diacritical marks. Because of the difficulty of typesetting them, however, all diacritics have been deleted. To Sylvia Farhi in Jerusalem and Valerie Bruce in Toronto, who studiously typed the manuscript, I owe my deep gratitude. I also thank my teacher and colleague, Professor Gabriel Baer, who was closely involved in the conduct of this project through its various stages; Abraham Alsberg, director of the Israel State Archives; and my friend and colleague Professor Moshe Maoz, whose support in the final stages of preparation has made this book possible. I would like to offer my deepest thanks to a dear friend and a patron of the Arts whose most generous financial contribution made the translation of this book possible. He has insisted on anonymity, however, and I reluctantly respect his wish. And last but not least, I thank all those residents of the West Bank and East Jerusalem who gave me so much of their valuable time and helped so much to fill the gaps in my knowledge about the functioning of their parties during the period under review. I am certain my hope is also their own—that this book will make some contribution, however modest, to the mutual understanding of the inhabitants of this troubled land.

AMNON COHEN

Jerusalem, 1980

*Political Parties in the
West Bank under the
Jordanian Regime,
1949–1967*

1. Some Empirical and Conceptual Considerations

THE HISTORICAL SETTING

The history of the Hashemite kingdom of Jordan was shaped, perhaps more than that of any other state in the Middle East, by modern warfare. The most important milestones in its modern (and only) history are two world wars and two regional ones. In the wake of World War I, Prince Abdallah of Mecca was stopped by the British in his march on Damascus, dissuaded from disrupting the unstable new political equilibrium, and subsequently, in March 1921, granted the emirate of Transjordan to satisfy both his personal ambition for power and the wounded pride of his family. It was not until twenty-five years later, after the conclusion of World War II, that this temporary arrangement solidified, the prince became a king, and his emirate was turned, in March 1946, into an independent state. As a result of yet another war, that of 1948–49, King Abdallah wholly incorporated the West Bank into his state. It was this same territory that was hastily evacuated by Abdallah's grandson, King Husayn, as a result of his miscalculated attempt to attack Israel in June 1967.

The years 1950–67 were of an importance that far surpassed their duration. It was at this time that a new element was introduced into the kingdom, namely the Palestinian Arabs. The territory of the West Bank, formerly a part of mandatory Palestine, was officially annexed to Jordan in April 1950, and its inhabitants formally became Jordanian citizens. This meant an addition of about 850,000 to the former population of 400,000 Jordanians. The demographic imbalance thus created was only one dimension of a new political reality. The Palestinians were not only traditionally anti-Hashemite (although there were some Palestinians who had traditionally supported the Hashemites), they also regarded their new partners as intellectually, culturally, and socially inferior.

There may have been more than a grain of truth to this claim. The Palestinians did have a higher level of literacy and greater political experience (more activity, parties, newspapers, and so forth) than the nomad East Bankers, and therefore had much more to offer—and thus demand—than what they actually gained.

In an effort to overcome these tensions, the king granted the Palestinians full rights, and they were formally regarded as equal political partners. A constitutional framework was elaborated, whereby half the seats of both houses of parliament were allotted to Palestinians, and ministerial portfolios were also usually equally split between inhabitants of the East and West Banks. But these initiatives could not easily abate the sense of alienation shared by many of the newcomers to Jordan. The alleged equality was regarded as a subterfuge that avoided any real, statistically justified representation. The various governments (headed by East Bankers in most cases) were blamed for deliberately diminishing the administrative importance of the West Bank (for example, Jerusalem's political and administrative importance, as well as its traditional economic centrality were undermined). This policy was matched by an alleged systematic economic and social discrimination against the Palestinians. The steady flow of inhabitants from the West Bank to the other side of the Jordan River mollified the situation somewhat, but for those Palestinians who remained, or for their families left behind, the lamentable state of affairs continued.

The socioeconomic problems, combined with increasing political stress, were further exacerbated by overwhelming tensions growing in the external affairs of the kingdom (the nationalization of the Suez canal, the tide of Nasserism, the war of 1956). During the period under review—and the years 1952-58, most particularly —the area underwent major cultural and political tremors which were felt almost everywhere and by everyone. Although these inter-Arab and international issues had milder repercussions among the Bedouin East Bank elements than among the Palestinians of the West Bank, they still concerned Jordan as a whole, and at times threatened to disrupt the entire fabric of state and society. Jordan, though assumed a loyal supporter of the West, was slowly moving away from Britain, its erstwhile ally. Part of a Middle East that had mostly divested itself of earlier associations with Britain, Jordan was following the general pattern: British military high command was dismissed (in March 1956); financial support was replaced by Egypt, Saudi Arabia, and Syria; and, finally, the treaty with Britain was abrogated (in March 1957). It appeared that Jordan was drifting toward a new focal center, with the government of Sulayman al-Nabulsi contemplating the establishment of close relations with the Soviet Union. A direct intervention by the king in spring 1957, however, stifled unrest in the army, replaced the government with a pro-Western one, and accepted financial and political aid from which ensured both American interests and the throne.

These developments should be viewed also in the context of Arab affairs. Jordan was being attracted intermittently toward either Egypt or Iraq. When King Abdallah opted for the annexation of the West Bank, he chose a position diametrically opposed to Egyptian policy: for unlike Egypt's occupation of the Gaza strip, which was deliberately regarded as temporary (the land eventually to be turned over to the Palestinians), Jordan *incorporated* the West Bank, implying that the act was final. In response, in the May–June 1950 vote, most members of the Arab League cast theirs for the expulsion of Jordan, but since Iraq (and Lebanon) abstained, this recommendation could not become binding. Jordan remained in the Arab League, but Egypt drew its lesson: since it could not expel Jordan, it tried henceforth to affect a major shift in the Jordanian foreign policy.

When King Abdallah was murdered by a Palestinian while entering the al-Aqsa mosque for the Friday prayer (on July 20, 1951), the event was interpreted as an indication of the displeasure of anti-Hashemite groups and of some Arab countries, at the annexation. Abdallah was succeeded by his son Tallal who tried to improve relations with parts of the Arab world, as well as provide the Palestinians a modicum of parliamentarism: the new constitution, which became effective in January 1952, while solidifying the omnipotent powers of the king, also made the government contingent upon a two-thirds confidence vote of parliament rather than on an arbitrary decision by the king. Tallal's failing mental health forced him to abdicate the throne, and in May 1953 his son Husayn was sworn in.

The political life in Jordan in the first years of Husayn's reign, between 1954 and 1956, though ostensibly an internal tug-of-war between the supporters of the king and his opposition, was largely influenced by developments in the Arab world. Egypt was actively involved in an attempt to prevent Jordan from participating in the Baghdad Pact, which was branded anti Arab unity and pro Western imperialism. An increasing number of Jordanians, mostly (though not exclusively) West Bank Palestinians, were attracted by the pan-Arab policies of Abd al-Nasser. The latter gradually became antithetical to Husayn's predominantly pro-Western policies. The growing support for the new "Egyptian dream" was best expressed in public manifestations in 1956, vociferous and violent in the streets, constitutional and no less impressive in the polls. The Sulayman al-Nabulsi government of late 1956 took steps to bring about a political and military volte face. Husayn, however, successfully outmaneuvered his internal opponents and external rivals. In spring 1957 he ousted the prime minister, arrested and banished many of his adversaries, and put an end to the ambiguity of Jordan's international position. This position became even more clarified after the creation of the United Arab Republic: to counterbalance the new Egyptian-Syrian bloc, Jordan joined Iraq in the Arab Union (on February 14, 1958). The experiment was even shorter-lived than its model, and the eruption of the Iraqi revolution later that year brought it to an end.

The end of the pro-Western alliance between Jordan and Iraq in 1958 did not, however, alter any of the basic political truths established earlier by Husayn and Abdallah: Jordan continued its pro-Western policy and maintained (successfully on most occasions) an aloofness from Egyptian overtures or threats, while attempting to consolidate a unified state and an integrated society. Throughout the period despite recurring references to the "Hashemite family," the split between Jordan's two populations was obvious, even in the face of formal equality. The Palestinians, most of whom were still concentrated in the West Bank, were discontent with this state of domestic affairs and foreign relations. Though Jordanian by nationality, many Palestinians felt a growing sense of alienation from some of the regime's most fundamental tenets; and questioned the ethicalness of its formal parliamentarism. Protest began, and perhaps its most typical form, elaborated by the Palestinians, was the political party.

"POLITICAL PARTIES"?

Although the Arabic word for political party, *hizb*, refers to a relatively new phenomenon in the Middle East, its etymology is rooted in the early years of Islam. Originally, *hizb* referred not only to the group of supporters of an individual or his ideas, but also meant "part" (it is in this sense that the word applies to one of the subdivisions of the Koran). In that it was only part of a larger whole, the concept "party" in Arabic, as in many other languages, has overtones of diminution, not only in terms of size, but also, perhaps, in terms of value. In the Koran, the word *hizb* is only twice used positively; in every other instance there is an unmistakable pejorative connotation,[1] an attitude that persisted into the present. In the years 1949–67, there appears to be both official and public disdain of political parties in the Arab world (to this day, *hizbi*, the adjective derived from the word *hizb*, is used derisively in Jordan and the West Bank). In Egypt, parties were regarded by Gamal Abd al-Nasser as unnecessary stumbling blocks to true democracy, and were despised in that country until the change wrought by Anwar al-Sadat in 1978, when political parties were resurrected and some of them restored to public favor. In other Arab countries, political parties were outlawed, their place being taken by mass movements organized by the regime—a move that further diminished the image of parties in the eyes of the public. The grafting of the western-style parliamentary system on Middle Eastern societies that were not ready for it and that were unable fully to understand its workings led to deep-seated misconceptions about the true role of parties in a parliamentary democracy. Moreover, the failure of the system to live up to the aspirations of these societies could only further discredit the hapless parties, which were an integral part of a system that imitated precisely those western countries—Britain, France, the United States, and Israel—which the Arabs considered their arch enemies.

Political parties, then, made their appearance in the Arab world relatively late, and when they did appear they did so hesitantly, on a limited scale, and only with the sanction of the regime. As such, they were artificial, rather feeble, creations. The strength which some of them later gained resulted from their struggle against an outside element (whether with the blessing of the regime, as in the case of Egypt, or without it, as in Syria). All this holds true for the emergence of political parties in Jordan. There, parties emerged very late (in the early 1950s), and were violently opposed to the dominant foreign power in the country, Britain. Much of this anti-foreign sentiment was directed against the Hashemite king, who was seen as inordinately reliant on his British overlords. The major parties in Jordan were, consequently, all opposition parties. Their emergence was due to two principal factors: the promulgation of the Jordanian constitution in 1951, and the new situation that had arisen with the formal annexation of the West Bank in the spring of 1950. The addition of a large new population, one which was more highly educated and more politically aware than most of the inhabitants of the East Bank, in the wake of the traumatic events of 1947–49, served to catalyze political activity in the country. What is more, the inhabitants of the newly annexed West Bank found it extremely difficult to owe allegiance to the Hashemite regime, which was alien to all of them and viewed with hostility by many. They were thus driven to seek other focuses for their political loyalty, and this led to the creation of several new parties on the West Bank.

Elie Kedourie, in analyzing the concept *hizb* in the *Encyclopaedia of Islam*,[2] discusses a wide selection of political parties in the Arab world. But he completely ignores—and not through oversight—the parties of Jordan. Kedourie questions the use of the term "party" to describe political organizations even in those Arab countries where political activity was more widespread and more deeply rooted, as in Egypt. Because it was the regime that dictated the composition and the character of the parliament in Egypt, Kedourie argues, political parties in that country were unable to function properly or in a manner that would justify the use of the term. The so-called political "parties" in Egypt could not, he pointed out, "function as coherent parliamentary and electoral organizations dedicated to the acquisition of popular support and the exercise of political power within a legislative assembly." Accordingly, Kedourie concludes, it would be more appropriate to call these bodies "movements" or "factions" rather than "parties." Similarly, the use of terms such as "parliament" or "democracy" with reference to the Arab world is also somewhat misleading and often quite arbitrary, for they have been borrowed from a political tradition alien to that of the Middle East and applied to phenomena only superficially resembling those to which such terms apply in the West. Nevertheless, if we accept the definition of a political party as "the articulate organization of society's active political agents, those who are concerned with the control of governmental power and who compete for popular support with another group or groups holding divergent views,"[3] there is clearly some justification for the use of the term in the Jordanian context. According to the above definition, the fundamental characteristics of a party are:

some form of structured organization; an aspiration to run the affairs of the nation, or, at least, to have a significant say in it; a coherent ideology; and the necessary machinery to acquire mass support for its ideas and aspirations. All these characteristics apply to the political parties examined in this book.

Admittedly, the role of the parliament in the political life of Jordan was extremely limited, and the validity of the elections to that body was often suspect. These limitations did, of course, greatly diminish the potential of Jordan's parties as agents of political or social change. But they did have a role to play, which they conducted with considerable vitality and resilience: they contested elections in the hope of acquiring a say in the decision-making process, and sometimes even succeeded in having their candidates elected (these occasions were few, however, and the elected opposition had little influence); they engaged in lively interparty rivalry for the support of the electorate, which was confined mainly to the politically aware urban intellectual elite; they drew up detailed ideological platforms, which, for all their defects and absurdities, often displayed a considerable (even exaggerated) degree of consistency; and, finally, they were locked in a constant struggle with the authorities who closely surveiled them and attempted to circumscribe their activities, which often led to harsh suppression.

The fact that the parties continued to exist in Jordan even after being outlawed was not entirely due to the forbearance displayed by the authorities. Rather, it was due primarily to the existence of dedicated, committed party activists who were prepared to keep their organizations alive and the presence of a reservoir of supporters who were unable to find alternative focuses for their loyalty and allegiance. Regardless, however, of whether these groups called themselves "movements" or "associations," it seems the term "party"—with both its negative and positive connotations—can legitimately be used to describe them.

We have now to consider another criticism that has been leveled against political parties in the Arab world: that while they may be parties in the fundamental sense of the word, they are deficient, outdated, and backward. This criticism seems, however, at least with respect to parties in Jordan, quite unfounded. One writer, for example, has this to say about political parties in Jordan:

When parties have been established or permitted in Jordan, they heavily have involved this personal factor, with most parties involving a loose grouping, around a leader who shares whatever successes he has with those around him. A pattern of family rivalry and feuds characterized much of political life.[4]

While this description might apply to a few small groups of politicians who chose to call themselves "parties," most of which were created by the Hashemite regime in an effort to create an impression of democratic support for it and soon disappeared, it does not by any means apply to the larger parties which functioned in Jordan in the 1950s and 1960s. M. Duverger's generalizations about political parties in the Middle East are also unsatisfactory, and he misses the mark in terms of Jordan. Speaking of the "archaic and prehistoric" parties one is apt to encounter in the Middle East, Duverger concludes that "these are but followers grouped around an influential protector, clans formed round a feudal family, camarillas united by a military leader."[5] This description applies to few political parties in the Middle East, and certainly not to any in Jordan.

The major parties that functioned in Jordan during the 1949-67 period can be seen to have included, quite unmistakably, all the basic elements mentioned by Duverger in his general description of modern political parties. Duverger traces a typical trend in the development of political parties in the Western world away from small decentralized parties toward large, centralized, and highly disciplined ones—that is, away from cadre parties toward mass parties.[6] One cannot, of course, really speak of "large" parties in Jordan, where the number of formally educated and politically aware inhabitants was very small, and where political activists were incessantly hounded by the authorities. But, except for size, all the other characteristics of a mass political party hold true. The larger parties in Jordan all had a highly developed organizational structure and a fixed hierarchy. Their degree of centralization compares favorably to that of parties in Europe,[7] especially considering the fact that they functioned for most of these years outside the framework of parliament, whether by choice or government ban. The more socially radical parties (the Communists, the Qawmiyun, and the Baath) were all modeled along the hierarchical lines of Communist parties elsewhere in the world (the basic unit was the cell; the lines of communication were vertical, befitting the clandestine nature of such parties; great selectivity was displayed in accepting new members; dues-paying members were required to undertake a wide range of obligations.[8] The more conservative, right-wing parties were organized somewhat differently. The Moslem Brothers, for example, which in Egypt was organized along strictly hierarchical lines and ran a highly trained fascist-style militia, was much less highly centralized in Jordan, where it possessed no paramilitary arm at all. The individual branches tended to function autonomously (albeit within the general guidelines laid down by the movement), and obligations such as the payment of subscription dues were much less rigorously enforced than they were in the radical parties in Jordan or, for that matter, than they were by the Moslem Brothers in Egypt. While the Brothers in Jordan tried at least to imitate the Egyptian model to some extent, the Liberation Party had no such model and was even more decentralized. Nonetheless, the socially conservative Liberation Party did display the characteristics listed by Duverger in his description of parties based on local branches (which, he argues, was the original model of most socialist parties): a great stress on the dissemination of its ideas and on political indoctrination, and little concern for the quality of its membership with greater interest in attracting a mass following. The absence of an organized hierarchical structure, a high degree of decentralization, and, above all, the lack of any obligation to pay subscription dues as a matter of principle, Duverger points out, are all features that characterized the middle-class parties in Europe.[9] Although the bulk of the members of both the Liberation Party and the Moslem Brothers came from the lower and more traditional levels of the middle class, these two parties were unquestionably the most right-wing of all the major parties in Jordan. The structure of the various parties as well as the patterns of their activity were, therefore, closely related to their political ideology.

Total membership of the different parties in Jordan was never very large, even at the peak of political activity in that country, to say nothing of the years of the banning order, and the success of their candidates at the polls was quite unimpressive. What is more, none of the major parties originated in Jordan, and they were all to a greater or lesser degree subordinate to their larger, better-established brother parties in the neighboring Arab countries (or even farther afield). Even so, the parties should not be regarded as a marginal phenomenon in the political life of Jordan, and especially of the West Bank. In the first place, they proved to be extremely resilient, and their ability to survive the constant harassment and the often brutal repressive measures taken against them by the regime is ample proof that they were *not* artificial, ephemeral creations, but rather authentic expressions of ever-present, active undercurrents of political sentiments and thoughts. Second, given the political and constitutional realities in Jordan, it was quite impossible for any opposition party to gain control of the country by parliamentary means, and none did, in fact, at any time constitute a serious threat to the ruling Hashemite regime. The regime also proved to be quite adept at manipulating some of the parties (particularly the Moslem Brothers) for its own purposes. But the turbulent events of 1956 and 1957 soon showed just how susceptible large sections of the population were to the type of radical pro-Egyptian sentiment that threatened the Jordanian state in its existing form. The government of Sulayman al-Nabulsi, although formed by his short-lived National Socialist Party, lost little time in jumping onto the pro-Nasserite bandwagon in 1956, and soon garnered the support of the left-wing radical parties in Jordan. At about the same time, there were growing signs that these radical parties were seriously planning to seize power in Jordan by force. The drastic measures taken by the regime against the parties in 1957 clearly indicate the seriousness with which the security authorities in Jordan viewed the potential threat posed by the parties outside the strictly controlled parliamentary arena.

Two important questions have yet to be considered: to what extent were the parties effective as agents of social and political change in Jordan, and what was the place of these parties on the political map of the Arab world? The political platforms of all the major parties in Jordan stressed the importance of social change. Little need be said of the economic and social changes advocated by the Jordanian Communist Party; the Qawmiyun adopted an increasingly socialist position, which by the mid-1960s had become central to their political ideology; the Moslem Brothers and the Liberation Party advocated a radical program of social change based on a fundamentalist view of a future society incorporating the values and mores of early Islam. But it is quite clear that each of these parties, especially the Communist Party and the Qawmiyun, placed much greater stress on political issues than they did on purely social matters. The twin specters of imperialism and Israel were of far greater importance to all parties than, for example, the problem of poverty or illiteracy; and the vision of Arab unity was more compelling than the elimination of social inequality. Even the two fundamentalist parties, the Moslem Brothers and the Liberation Party, were rather more interested in the establishment of a society based on Islam as a future political goal than in addressing themselves to the immediate social task of adapting traditional values to the needs of a modern society. In other words, these were all fundamentally *political* parties, whose main concern was to find answers to the pressing political problems besetting Jordan, rather than coming to terms with the economic, social, or even religious issues affecting its inhabitants, and in this sense, they were no different from political parties elsewhere in the Arab world.

All the major parties in Jordan were, in fact, originally established as local branches of larger parties that had their centers in Egypt, Syria, or Lebanon. But, as will be shown in the course of this book, they were by no means mere copies, or offshoots, of their counterparts elsewhere in the Arab world. The Liberation Party, for example, did have branches outside Jordan, and its leaders were based abroad for much of the time; but there can be little doubt that it was an essentially Jordanian party, and the bulk of its activities were carried out in Jordan. The Moslem Brothers, because they were officially sanctioned in Jordan, evolved as a much more moderate, less militaristic movement than their counterparts in Egypt, who were outlawed by the authorities there. Al-Qawmiyun al-Arab, for all their adulation of Gamal Abd al-Nasser, were careful to keep their movement's secrets strictly to themselves, and proved to be considerably more radical and militant than their counterparts in Lebanon. Even the Communist Party, while it was closely modeled on other Communist parties both in the Middle East and abroad and often took its cue from these parties, displayed a degree of idiosyncracy in Jordan (where, unlike in most other countries, it concentrated its efforts on the intellectual elite, and paid little or no attention to the peasants or even to the country's workers). Furthermore, the Communists in Jordan also displayed considerable independence of thought, and this was most apparent in their commitment to the idea of Arab unity throughout the 1950s, long after it had become passé in other Arab Communist parties. The adherence of the Jordanian Communist Party to the pan-Arab ideal, like the Marxist influences that brought themselves to bear on the Qawmiyun or the preoccupation of the Liberation Party and the Moslem Brothers with the Palestine problem while ignoring political events elsewhere in the Arab and Islamic world, is indicative of the very considerable degree of flexibility all political parties displayed in Jordan. They were not adverse to shifting their ideological positions (sometimes with the result of severe distortion and even contradiction) to accommodate the political realities of the society in which they had to function. Arab unity, spearheaded by Nasserite Egypt, was seen throughout the 1950s not only as the surest way to combat imperialism in the Middle East, but also as the most effective way to solve the Palestine problem. Accordingly, the concept had an irresistible fascination for all political parties in the West Bank, even those parties whose self-proclaimed ideal was primarily a new social or religious, rather than national, order in the area. Just as socialist principles had influenced the thinking of the Qawmiyun and pan-Arab particularism had infiltrated the ideology of the Jordanian Communist Party, so the concept *"jihad"* ("holy war") took on new, unaccustomed overtones in the thinking of the fundamentalist parties in Jordan. All political parties in Jordan saw the Palestinians of the West Bank as a prime reservoir of support for their opposition to the status quo, and all were prepared to shift and sometimes even distort their ideological positions in an effort to accommodate the sensibilities of that population.

During the years 1950–67, the political pendulum in Jordan and the West Bank swung between the striving for far-reaching political and social change that would improve the lot of the Palestinians and the growing acceptance that the Palestinians would have to realize their aspirations not through radical change of the existing political order but within the framework of the Jordanian state. This spectrum of opinion was, as we shall see, reflected in the ideologies of the major parties in Jordan during that formative period.

2. The Communist Party

ACTIVITIES

The National Liberation League (Usbat al-Taharrur al-Watani)

The Communist movement had been active in Palestine for several decades prior to 1948. The events that shook the country in 1947–48, however, galvanized the movement into heightened activity. A number of key Communists moved into the area controlled by Abdallah and began working among the refugees, many of whom had been familiar with the movement in their native towns and villages, as well as among the population of the larger towns in the West Bank. The Communists believed that the new situation provided them with an ideal opportunity to gain new sympathizers and recruit new members: part of the West Bank population, at least, was antagonistic to Abdallah, and so shared common cause with the Communists; the harsh military administration instituted by the occupying Egyptian and Transjordanian armies had led to widespread dissatisfaction, which could be usefully exploited; and, above all, tens of thousands of homeless refugees were anxious to improve their material, no less than their political, lot.

In the years 1949–51, the Communists in the West Bank distributed leaflets, set up new cells and party branches, and organized open protests in the larger towns and villages. A central objective of the Communists at this time was to secure the immediate withdrawal of the occupying armies, and the League sought to achieve this by appealing not only to the local population (leaflets were distributed in Nablus and the surrounding villages, as well as in Jerusalem, Bethlehem, and Beit Sahur), but also to the soldiers serving in the various Arab armies. Thus, for example, leaflets were distributed to soldiers of the Iraqi expeditionary force calling on the Kurds among them to desert in protest of the crimes being committed by the Baghdad government against their brethren at home.

The Communists' opposition to foreign occupation—even if the occupying armies happened to be Arab—stemmed from their declared commitment to the implementation of the United Nations partition plan, and their concomitant rejection of any attempt to annex the West Bank to Transjordan. When, at the beginning of 1950, Abdallah announced that he intended holding general elections in the West Bank—clearly part of his design to unite the two banks of the Jordan in a single state—the League directed most of its efforts toward fighting this eventuality. Through its newspaper and leaflets, the League called on the West Bank population to boycott the elections, and there were also reports that it intended to disrupt the polls by holding a mass demonstration in Nablus. It even sent threatening letters to several candidates, in an attempt at intimidation. But, these letters notwithstanding, the League refrained from engaging in any actual violence or terrorism; its overriding concern at this time was to organize itself and build up the party.

In Jerusalem, the League sought recruits among those people who were openly critical of Abdallah, but most of its activities during this period took place in the north. A branch was set up in Nablus as early as 1949, with Ridwan al-Hilu, a veteran Communist, playing a key role. Fahmi Salim Awwad returned to his native village, Salfit, after serving as secretary of the party's central committee in Gaza, and began to organize branches in the village and its surroundings. At first, the coffeehouse run by his cousin served as a regular meeting place, but when the authorities began to harass him, Fahmi and another cousin left the village and began to operate covertly.

A number of demonstrations were staged at the end of 1949 (in Tulkarm, for example), and although these were not actually organized by the League, they received its official blessing after they had taken place. The first demonstration planned and staged by the League was in Nablus, on March 31, 1950. Held to protest Abdallah's elections, about fifty people took part. All were arrested, shackled, and forced to walk to Amman. One died on the way, and the others were jailed for two months. Among those arrested were the main activists at that time in Nablus, Salfit, Rafidya, Beit Iba, and Farkha (these included Ridwan al-Hilu, Hamza al-Zirr, Rushdi Shahin, Raja Ghanim, Abd al-Rahim Ershid, and Sami

Ghadban). Ridwan al-Hilu had been arrested previously, at the end of 1949, for being in possession of Communist literature, and another party activist, Fuad Nassar, had been served with a detention order at about the same time. But the demonstration in Nablus constituted a significant landmark: it was the first time that Communists in the West Bank had openly challenged the authorities; their overt activities up to this time had been restricted primarily to the distribution of leaflets.

During 1950-51, Communist activities in Jerusalem and Nablus increased significantly. In Ramallah, the League successfully infiltrated the local Workers Association and managed to seize control of it. But, encouraged by its success, the League began to overreach itself: on the eve of May 1, leaflets were openly distributed in the streets of Ramallah and a reception was held at the Workers Association, where party members delivered pro-Communist speeches. The following day, May 2, about forty people, including several students, demonstrated in front of the offices of the administrative governor and district military commander, bearing placards calling for bread, work, and international peace. The Association was immediately outlawed and the organizers of the demonstration were imprisoned in Amman. Other demonstrations took place in Nablus and Jericho, and these too resulted in arrests. Several activists were arrested in Jerusalem, Bethlehem, and Beit Sahur also.

The arrest of some of its leading activists in Jerusalem and Nablus, the tighter overall controls imposed by the authorities on teachers and Communist sympathizers, and the uncompromising policy of suppressing any attempt to organize anti-Hashemite demonstrations brought the League to a crucial point in its history. Those who believed that the party should continue to orientate itself toward the country's workers found their traditional view seriously challenged. The failure in Ramallah lent support to growing opinion that the party's main efforts should henceforth be directed toward the intellectuals—even if this was not entirely consistent with its traditional doctrinaire stand on class conflict. The argument put forward by traditionalists such as Ridwan al-Hilu was that the intellectuals, because of their social position, were not sufficiently class conscious and were thus likely to undermine the coherency of the party. It is quite possible that this difference of opinion was also somewhat colored by personal rivalry: Ridwan al-Hilu was forced out of the party in 1952 after being accused of plotting against Fuad Nassar, while another similarly minded traditionalist, Harb Harb, became embroiled in personal disputes with other party members and was pressed into leaving in 1953. It was already clear in 1951, however, that men like al-Hilu and Harb were in the minority, and that the stand taken by Fuad Nassar and his supporters would prevail. Nassar held that as long as the proletariat in Jordan remained relatively small and insignificant, the party should be realistic and direct its efforts toward the country's intellectuals.[1] The party was also forced to come to terms with the undeniable fact that the two banks of the Jordan were now effectively united following the elections to the House of Representatives in Amman. Moreover, the establishment of the Baath party and its growing strength in Jordan presented the League with another serious challenge, and demanded a fundamental reorganization of the party. Fuad Nassar became its undisputed leader, and under him the reorientation of the party toward the intellectuals was effected. It was also decided that the name of the party should be changed, and from June 1951 it ceased to be called the National Liberation League, taking the name Jordanian Communist Party (JCP).

1951-1956

The 1951–56 period was characterized by the slow growth of the party, in the face of incessant harassment by the Jordanian authorities. The party followed a two-pronged strategy in those years. Its main efforts were directed toward the establishment of new cells and branches, the dissemination of Communist ideas, and the extension of its activities into areas it had failed to penetrate in the past (mainly Hebron and the surrounding villages). At the same time it sought to reach a wider audience through various "front" organizations such as the politically innocuous Peace Partisans (Ansar al-Salam). The Peace Partisans were associated with the international Communist-inspired antinuclear campaign of the early 1950s. While there was some opposition on the JCP central committee to working through them, Fuad Nassar argued that the alliance was essential, for apart from broadening its base locally, it was important for the newly reconstituted party to engage in political activity on the international level. Nassar's view prevailed, and the JCP became the main force behind the Partisans, giving considerable prominence to their activities in the various JCP publications. It was in the interest of the party to exaggerate the significance of the Partisans (a report in the party's organ claimed that some 40,000 people had signed a petition organized by the Partisans in 1952,[2] a figure discounted as highly inflated by several activists of the period), if only to press its claim to mass support far beyond its actual membership. The authorities appear to have been aware of this, and effectively prevented the Partisans from establishing themselves nationally,[3] although several local branches were set up.

But the authorities were also aware that, in spite of the importance of restricting the activities of the Peace Partisans, the real danger lay in the JCP's covert organizational and propaganda activities. Accordingly, at the end of 1951 and the beginning of 1952, acting on a tip-off from an inside informer, the authorities struck two crippling blows at the party. On December 29, 1951, Fuad Nassar, the secretary-general of the party, was arrested in Amman along with four other activists.[4] A large quantity of propaganda material was also seized, together with the JCP's sole printing press. Nassar was sentenced to ten years in prison, and the other four members to six years each. The imprisonment of several of its key members was unfortunate enough, but the loss of its printing press severely restricted the party's activities and set it back at least two years. Then, at the beginning of March 1952, one of the most active cells in the Nablus area was uncovered, two of its leaders were arrested,[5] and the duplicating machine used to put out the party's leaflets was confiscated. By this time, however, the party was sufficiently well established and resilient to continue functioning: Rushdi Shahin went underground and took over the running of the party and its newspaper (which continued to appear in an improvised form); a large demonstration was held in Amman at the beginning of August 1952, attended by many activists from the West Bank, followed by two more demonstrations in Nablus in September and November; leaflets continued to be distributed in Nablus and Tulkarm; and in Salfit, more than fifty people signed a petition in October 1952 calling on the prime minister to release all political prisoners.

An internal circular put out by the JCP in September 1952 proclaimed 1953 to be the year in which the party was to be put on a "mass popular" footing, that is, it would concentrate on attracting a large number of supporters instead of following its earlier preference for a hand-picked, limited group. While this was clearly a long-term objective, the party did make significant progress in this direction during 1953. The party newspaper began to appear regularly for the first time and was distributed in all the principal towns of the West Bank, as well as in many villages. Many new cells were established among high school students, especially in Nablus and Jerusalem. Activities were intensified in Tulkarm,[6] Ramallah, and al-Bira, while special efforts were made to establish new branches in the Hebron area. The veteran Hebron Communist Mukhlis Amr was in Gaza at this time, and the task of organizing the party in the area fell to Fakhri Maraqa, who was ably assisted—unbeknown to the authorities—by Dr. Abd al-Hafiz al-Ashhab. The religious conservatism that characterized the Hebron area made it extremely difficult for the party to establish itself there, and Maraqa recognized that its best strategy would be to organize trade unions and other fronts which could covertly advance the aims of the party. Thus, for example, a branch of the Peace Partisans was opened in Hebron in the second half of 1953 and held regular weekly meetings. Attempts were made to organize a petition in Hebron protesting the new anti-Communist legislation, while other petitions were organized in the nearby village of Surif. The distribution of Communist leaflets, which had long been widespread in the towns of the West Bank, was still a novelty in Hebron, but during 1953 it became increasingly common. The local chief of detectives reported at the end of the year that there was no longer any Communist activity in his district;[7] but from even these few examples it is clear that although the JCP's activities in the Hebron area were not as numerous as they were elsewhere, they were clearly on the rise in 1953, with several new cells having been established in the town itself as well as in the surrounding villages.[8] It was hardly surprising, therefore, that in July 1953 three public figures identified with the party[9] visited Hebron in the course of their tour of West Bank towns, and tried to get residents to sign a petition calling for the release of political detainees, permission to establish trade unions, and support for the Peace Congress in Bucharest. It would seem that their appearance in Hebron was the last straw for the authorities, who had ignored similar visits the three had made to Jerusalem and Nablus the previous month. They were arrested on July 18, 1953, and expelled to the East Bank. This did not, however, deter Hebron activists from attending the Bucharest meeting, along with delegates from other towns in Jordan.[10] The participation of Jordanian representatives in pro-Communist congresses abroad testified to the growing strength of the JCP, while the election of several prominent party members and sympathizers to the World Peace

Council in July 1953[11] testified to the greater interest of Communists abroad in the activities of their comrades in Jordan.

Another indication of the growing strength of the JCP was the perceptible toughening of the authorities' attitude toward the party. The series of detentions in the notorious al-Jafar Prison, the various forms of official harassment, and the attempts to turn the country's religious establishment against the party[12] appear to have had little effect. On December 1, 1953, a new, tougher anti-Communist law was promulgated by the parliament in Amman. This prescribed imprisonment, with "temporary" hard labor, for any member of the Communist Party, as well as for anyone engaged in the printing or distribution of Communist propaganda—or even being found in possession of Communist leaflets for propaganda purposes. Under the law, which superseded the previous (1948) anti-Communism law, anyone contributing to a Communist organization, printing or selling Communist literature, or distributing Communist leaflets could be jailed for up to three years.[13] The very fact that such a draconian measure was deemed necessary reflected not only the determination of the authorities to oppose the JCP but also, and perhaps more significantly, their growing awareness that only severe deterrents would be able to abort what they recognized to be a potentially powerful mass movement.

During the 1954–55 period, the JCP continued to pursue its two-pronged strategy, pressing on with the covert organization of new cells and branches while at the same time trying to extend its influence into various broad-based movements which were not necessarily Communist. In the spring of 1954, attempts were made to establish in the larger towns of the West Bank (Nablus, Jerusasalem, Ramallah, and Bethlehem) a popular youth movement called the Democratic Youth Association. In the Ramallah area, party activists sought nonpolitical outlets for their activities, such as setting up trade unions. At Salfit and in villages surrounding Nablus, JCP members organized a petition among the fellahin, calling on the government to improve their conditions and to permit the establishment of a Fellah Reform Association. In an attempt to realize a long-standing party principle, the JCP worked for the establishment of the so-called National Front (al-Jabha al-Wataniya), an organization that included in its ranks such Communist leaders as Fakhri Maraqa of Hebron and Dr. Abu Hajla of Nablus.[14] The Front was finally established in May 1954. With the approach of the general elections the following October, Communist activists campaigned on behalf of the Front in several West Bank towns and villages. The authorities were sufficiently worried by the emergence of the Front to order the arrest of several of its candidates (these included such prominent Communists as Dr. Yaqub Ziyadin and Naim al-Ashhab). Despite this, the National Front managed to get its Nablus candidate, Abd al-Qadir Salih elected. Notwithstanding the very low poll (about 50 percent), Salih received some 36,000 votes to the 12,000 polled by his National Socialist Party opponent, Hikmat al-Masri.[15] Salih, a large landownder in the Nablus area, was never a Communist, but the moment the JCP came out in support of him, he was identified with the party in the eyes of the public. Thus his election to the House of Representatives was in effect further proof of the growing strength of the JCP in the West Bank, particularly in Nablus.

The party made notable progress in other West Bank towns as well. An internal report circulated by the central committee in February 1954, for example, congratulated the Jerusalem branch on its achievements, particularly in the field of indoctrination. The major emphasis, both in Jerusalem itself and in the surrounding villages, was on high school students.[16] This led one of the city's leading religious figures, in the autumn of 1955, to call on all true believers to fight the party and prevent it from making further inroads in the area.[17] Several cells were set up in schools in Jerusalem, Hebron, Salfit, and Tulkarm (where there were twenty cells at the end of 1954) and several refugee camps (Ayn al-Sultan, for example). Both students and teachers were involved. The activities of the students were generally anti-establishment and anti-"imperialist," and being Leftist in tone, were described as "Communist." In actual fact, however, the wave of student demonstrations that took place in November 1955 in Jenin, Tulkarm, Salfit, and Nablus drew support from a wide variety of sources, but the JCP, the most highly organized body, claimed full credit for the demonstrations as expressions of support for its own aims and ideals.

Following the success of the National Front in the recent elections, members of the JCP tried to broaden further the base of the Front. In Tulkarm at the beginning of 1955, there were numerous reports that the JCP tried to draw closer to the Baath party; in Jerusalem at the end of the year, they approached the Islamic Liberation Party, stressing their similarities in aims. But in both cases the JCP's overtures were spurned.

1956–1960

The JCP enjoyed its greatest successes in Jordan during 1956 and early 1957. Its public activities during this period were manifold. Petitions were organized in the main towns of the West Bank, usually against the background of some major political development affecting the area (against the treaty with Britain, for example, which prompted three separate petitions in Nablus alone, in June, August, and October).[18] In the second half of 1956 preparations began for new elections to the House of Representatives in Amman, and once again the JCP lined up behind the National Front. Attempts to bring the Baath into the Front failed, as they had before the previous elections, and this marked the start of a bitter rivalry between the two parties (especially in Nablus and Ramallah), with the Baathists accusing the JCP of supporting Israel.[19]

While in 1954 the Front's major effort and only real success had been in Nablus, this time the party devoted special attention to Jerusalem and Ramallah as well. In Ramallah, Fayiq Warrad was chosen as the party's candidate (in preference to Ibrahim Bakr, a veteran activist in the area). The campaigns conducted by Warrad in Ramallah and by Dr. Yaqub Ziyadin in Jerusalem were carefully and systematically planned. An office run by Warrad was opened in the town and made all the preparations for the coming elections quite openly. A mass rally in support of Warrad was held in Ramallah on July 8, 1956; buses and taxis brought close to 700 party activists from places as far afield as Jericho, Nablus, and Hebron, as well as from towns in the East Bank.[20] Tariq al-Asali toured several villages in the Jerusalem area, addressing numerous private meetings on behalf of Dr. Ziyadin, while other activists organized information meetings in Ramallah and the surrounding villages, a number of which were attended by Fayiq Warrad himself.[21] The campaigns fomented support in several instances by tying in with major political events. Egypt's nationalization of the Suez Canal sparked off numerous demonstrations in Jerusalem, Bethlehem, and Ramallah, attended by members of both the Baath and the JCP, as well as other groups. But the JCP was prominent at these rallies as a cohesive body, with its own separate slogans,[22] and in a number of cases it was the Communist activists who set the tone.[23] In Nablus, the party held a mass meeting on July 28, chaired by Rushdi Shahin, in support of the nationalization, while several members of the party sent personal messages of congratulation to Egyptian President Gamal Abd al-Nasser.[24] There were also several demonstrations supported by the Communists that were not directly related to important political events. The one held in support of Dr. Ziyadin in Jerusalem was attended, among others, by fifty party activists brought in for the occasion from Jericho and the Nuayma refugee camp. The demonstrators, apart from affirming their support for the Front's candidate, shouted slogans in support of Khalid Bakdash (the prominent Syrian Communist), the Soviet Union, and international peace.[25] As the elections approached, the candidates met with the electorate more and more frequently; Warrad held meetings in Ramallah, Dr. Ziyadin in Jerusalem, Jericho, and the surrounding refugee camps, and other National Front candidates in Nablus.[26]

The carefully planned campaign paid off. In the elections, which took place on October 21, 1956, no fewer than three National Front candidates identified with the JCP were elected: Fayiq Warrad, Dr. Yaqub Ziyadin, and Abd al-Qadir Salih. With Sulayman al-Nabulsi as the new prime minister, the party began to act more openly—going so far as to publish an open letter in the press.[27] A number of party activists were released from detention and even from prison. One of the latter was Fuad Nassar, the former secretary general of the party, who was enthusiastically received on his return to Nablus.[28] The three Front representatives met frequently with Prime Minister Nabulsi, and while they came out openly in support of "the brilliant national policies of King Husayn," they also presented a number of demands of their own, including rapprochement with the Soviet bloc, and the abrogation of the anti-Communist law.[29] This law was still in force, but both supporters and political rivals became increasingly aware that legislation was not an effective styptic against the party.[30]

In January 1957, however, Rushdi Shahin published the newspaper *al-Jamahir* ("The Masses"), which was closed down by the authorities at the end of that same month. This signaled the start of a renewed drive against the JCP, spearheaded by King Husayn himself.[31] In reply to a cable sent to him by the Front's delegates in the Jordanian House of Representatives (following his meeting with the American ambassador concerning the Eisenhower Doctrine), the king sent a message which said, among other things: "We, as a nation having certain noble goals and ideals, cannot countenance those among us who propound materialism and other prin-

ciples which oppose our religion."[32] Abd al-Qadir Salih (representing the JCP though not a member) contemplated resigning his post
as agriculture minister in the Nabulsi government in protest against
the king's attack. The party, however, persuaded him to stay on,
recognizing the clear advantages to be gained from his remaining in
office: on the one hand, he could continue to inform the party of
the government's actions and, on the other, he could work from
within to forestall any attempt to curtail party activities.[33]

The "institutionalization" of the party following its successes in
the 1956 elections did not deter it from continuing its traditional
public activities. In the spring of 1957, for example, it organized a
student demonstration in Hebron to protest against the treaty with
Britain, and to call for the establishment of diplomatic relations
with the Soviet Union. Before this, at the end of February, it had
held a mass picnic at the Dead Sea, in which scores of students and
party activists from Jerusalem participated. While for many it was
simply a pleasant outing, there were also speeches delivered by several prominent party leaders, including Fuad Nassar, Jawda Shahin
and Dr. Yaqub Ziyadin. A month later, in what was evidently an
attempt to boost the party's membership in Jericho, a large rally
was held in the town, attended by many members and supporters
brought in especially from Jerusalem.[34] Dr. Ziyadin continued to
keep in close touch with his constituents, frequently addressing
audiences in Jerusalem, Jericho, and the surrounding refugee camps
in an effort to keep them informed of the party's stand on various
issues. Fayiq Warrad addressed similar audiences in Ramallah and
the surrounding villages. The speeches of both men were subsequently printed and distributed as official JCP publications. Soviet
literature, primarily translations from Tass, were widely distributed,
either by mail from Damascus (to Ramallah) or through al-Qutub's
bookshops in Nablus and Tulkarm.[35] But the party was already
planning its next step: in 1957 it began secretly to build up arms
caches, something it had not dared to do before. It is not clear
when exactly this process started, but by the second half of 1957,
a steady stream of weapons was finding its way to cells in the Hebron area, smuggled across Israeli territory from the Gaza Strip
and, on a somewhat smaller scale, from Syria.[36] In a newspaper
interview in mid-1957, King Husayn claimed that the JCP had even
begun to infiltrate the army, indoctrinating certain officers.[37] Storing up arms and infiltrating the army were the logical outcome of

the party's development, fired by the growing influence of the Soviet Union in the area at this time and the greatly increased strength of the Communist parties in neighboring Iraq and Syria. Moscow's belated endorsement of the Free Officers in Egypt clearly also influenced the party in Jordan, causing it to reappraise its opinion of the officers as reactionary lackeys of the king.[38] But this development was nipped in the bud by the authorities.

As mentioned earlier, Husayn denounced the party in January 1957. At the beginning of February, he spelled out his opposition even more forcefully in a message to Prime Minister Nabulsi.[39] That same month, all Tass publications were banned in Jordan and restrictions were placed on mail coming from Syria and Lebanon. There were signs that the steps taken against the party were on the king's own initiative and did not have the backing of Nabulsi, who declared at the end of February that Communism was not a threat in Jordan and that the rumors of Communist infiltration of the country were almost without foundation. When he dismissed the Nabulsi government, Husayn stated at a press conference that the prime minister had acted against his instructions and had permitted the JCP to "sow dissension throughout the country."[40] The party continued to function energetically, however, organizing petitions opposing the Eisenhower Doctrine and calling for close ties with the Soviet Union. The next blow came with the passage of the law disbanding all political parties on April 25, 1957. While the new law outlawed the JCP along with all other parties, the king, in a public broadcast announcing the legislation, referred only to the Communist Party, which he accused of maintaining ties with Israel, of treachery to the Arab cause by calling for peace with the Jewish state, and of threatening the religious and national integrity of the kingdom.[41] The authorities were fully aware that the party continued to function underground, and began to hound its leaders and main activists. They forced many members to renounce in the local press any further links with the party. During May 1957, detention orders were served against dozens of Jordanian Communists, many of whom were from the West Bank. In Nablus alone, 150 such orders were served against alleged Communists. Parliamentary immunity was lifted, and Warrad and Dr. Ziyadin were tried and sentenced to long prison sentences, of sixteen and nineteen years respectively.[42] Party activists were forced to go underground, seeking refuge in the hills around Salfit, or renting rooms under assumed identities.[43] Many used false identification papers to escape to the Gaza Strip or to Syria. The vigorous witch-hunt resulted in the arrest of many Communists, and the heavy sentences imposed induced many of those who managed to evade arrest either to leave the country or the party or at least to suspend their activities. The Supreme Muslim Council, headed by Shaykh Abdallah Ghosha, was asked to issue a public statement supporting the king's measures against the Communists, declaring their principles to be contrary to those of Islam, and calling for a continued crackdown on the party and its ideals.[44] Newspapers published reports, attributed to "official sources," that several Communists had fled to Israel, thus "substantiating" the claim that the JCP continued to maintain ties with the Israel Communist Party. The king, who repeated this assertion, attacked international Communism in the press and over the radio, accusing Communists abroad of trying to infiltrate their ideas into the kingdom through Tass publications and propaganda films, using its lackeys in the Middle East—the Syrian foreign minister, for example—as well as the Communist Party and its supporters in Jordan for this purpose.[45] In February 1958, a large public trial was held, in which several JCP members were accused of hoarding weapons and establishing terrorist cells. Other military trials were held in Jerusalem, Bethlehem, and Jericho, and Communist Party members were sentenced (frequently in absentia) to long prison terms.[46] All this had a toll on the party, which found itself in a more troubled state in the late 1950s than it had been for some years past. Many members and sympathizers deserted, while others continued to be arrested and jailed (Dr. Abd al-Hafiz al-Ashhab was arrested in 1959, drastically reducing Communist activity in the Hebron area). The mosques were also brought into the anti-Communist drive, with imams (in Nablus, for example) being instructed to attack the party and its principles in their Friday sermons.[47]

But the party was not broken. It continued to function, adapting itself to the new conditions. By signing the manifesto along with about sixty other Communist parties around the world to mark the fortieth anniversary of the Revolution, the JCP both defied the government and served notice that it was still alive. In the spring of 1958, the JCP instructed its members to refrain from entering into any public debate with members of other parties, to avoid them in case they might be provocateurs. At the end of the same year, those members who had fled to the neighboring Arab countries were ordered to return to Jordan, and any member wishing to leave the country henceforth first had to obtain the party's permission.[48] In Jerusalem especially the party was extremely active among high school students in 1958. Several cells were established at the al-Rashidiya, Coptic, al-Tur, and Ibrahimiya schools in the city.[49] There are indications that, in Jerusalem at least, the party's activities were connected with the Egyptian consul-general, who maintained contact with several of the party's key activists.[50] At the same time as it was secretly building up new cadres in the high schools, the party was also active in the streets, organizing demonstrations and distributing leaflets. But even these activities bore the the mark of the party's penchant for careful, covert preparation: the student demonstrators who took to the streets could do so only after receiving permission from the party. There was activity in the schools elsewhere as well: teachers in the Aqabat Jabir refugee camp disseminated the party's ideology and distributed leaflets to their pupils and colleagues, as did teachers in Jenin and Qalqilya.[51] There were, however, risks involved in recruiting teachers and pupils. At the end of 1959 a teacher in the village of Zawiya near Jenin was arrested after trying to recruit a pupil into the party, and he provided the police with information that led to the arrest of two key activists in the Nablus area. Despite the careful security measures taken by the party, an important network was thus uncovered (the teacher, it emerged, knew not only the code names of the party's main activists in his district, but their real names as well). The network was extremely well organized. Large sums of money were arriving from Amman,[52] which the party treasurer would distribute (through the National Front's deputy Abd al-Qadir Salih) in small sums to needy families, the families of political detainees and prisoners, and to party activists who had gone underground. The ring also distributed leaflets and other publications from Tulkarm and engaged in recruiting and indoctrination activities in Salfit, Deir Istya, Sannirya, and Burqin. The cells in Burqin, which were made up mostly of fellahin, were recruited and trained under the auspices of the party's Nablus branch, but received their ideological material from the Ramallah area (Mazari al-Nubani).[53] This far-reaching network, when it was uncovered, was described by the authorities as the principal network in Nablus; but they later discovered that, for all its importance, it was by no means the only one. The ring was characterized by the fact that it was headed by people whom the authorities had not known were active in the party.

There was also renewed activity among the families of detainees in Ramallah and al-Bira, with Emil and Dr. Alfred Tubasi particularly active.[54] New cells were also set up in the Bethlehem area, in the Daheisha refugee camp, and in Jericho, but most of these were uncovered by the police and their members arrested.[55]

By the end of the 1950s, then, the Jordanian authorities could claim, with some truth, that they had struck a crippling blow to the Communist Party. Its development and expansion had been effectively stemmed, its attempts to organize for an armed struggle were nipped in the bud, many of its cells were uncovered, several of its key members had been arrested and many others were deterred from active participation in the party. The public activity of the party was almost totally suspended, and the party was forced to concentrate once again on its infrastructure. From 1960 on, the party kept off the streets and its public activities were kept to a minimum. Instead it directed its efforts toward slowly building up carefully trained and thoroughly committed cadres who, although few in number, were preparing themselves to infiltrate the country's schools and trade unions when the time was ripe.[56] The party newspaper, *al-Muqawama al-Shaabiya*, continued to appear regularly, however, serving as a beacon to the party faithful, and all attempts by the authorities to discover where it was being printed failed.[57]

STRUCTURE AND MEMBERSHIP

Hierarchy, Communications, and Covert Activity

The structure of the party was basically hierarchical, and remained unchanged during the period under review. At the head was the central committee (*al-lajna al-markaziya*), which was sometimes known as the general central committee (*al-lajna al-markaziya al-amma*). This committee was responsible for the party's activities throughout Jordan, and was thus made up of members from both Banks—although the most prominent were almost invariably from the West Bank. The central committee was headed by the secretary-general, Fuad Nassar, and comprised seven members, each representing his own area. One of the members, Rushdi Shahin, served as treasurer (*amin al-sunduq*), while another, Fahmi al-Salfiti, was responsible for propaganda. The members of the central committee in 1957 (and, indeed, most of the following sat on the committee throughout the entire period under review)[58] were: Fakhri Maraqa (Hebron), Salih Haddadin (Karak), Fahmi al-Salfiti (Salfit), Fayiq Warrad (Beitin), Rushdi Shahin (Nablus), Dr. Yaqub Ziyadin (Jerusalem), and Fayiz al-Rusan (Irbid). The central committee included the politburo (*maktab siyasi*). While the central committee met only a few times a year, the politburo was responsible for the everyday running of the party. It comprised three or four members of the central committee; these were not elected but chosen by agreement within the committee itself. In 1953 the politburo members were Fuad Nassar, Fahmi al-Salfiti, Harb Harb, and Rushdi Shahin.

At the next level stood the central, or district, committees (*lijan markaziya* or *lijan mantiqiya*). Each of these committees represented one of the areas represented on the general central committee, and contained between three and five members (the Nablus committee, however, included as many as eight members in 1954, one of whom was in charge of the Tulkarm district.[59] Some members had clearly defined duties, such as treasurer, propaganda supervisor (sometimes called "teacher" [*mudarris*]), coordinator of students, or coordinator of fellahin and workers. These positions were not permanent and often changed hands, either as a result of a member being exiled or jailed or falling from grace in the party.[60] There were about ten such committees (at the beginning of the 1950s these were in Jerusalem, Nablus, Jericho, Bethlehem, Ramallah, Irbid, Amman, and Karak. Hebron was represented by a local committee until about 1953, when a regional committee was established

At the third level were the local councils (*mahalliya*), which were established in all the principal towns and even in some villages. These also comprised three or four members, each charged with a specific function (treasurer, ideological commissar, secretary [*jihaz*] who was responsible for distributing leaflets). The members of the local committee in Hebron in 1956 were Dr. Abd al-Hafiz al-Ashhab (secretary), Amr Khalil Abu Iyash, and Zuhdi Sultan.

The lowest organizational level was the cell (*khaliya*), made up of between three and six members ("comrade" or *rafiq*). At the head of each cell stood the commander (*qaid*), who was also responsible for distributing leaflets (sometimes referred to as "servant" [*khadim*]).

In the larger towns there was an intermediate level between the cell and the local or district committee, dealing with specific sectors such as students or fellahin and workers, each headed by a member of the district committee.

The central committee led the party, laying out its operational guidelines and organizing its finances. It was also in charge of over-all propaganda, putting out the party's various publications and leaflets. The day-to-day administration of the party was the task of the politburo, with most of the burden falling on the secretary-general. The district committees were charged with coordinating the party's activities in their own areas, being responsible for the distribution and sometimes even the publication of leaflets. They served the vital function of channeling instructions from the general central committee to the local committees and through them to the cells. The basic task of the district committee, however, was to organize and plan the activities of the cells in its area and to rebuild the network when it was uncovered by the authorities. Information, requests for instructions, and membership dues were channeled upward from the cells, through the local and district committees to the general central committee.

The individual cells held weekly meetings, both to discuss and plan activities and, more frequently, to debate ideological issues and current political problems (these meetings were also devoted to self-appraisal and self-criticism—a practice strongly advocated by the district committees). The commander of the cell would present the party line as he had received it from the local or district committee—which necessitated careful maintenance of un-broken communication among the various levels. This direct contact was important, as the publications put out by the party were relatively infrequent. The commander ran the cell meetings, and the individual members knew each other by name. Contact with the local committee was through the cell alone, but even then with only one specific member. Regular contact was made in writing; face-to-face meetings were extremely rare. The commander could not make any decisions on his own, and had to address any questions he might have to his local committee. Cell members were bound by a strict disciplinary code which affected not only their political activities but their personal lives as well: a member who wished to move to another town or village, for example, could not do so without permission from the party. Moreover, a member could even be asked by the party to change his place of abode or employment. The party would be especially anxious to keep members who were wanted by the authorities out of view, and sometimes moved them to remote villages, taking care of their livelihoods until the storm passed. Any member who refused to obey party instructions was tried by the cell commander or the local committee, and if he was found guilty, could be banned from further meetings or even expelled from the party. The expulsion of a member was usually reported in the party newspaper, both for security reasons and so that he might serve as an example to others.

The party continued to remain responsible for its members even after they were arrested. Couriers maintained regular contact with their families and provided them with material aid when needed. If sufficient funds were not available locally, they were obtained from the central committee. At the end of 1959, for example, a sum of about one hundred dinars was transferred to Nablus from Amman via Jerusalem and distributed by a party member, (Dr. Adli Dallal) in sums of three to five dinars a month to the families of imprisoned or ill members.[61] The prisoners themselves also received financial aid, smuggled to them in prison by their relatives (usually women). In prisons where there were a large number of Communist detainees, such as al-Jafar in 1957, a special committee was set up in the prison (*lajna qiadiya*) to handle the distribution of these funds. If a member died, the party assumed responsibility for his family until it could support itself.

Structure of the party

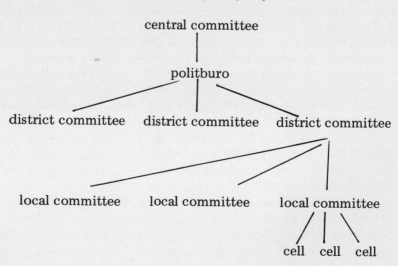

As in other Communist parties operating underground, contact between the various levels was always vertical—that is, there was never any contact between individual cells or individual local committees. Contact was maintained through couriers (*murasil*). Communication between the central committee and the district committees was through two veteran and highly reliable couriers. Most communication, however, took place on the district level, with couriers transmitting material and instructions from the district to the local committees, which, in turn, used their own couriers to deliver these to the individual cells. One specific member in each cell was responsible for receiving these communications, and passing them on to his comrades in the cell. It was also his function to distribute leaflets and other publications to sympathizers who were not actually members of the party and to the public at large. At the higher levels, the principle of "compartmentalization" was strictly observed (when the cells were reorganized following the publication of the emergency regulations in 1957, for example, and the party's Bethlehem representative traveled to Jerusalem to receive instructions, he was not permitted to contact any member of the district committee; instead, he met with a representative of the committee, and all further instructions were conveyed to him through another courier). Within each district, however, this principle was less strictly adhered to. Umar Iyash, for example, who served as the main courier between Jerusalem-Ramallah and the Hebron area, though he did not himself distribute materials he received, did meet the courier charged with that duty, Zuhdi Sultan, in his own home. Moreover, on one occasion, following the reorganization of the party at the beginning of 1958, Iyash permitted Sultan to be present at a meeting he had in Ramallah with a representative of the party leadership. The courier worked in both directions, distributing material and instructions from the center to the periphery and transmitting messages and membership dues from the periphery to the center. (There was, however, a departure from this procedure in Salfit in 1954, when the secretary of the local committee in the village, Hamza al-Zirr, was responsible for remitting money to Nablus—in addition to this organizational and ideological functions—while the courier in the area delivered leaflets and other literature from Nablus to Salfit).

But the party also had more sophisticated and efficient ways of preserving secrecy. Members and villages were given code names or numbers, which in some cases were changed every few months (in 1952, for example, Fuad Nassar was known as "Khalid," or "Abu Salam;" Rushdi Shahin, as "Bashir;" and Fahmi al-Salfiti, as "Fahd"). Members were instructed never to mention real names in their dispatches and reports. In order to reduce further the danger of discovery, compartmentalization between the individual cells was strictly followed. Cell members were repeatedly warned not to contact party members from outside their own town or village, and under no circumstances to reveal their identities to non-party members. It was, of course, not possible, given the traditional social structure of the villages and even of the towns, to adhere completely to these instructions; nonetheless, on several occasions, the security authorities complained that the discovery of one cell did not usually lead to the discovery of others. "Despite all our efforts," read one report, following the interrogation of apprehended cell members, "they would say nothing beyond admitting that they were, in fact, Communists."[62] The system was indeed so effective that on one occasion, following the arrest of a courier, certain cells complained that they were unable to trace other cells that they knew to exist in their vicinity.

The party, which had been hounded from its inception by the Jordanian authorities, also devoted considerable effort toward training its members how to conduct themselves if they were arrested. Members were instructed to destroy all documents after they were interrogated and to avoid all contact with comrades from cells other than their own. They were given special instruction in how to behave in prison (a pamphlet on the subject was printed at the beginning of 1954). The party drew a distinction between two stages: (1) Arrest and interrogation, when the member was instructed not to admit his membership in the party, even if he were presented with indisputable proof of it; not to attempt to defend his ideals; not to succumb to torture or threats; not to be deceived by provocateurs, whom the police might attempt to plant in his cell; and not to cooperate with anyone. (2) The trial, when the member was instructed to admit the charges, to make use of legal aid, and, above all, to exploit the occasion to expound the party's aims and ideals. In general, the party's internal circulars repeatedly stressed the fundamentals of secrecy: to keep tight-lipped, to beware of provocateurs, and never to have any incriminating material on one's person or at home.

The transfer of documents and party literature was usually carried out from hand to hand, but in some cases (particularly when the authorities intensified their harassment, the material was simply deposited in predetermined places, to be collected later. The cells frequently met outside the town or village itself (in the orchards or vineyards around Hebron, for example). Alternative venues or dates were not usually set. While members would sometimes call at one another's homes, they did not do so if a member failed to show up at a prearranged meeting and it was feared that he might have been arrested—at least not until it had been established that this was not the case, and even then the member's house was carefully staked out before a visit took place. In the larger towns, meetings were often held in local bookshops (Saadi Shahin's bookshop in Nablus, and "al-Maktaba al-Shaabiya" in Ramallah, for example, in 1955). These were not official meeting places, or party clubs, but simply convenient.

Other steps taken by the party to increase its security included the following: (1) "Safe houses" were maintained in the larger towns, especially in Jerusalem and Nablus. These were carefully investigated, with the identity of the owner and the neighbors thoroughly checked. Wherever possible, safe houses were not rented in the name of the person most likely to be using them. (2) Procedures existed to transfer members, usually from the larger towns to isolated villages, when the authorities were pursuing them. The party was careful to provide fugitives with proper clothing and financial support. (3) Senior members of the party were provided with false identification papers and often with false passports as well. (4) In certain cases, fugitive members would go underground in uninhabited areas, taking refuge in caves for several months at a time (this was particularly common in the Salfit area). (5) Members were asked to provide themselves with two distinctively different sets of clothing, so that they could change their outward appearance if they needed to escape from the authorities.

Recruitment

Despite their strict code of secrecy, and to some degree in contradiction of it, party members saw themselves as charged with a mission to spread the party's message to as wide an audience as possible. Thus members would espouse their personal ideas to friends and acquaintances, and if they seemed responsive would pass their names on to their local committees. These recommendations would be accompanied by a detailed report, outlining the prospective candidate's background and qualifications and the contribution he would be able to make to the party. If the local committee approved, after thoroughly investigating the prospective candidate, the sponsor would be authorized to approach him and ask if he would like to join. His actual induction would be carried out by someone known to the candidate, sometimes by his superior at work. A new recruit was required to demonstrate his loyalty to the party in two ways: by paying his dues and by distributing leaflets. The latter, which would continue for several months, was designed to test both the recruit's willingness to take risks on behalf of the party and his aptitude for undercover work. Simultaneously, the recruiting officer would instruct the new member in the party's basic ideology before attaching him to a cell. In isolated cases, mostly in the early 1950s, the candidate would be asked to submit his application for membership in writing (*waraqat intisab*), to be endorsed by two veteran party members. This procedure was apparently designed to test the candidate's seriousness, but more commonly applications were made orally. Even after the candidate had been approved by the local committee (and sometimes even by the district committee), the member who had sponsored him was held responsible for him—a procedure designed undoubtedly to deter hasty and hence hazardous induction of new members. After Fuad Nassar and four other leaders were arrested in Amman at the end of 1951, it emerged that they had been betrayed by a new member, Daud Dhib Abu Shamis, who had been recruited not long before in Nablus. Shamis' sponsor, Rushdi al-Habbab, a highly respected and senior member of the party, was held responsible for the leak and had to submit in writing to the central committee a lengthy apology and explanation of how he had been deceived by his protégé's "proletarian origins." (Al-Habbab paid dearly for his error in judgment when he himself was arrested three months later).

Finances

One of the first acts of a new member was to pay this subscription dues (*ishtirak*). Ranging between 150 and 500 fils, they were paid once a month. Dues were collected in each cell and transferred to the treasurer on the local council, who in turn would remit them to the district committee. The treasurer was obliged to keep accounts, showing precisely what proportion of the dues collected went on running expenses. In addition to their monthly dues, members were sometimes asked to make somewhat larger contributions, usually to help out detainees and their families. Sympathizers of the party constituted an important source of income, but their contributions were made on a personal basis and most often they were not told what the money would be used for. Even former members who had been expelled from the party often continued to contribute as a way of keeping involved in the cause. Additional funds were raised by the sale of the party newspaper, which members were required to pay for. Nevertheless, from various documents seized by the authorities it was clear that the party suffered from a chronic shortage of funds. At least until 1953 the party did not receive any outside help, and as a result its activities were seriously hampered. Following Fuad Nassar's arrest in 1951 and the confiscation of the party's printing press, its paper, *al-muqawama al-Shaabiya*, was published in improvised form on a simple copying machine; it was not until 1954 that the party was able to raise enough money to acquire a new press. When finally the paper returned to its old format, it printed a touching appreciation of the contributions that had made the purchase of the new press possible. There were rumors in the mid-1950s, not altogether baseless, that the party was receiving substantial financial support from its brother party in Syria.

Reportage

Each cell and local committee was required to submit a regular report each month to the district committee in addition to the ad hoc reports they submitted whenever necessary. The district committees were required to submit both an administrative report and an operational report, the latter detailing the decisions taken at its own meetings and the activities of the cells.

Each cell had to report on the situation in its area or sector (the prevailing mood among students or workers, for example). Occasionally, the local committees would be asked to collect information following some unusual political event in the area. This material enabled the district committee to assess the situation and report it to the central committee, in addition to providing information for its own publications.

The central committee issued two types of communication: typewritten background papers (*risala dakhiliya*), which analyzed the political situation and spelled out the party line, and internal communiques (*risala hizbiya*), typewritten sheets outlining the committee's response to the reports it had received, giving guidelines for future activities, and sometimes providing ideological commentary on current events.

Publications

The JCP was the only party in Jordan which, from 1948 on, tried consistently to put its message across to the public at large. Unlike other parties, the JCP viewed this as one of its most important public activities, and hence went to great lengths despite constant harassment by the security services to keep communication lines open. There were no doubt ideological reasons for the party's preoccupation with keeping its publications appearing regularly. One was perhaps its desire to reach the widest possible audience, particularly the country's intellectuals. Another was that the preparation and distribution of party literature constituted an important test of its members' loyalty, enthusiasm, and initiative. With the authorities determined to stamp out the publication of Communist literature—by trying to seize the party's printing equipment and disrupt its distribution apparatus, and even making possession of such literature illegal—this activity became the most common battleground. As the authorities escalated their efforts to disrupt or suppress the party's publishing activities, the party in turn stepped up its efforts to prove that in this area at least it had the upper hand. Its ability to continue putting out its publications became for the party a symbol of its vitality and a promise of things to come.

The JCP's most important publication, from mid-1949 on, was its official organ, *al-Muqawama al-Shaabiya* ("The Popular Struggle"). It usually appeared monthly, but on occasion would be put out more frequently. The journal bore the hammer-and-sickle emblem on its masthead over the legend; "Organ of the National Liberation League in Palestine." Beginning in late 1951, after the party changed its name, the legend was changed to "Published by the Central Committee of the Jordanian Communist Party." The paper cost five mils when it first appeared, went to ten mils in August 1949, and fifteen fils from mid-1951 on.

The format of the publication varied: at first, it comprised just two pages each having two columns, expanding to six pages of five columns in 1951. During 1952–53, after the party's printing press was seized and the paper was produced on a duplicating machine (at first from handwritten and later from typewritten stencils), its size varied between four and ten pages. From 1954 on, after the acquisition of a new press, the paper was once again printed but in a smaller format of two five-column pages (this was doubled to four five-column pages during 1956, when the fortunes of the party were at their height, but returned subsequently to the smaller format). The paper regularly contained a long leader which took up between 15 and 40 percent of its space and most often presented the party's position on the major political events of the period. About 50 percent of the paper was devoted to coverage of political events in Jordan, while at least 10 percent (often much more) was given over to translations from the Soviet press, excerpts from the speeches of Soviet leaders, and articles dealing with major developments in the international Communist movement. Less attention was paid to developments in Communist countries other than the Soviet Union, but from time to time long excerpts from statements issued by Communist parties in the neighboring countries (including Israel until the early 1950s) were printed. Only sporadic reporting was done on social and economic issues, and no attempt was made to provide systematic analysis in this area. The Gaza Strip[63] and the Arab world in general were largely ignored, although this attitute changed somewhat in the late 1950s. The paper addressed itself primarily to a politically aware readership, which it sought to enlighten and guide. It stressed its Jordanian-Arab (and Palestinian) orientation, but continually impressed on its readers the party's ideological ties with the Soviet Union. The paper did not direct itself to the masses, and gave only superficial notice to issues affecting the country's workers, fellahin, and, of course, the refugees.

Far greater attention was given to current news events in the journals that began to appear in the larger towns in the mid-1950s (*Nidal al-Shaab* in Jerusalem, *Sawt Jabal al-Nar* in Nablus, and *Kifah al-Shaab* in Amman).[64] *Nidal al-Shaab* ("The Popular Struggle") and *Kifah al-Shaab* (which also translates as "The Popular Struggle") began to appear in the middle of 1955. They comprised four or six pages, rolled off on a duplicating machine from typewritten stencils. *Sawt Jabal al-Nar* ("Voice of the Mountain of Fire") began to appear as a six-page monthly in the middle of 1956. All three publications were subsequently reduced to just two pages. They were put out by the local committee in each town, selling at first for ten fils, later rising to fifteen. Their major concern was to give in-depth coverage to local events in and around their respective towns. But the local journals also contained leading articles that dealt with broader, ideological subjects, similar to those appearing in *al-Muqawama al-Shaabiya*. Published when the party was at its most active, these local papers seemed designed to reach a far broader, less politically aware audience than the official party organ. In order to strike a response in this audience, the papers had to deal with matters that were most relevant to them—but even so, never at the expense of the party's basic ideological line.

While the permanent publications were aimed primarily at the party's members and sympathizers, leaflets were used to reach the public at large. Each major political event in Jordan or the Middle East occasioned the printing of leaflets presenting the JCP's view of that event. Leaflets were also printed to mark significant anniversaries—May 1, the October Revolution, and even Christmas—and distributed in all the larger towns and villages. (On May 1 there was frequently a cat-and-mouse game between the police and the party: the police took special precautions to prevent the distribution of leaflets on the international Labor Day, and the party evaded them by distributing their leaflets either immediately before or after the day itself.) The leaflets, generally comprising one or two pages, were always dated. At first they were signed by the National Liberation League, and after mid-1951, by the Jordanian Communist Party. Although they were usually printed on the party's press, sometimes they were duplicated from typewritten or even handwritten stencils (this latter method was employed by the local branches to put out leaflets dealing with local events). The leaflets were directed at the Jordanian and Palestinian public and presented in simplified form the party line as given in far greater depth in *al-Muqawama al-Shaabiya* and the other regular publications.

The same network used to distribute the official party organ also served the local publications and leaflets. But while the regular publications—*al-Muqawama al-Shaabiya* and the local papers—were distributed by party members, leafletting was often entrusted to youths and even to children (who did not know the content of the leaflets and agreed to do the chore in return for a small fee).[65] The usual procedure was simply to distribute the leaflets in the main streets of the town or village or leave them in piles at the entrances to schools in the hope that at least some of them would find their way into the hands of the public before they were collected by the regular police patrols. A less common method was to mail the leaflets to senior officials, intellectuals, and prominent political figures (this was done in Nablus at the end of 1955). At the beginning of 1956 there was even an attempt to mail leaflets to officers in the army. This method of distribution was highly inefficient, however, and toward the end of 1955 the party decided to distribute its literature hand-to-hand. This move coincided with the party's increased efforts in 1956 to reach the greatest possible number of people in the West Bank.[66] The police were rebuked for failing to prevent the party from distributing its literature in this way, and as late as 1958 there were still reports of Communist publications being passed from hand to hand. The leaflets and other publications were usually distributed from one specific center, but were not actually printed at that center. The security services were able to trace the party's printing press on only one occasion, in 1951, and despite unceasing subsequent efforts to trace party writers and printing equipment (their files record several such attempts), they were never again successful. It was even suggested in the late 1950s that the leaflets were printed in Israel (a claim repeated in 1956), and the Jordanian military intelligence reported that they were printed in Syria.[67]

Nablus was the distribution center for all publications in the north. From there, material was sent out to Tulkarm, Qalqilya, Jenin, and Salfit. There are also indications that Jerusalem may have served as a distribution center for the entire West Bank, disseminating material through Nablus and Hebron. In mid-June 1953 hundreds of copies of *al-Muqawama al-Shaabiya* were discovered in a taxi going from Jerusalem to Nablus, and in April 1954 a similar consignment was found in the trunk of a taxi en route from Jerusalem to Hebron. There are reports of similar discoveries in the late 1950s. It is hardly surprising, therefore, that the security services' most intensive efforts to trace the party's press were concentrated in the Jerusalem area, particularly following reports at the end of 1954 and again in 1956 that it was situated either in al-Tur or in the Coptic monastery in the Old City.[68] But all these efforts, both in Jerusalem and elsewhere in Jordan, proved to be in vain.[69]

Social Characteristics of the JCP

The Jordanian Security Services kept a close watch on all JCP activists. Lists were compiled and constantly updated, always on hand should the police decide to crack down on the party. The people on these lists were often so well known to the police that there was no need to keep a record of their exact addresses: their names, professions, and hometown or village were usually sufficient. Party activists were graded into three categories (A, B, C) according to their importance. Most of these lists date from the mid-1950s, when the party was at the peak of its power. They are extremely useful in attempting to establish the social makeup of the party, not only during the mid-1950s but also during the entire period under review.

There are, however, a number of difficulties in compiling this sort of picture. The security services' data concerning place of abode (town, village, or refugee camp) and civil status (refugee or permanent resident) are satisfactory (in the Nablus district, for example, we can establish the place of abode of 432 of 443 members in the area, and the civil status of 397 of them). This information is relatively reliable and can be used reasonably as the basis for a number of sociological generalizations. Data on profession, however, in a high percentage of cases was not known by the authorities (in Nablus, for example, the professions of only 92 of the 443 members, about 20 percent, are listed, and the same applies to other areas of the West Bank). Thus all we have to say about profession should be viewed as tentative. We can make only a few generalizations, which become less and less reliable as the importance and standing of the member in the party descends. Our method has been to base our conclusions for the *entire* membership on the 20 percent of party members whose professions are known. Finally, we define "Grade A Members" as those fully active in the party. They numbered between three and four hundred. The remainder (Grades B and C), rather less than two thousand, were either supporters of varying degrees of commitment or members who were not very active in the party.

Place of Abode

Perhaps most striking is the nearly complete absence of members in the refugee camps. Those party members whose civil status was refugee did not actually live in the camps but in the towns. The situation in Nablus is typical: of the 432 members in the area whose place of abode is listed, 323 lived in the town itself and only 14 in the nearby refugee camps. In most other areas there were no members at all in the camps. (The one outstanding exception was in Jericho, where about 70 percent of the members lived in the camps.

The refugee camps were of far greater importance in the Jericho area than elsewhere in the West Bank: the population of the camps far exceeded that of the town and educationally and economically was equal if not superior to that of the town. As a result, the camps constituted an important focus of the party's activities in Jericho). Given the negligible number of members in the refugee camps, and the fact that many of these camps had become effectively integrated into the towns these members should be regarded as urban.

In the West Bank as a whole, the place of abode of 2,018 of the 2,282 party members (that is, about 88.5 percent) can be established. Of these, 75 percent lived in towns and the remaining 25 percent in villages. Of Grade A members (the party's leading activists), some 78 percent were urban and 22 percent rural. The ratio for Grade B members (numbering about 1,670) was 60 percent living in towns and 40 percent in villages. A breakdown by district shows that in the north (Nablus, Tulkarm, Jenin, Qalqilya, Salfit, Tubas, and Anabta), of the 939 members whose place of abode is known to us, 74 percent were urban and 26 percent rural; in the central area (Jerusalem, Bethlehem, Jericho, and Ramallah), of the 940 members whose abode is known, 78 percent were urban and 22 percent rural; and in the south (the Hebron area), urban members slightly outnumbered rural members (54 percent to 46 percent). In the northern and central areas, there was no significant difference in the urban-rural breakdown of Grade A and Grade B members, while for all grades, the breakdown was close to the West Bank average. A comparison of the various towns in the central area reveals a number of interesting features: while in Jerusalem the urban-rural breakdown was close to the West Bank average, in Jericho (were refugee camp members are classified as urban) and Bethlehem there were almost no rural members, and in Ramallah (which has a greater rural population than anywhere else in the West Bank), the proportion of rural members came to some 63 percent. The Hebron area differs somewhat from other parts of the West Bank in that its population is almost evenly divided between urban and rural elements. This accounts for the near parity in urban and rural members in the area, although it should be noted that in the Grade A grouping, urban members did in fact significantly outnumber rural members. The fact that several members who worked in Hebron still lived in their native villages may also have contributed to the somewhat unusual breakdown in the town.

Civil Status: Refugees and Permanent Residents

Our data for the West Bank as a whole provides information on civil status for about 80 percent of all members. Of these, 19 percent are listed as refugees (although most did not actually live in the camps) and 81 percent were permanent residents. The proportion of refugees was somewhat smaller in the Grade A group, 15 percent, and marginally higher, 20 percent, in the Grade B group. This breakdown (a greater proportion of refugees in the Grade B than in the Grade A group) remains basically the same in the various districts, but may be partially due to incomplete information. There are only minor differences between the breakdowns for individual regions: in the north, refugees accounted for 13 percent of all members; in the central area, for 22 percent; and in the south, for 14 percent. The overall picture, then, is that there were far fewer refugee members than permanent resident members, and that the proportion of the former to the latter decreased in the higher levels of the party membership.

Occupation

For the sake of simplification, I have included under the single heading "intellectuals" a wide variety of groups: teachers, clerks, professionals, students, and security personnel. The most numerous group were the teachers (who comprised about 60 percent of the intellectual members in Nablus), while the smallest group were members of the security forces, which the party had very little success in penetrating. Students were an important group in Jerusalem, Tulkarm, and Hebron (though insignificant in other areas), but they were always classified as Grade B members, presumably because of their age. Laborers and the unemployed were grouped together on the assumption that most of the unemployed were unskilled or semiskilled laborers (they certainly weren't fellahin). Because of the paucity of the data on the breakdown of party membership by occupation, no differentiation was made between Grade A and Grade B members. For the West Bank as a whole, the breakdown by occupation is as follows: intellectuals, 51 percent; property owners, 0.5 percent; artisans and merchants, 13.5 percent; laborers, 25 percent; and fellahin, 10 percent.

By region, the following picture emerges: in the north, 41 percent of members whose occupation was known were intellectuals, one percent were property owners, 17 percent were merchants and artisans, 29 percent were laborers, and 12 percent were fellahin; in the central area, 48 percent were intellectuals, 13 percent were merchants and artisans, 27 percent were laborers, and 12 percent were fellahin; and in the south (Hebron only, excluding the surrounding villages), intellectuals constituted 83 percent, merchants and artisans 7 percent, and laborers 10 percent. The apparent lack of fellahin among party members in Hebron is actually somewhat a distortion of the truth, which seems to arise from the fact that the lists compiled by the security services included members only from the town of Hebron and ignored those in the surrounding villages. Of the three major towns in the West Bank, it emerges that Hebron had the greatest percentage of intellectual members, followed by Jerusalem and Nablus. On the other hand, Nablus had the greatest percentage of merchant and artisan members (20 percent), followed by Jerusalem (12 percent) and Hebron (7 percent). The percentage of laborers was roughly the same in Jerusalem and Nablus (a little under 30 percent), and much lower in Hebron (10 percent).

The most outstanding feature of the party's occupational breakdown is the relatively small percentage of laborers and fellahin in its ranks, and the large percentage of intellectuals. This group not only was much larger than any of the other occupational groups (comprising more than half its membership for whom we have information), but also constituted a formidable bloc within the party and left its mark on the party's activities and its organizational structure.

These findings, although based on very incomplete data, do seem to conform with the nature of the party's activities and with its ideology: despite the lip service it paid to the country's laborers and fellahin, the main thrust of the JCP was clearly toward the intellectuals. The significant percentage of merchants and artisans in the party's ranks explains the attention paid in its various publications to events affecting these groups, even though they weren't "typcial" of the groups the party chose to work with.

General Observations

The JCP was the most powerful political party in Jordan in the 1950s. One or another of the other parties may have claimed a greater number of members and supporters in the mid-1950s, but this has yet to be proven. The JCP managed to have three candidates elected to the House of Representatives in the general elections of 1956—the least "rigged" elections that had ever taken place in Jordan—an achievement no other party matched. One point conceded even by its political opponents was that the degree of indoctrination and organization in the JCP was so great that even if it did have relatively few members, the party possessed a strength and resilience far greater than its actual membership.

It is difficult to establish the precise numerical strength of the party. Because of its secret mode of operation, the party itself kept no centralized lists or statistics. The only information available to us is that collected by the security services, or recollected by party activists. At the beginning of the 1950s, the JCP had about two hundred members in the West Bank, and another one hundred or so in the East Bank, the majority of the latter being Palestinians. The total membership dropped considerably in 1958, to between one hundred and two hundred in all. Even at its peak (1956–57), according to the various sources, the party never had more than one thousand active members. The lists compiled by the security authorities placed the number at about two thousand, a figure genererally considered inflated.[70] The security authorities tended to exaggerate the numerical strength of the party, and included in their lists the names of persons who had long since left its ranks, as well as persons who were sympathizers or in some way connected with the party without actually being members. We can, therefore, only assume that at its height the JCP's membership in the West Bank was between one thousand and two thousand (probably closer to the former).

Cells were set up not only in the main urban centers of the West Bank but also in several villages. Jerusalem and Nablus were easily the two most important centers and closely coordinated their activities, with key members sometimes moving from one town to the other. A third important center was the village of Salfit, near Nablus. From the late 1940s, Salfit was prominent not only as the native village of several leading party activists (Fahmi al-Salfiti, Hamza al-Zirr, Arabi Awad), but also for the large and highly active branch which had grown up there. The reasons given for this somewhat unusual phenomenon are not completely convincing. One explanation is that although it was not situated on a major artery and therefore fairly isolated, Salfit was still relatively close to Nablus and Ramallah. Another reason perhaps was Fahmi al-Salfiti's long Communist experience. Other explanations include the fierce clan rivalry in the village which, it is argued, expressed itself in extreme ideological polarization; the relatively quiet early years when the village escaped the scrutiny of the security services and was able to build up its cadres without harassment; and the very considerable influence of Dr. Abu Hajla, whose family owned large tracts of land in the area. There is undoubtedly an element of truth in all these explanations, but far more penetrating research into the sociopolitical makeup of this highly unusual village is required before any final conclusions can be drawn. Nevertheless, Salfit provides a unique case of a village in the West Bank becoming a major center of Communist activity.

The primary reasons for the party's strength in the West Bank were the painstaking attention to detail displayed by its leaders in building up the party apparatus; the strict code of secrecy which governed its activities at every level; its unceasing indoctrination efforts; the considerable revolutionary experience of its leading members; the deep conviction in the rightness of its path; and, undoubtedly, the accumulated experience of the international Communist movement. The party gained considerably from the sense of disillusionment and frustration that had set in among the population with the failure of the Arab armies to destroy the nascent state of Israel in 1948. This mood gradually made less abhorrent the party's early stand on the Palestine issue, its acceptance of the UN partition plan, and its de facto acceptance of Israel's existence, especially in the mid-1950s, when the JCP shifted its position somewhat and made some effort to disassociate itself from this early "heresy." The Czech arms deal in 1955 and the growing rapprochement between Egypt and the Soviet Union (which strengthened the position of all leftist-oriented groups in the area) enabled the JCP to enjoy the best of both worlds: it could simultaneously openly declare its support for Egyptian President Gamal Abd al-Nasser and thereby affirm its commitment to the Arab nationalist cause and also flaunt its alliance with the Soviet Union, now the champion of the Arabs, and justify the path it had followed in the past. It is hardly surprising, therefore, that the years of the Moscow-Cairo close cooperation (1956–57) and the attendant enthusiasm for the Soviet Union in the Middle East coincided with the peak period of the JCP's success in the West Bank. The Soviet agreement to finance the construction of the Aswan High Dam in Egypt in 1958 gave a further boost to pro-Communist sentiment in the area, and enabled the JCP to survive the unremitting harassment it was then undergoing by the Jordanian Security Services.

In retrospect it is evident that it was the nature of the party's early public activity that determined the path it followed in later years. The proletariat—workers and farmers—was in the early 1950s, as we have seen, largely written off as insignificant. Thus little effort was directed toward recruiting new members from its ranks, and socioeconomic subjects were, though not totally neglected, given secondary importance in the party's debates and publications.

The high percentage of teachers in the party's ranks was not only a function of the relatively high level of education needed to fully understand and appreciate its ideology but was also the direct result of the deliberate attempt to recruit new members from the schools. The party saw a number of advantages in recruiting teachers. First and most important, it was the safest and most effective way of penetrating the schools and bringing party influence to bear on the students. The party had a two-fold interest in the students: in the short term, students played a major part in distributing the party's leaflets and pamphlets in the towns; in the longer view, the students, young, impressionable, and open to new ideas, were an ideal source of future recruits (although many students lost interest and grew away from the party as soon as they left school). Second, it was government policy to transfer teachers from place to place every few years, thereby unwittingly helping spread the party's influence to areas it might otherwise never have reached. Finally, emigration of teachers (and intellectuals in general) to the surrounding Arab countries enabled the party to disseminate its ideas and gain recruits throughout the Arab world (according to one source, an estimated one thousand new activists were acquired in this way).

One of the ways in which the party tried to influence those groups which most interested it (that is, the intellectuals) was to project a suitable image—having among its leaders a number of highly educated men, several of whom were doctors. This public relations tactic was not universally approved by the party leadership. The recruitment of Dr. Nabih Irshidat and Dr. Yaqub Ziyadin in the early 1950s met with some resistance, less so in the case of Dr. Ziyadin, who was well liked by the local population for the free treatment he offered the needy, but certainly in the case of Dr. Irshidat, who was a considerable property owner. Some people, however, considered Irshidat's property ownership an advantage, as his wealth enabled him to acquire considerable support. This attitude applied also to Rushdi Shahin, who owned large tracts of land in Beit Dajan and Beit Furiq.

The most higly regarded of all the other party leaders was the secretary-general, Fuad Nassar. Nassar was idolized by the party's rank-and-file for his honesty, his shrewdness, his fine oratory, his powerful personality, his deep commitment to his ideals, and, above all, his unassuming image as a "man of the people." He owed his prominence in the party to these leadership qualities alone, and unlike Ziyadin or Irshidat had no formal education, owned little property, and came from humble origins. Even the fact that he was a Christian failed to detract from his paramount position in a party whose membership was primarily Muslim. (Here, Nassar was something of a phenomenon: in most Communist parties in the Arab world to be other than a Muslim Arab was an almost insurmountable obstacle to powers, and on several occasions a Christian or non-Arab leader found himself ousted and replaced by a Muslim Arab. It was Nassar who, as we have seen, determined the party's orientation toward the intellectuals in the early 1950s, his view prevailing over that of Ridwan al-Hilu, another veteran leader, who was subsequently forced to leave the party (although he continued to remain one of its most loyal sympathizers and supporters).

Even in retrospect it is difficult to single out any serious tactical mistake made by the party. The factors that prevented the party from achieving more than it did were largely beyond its control. The constant hounding and harassment by the authorities undoubtedly played a major role. The party's unpopular stand on the Palestine question, to which it was ideologically committed and which it could not easily reject without losing credibility, must also have impeded its progress. The party's deliberate decision to neglect the workers and concentrate on the intellectuals must have cost it some support among the proletariat, but this was more than counteracted by the gains it made among the intellectuals. The Baath drew away some of the JCP's potential supporters by appealing to the same sectors of the population, enjoying what among certain groups was the advantage of not being associated with the Soviet Union. The serious rift between Abd al-Nasser and the Kremlin in the late 1950s also probably cost the party some support, as Nasser was at the peak of his popularity in the Arab world at that time. The antireligious tenets inherent in the Communist ideology undoubtedly greatly hampered the party's progress in an area which was still largely conservative, although, at the height of its rivalry with the Baath in the mid-1950s, party activists were instructed to refrain from openly expressing antireligious sentiments, to avoid drinking wine in public, and to keep women veiled.

IDEOLOGY

Anti-imperialism

The source of all the problems that had afflicted the Arab world, and especially Palestine, was "imperialism" (*al-istimar*). The term clearly referred at first to Britain, although this was not usually spelled out. It was the British who had turned the Jews and the Arabs against each other in Palestine, and who had practiced a policy of racial discrimination in wages, work conditions, and other areas. It was the British who in 1948 had tried to undermine the UN partition plan (which the Communists supported), who drove the Arab League and the Palestinian leadership to oppose the plan, resulting in the flight of Arabs from the area allocated to the Jewish state and thwarting any possibility of economic and perhaps even political cooperation between the two states which were meant to be created in Palestine.[71]

The crimes of imperialism were not, however, relegated to the past. It was the party's view that imperialism was still an active policy, being applied in new and various ways toward the same end: to extend the influence and control of imperialism over the Arab countries and, in particular, to regain its position in those Arab countries from which it had been evicted (Egypt, after 1955; Jordan, in 1956;[72] and Syria, after 1958). The ultimate aim, the party held, was to turn the Middle East into a huge arsenal and base from which to launch an attack on the Soviet Union.

The arch-imperialist power was at first considered to be Britain. Later, however, the United States was also condemned, and "Anglo-American Imperialism" became a catch-phrase in the party's literature. The two imperialist powers were held to have clearly defined spheres of influence in the area: Britain's being Jordan (which it wished to turn into a "British colony"[73]) and America's being in Israel. Abdallah, Britain's "lackey" in the area, was assassinated by U.S. agents,[74] the party maintained, in order for the U.S. to set up its own puppet in Jordan, Abdallah's son Talal. America thus took over Britain's role in the country, issuing daily orders to Talal through the U.S. ambassador in Amman "and other experts in reactionary subversion."[75] Thus despite their common objectives in the area, the two imperialist allies were sometimes engaged in open rivalry. The dispute in the Arab League concerning the annexation of the West Bank to Transjordan was, in the party's view, another instance of this rivalry, with the U.S. opposing annexation, through Egypt, and Britain favoring it, through Transjordan.[76] The party saw this internal rivalry as a fundamental weakness of the imperialists which would ultimately result in their downfall. When this happened, the Palestinians—the prime victims of imperialism— would be the main beneficiaries. All this was viewed in the broader international context, in which the imperialist camp was seen as growing progressively weaker while the democratic camp headed by the Soviet Union was becoming progressively more powerful. Accordingly, it was in the Arabs' interest to ally themselves with those who were on the ascendant—despite the fact that with its inevitable eclipse, imperialism would eventually lose its influence in the area anyway.

While this international scenario was being played out, the im- perialists addressed themselves to forwarding their aims in the area itself. After achieving their first objective, preventing the imple- mentation of the UN partition plan, they turned to their next: that of forging an alliance between Israel, the Arab countries, and Tur- key. This was part of their plan, the party believed, to build up a base in the area for aggression against the Soviet Union. It was in this context that the party viewed the tripartite declaration in 1950, the Baghdad Pact in 1955, and the Eisenhower Doctrine in 1957. From the failures of imperialism in the past, the party drew conclusions concerning the fate of its future designs, stressing that these were inimicable to the Arabs' interests and would thus be vigorously opposed by the Arabs.[77] In order to get the Arabs to cooperate with their various plans, the party charged, the imperial- ists made use of their lackeys in the area—such as the king in Jor- dan. The imperialists advanced this objective, furthermore, by build- ing up military power in Israel (Israel, the party noted, had a large army on the Jordanian border and periodically launched massive strikes against villages, such as Qibya and Nahhalin, in the West Bank) to show just how weak the Arabs really were. This, accord- ing to the argument, would bring the Arabs into greater reliance on the imperialist powers, and perhaps even into a security pact with Israel. The role of the Soviet Union in the creation of the Jewish state was conveniently ignored from the early 1950s on, and Israel was seen exclusively as an "imperialist creation" and an "illegal state,"[78] whose sole purpose was to serve imperialist inter- ests in the Middle East.

Imperialism was at work throughout the world, the party charged, and consequently its successes as well as its failures elsewhere were of significance for the Middle East. Its machinations in the Arab world, the party pointed out, extended from North Africa through Amman to Baghdad. It is interesting to note that, while the JCP fully supported the Arab revolts against the French in North Africa, France was never specifically singled out for the type of censure reserved for the arch-imperialist powers, Britain and America.

The Soviet Union

The antithesis of imperialism, according to the JCP was, naturally, the Soviet Union and the socialist camp. In the view of the party, the socialist countries, spearheaded by the Soviet Union, being locked in a global conflict with the imperialists, headed by Britain and the United States, were eager to help and support those regimes that were working to throw off the imperialist yoke. Furthermore, as the champion of the democratic cause throughout the world and the true friend of the people everywhere, the Soviet Union was ipso facto also the true friend and champion of the Arabs (and, for that matter, the Jews).[79] Finally, there existed a clear community of interest between the socialist countries and the Arabs in the advancement of world peace. In Jordan, for example, some forty thousand signatures were collected on a petition calling for world peace—indisputable proof, the party argued, of the extent to which the Jordanian people (as opposed to their rulers) identified with the aims of the Soviet Union.[80] But in addition to all these ideological reasons, there were sound pragmatic reasons for the party's pro-Soviet orientation. The Soviet Union, after all, bordered on the Middle East, and was commonly referred to as "our generous neighbor."[81] Even more common was the argument that the Soviet Union had on several occasions in the past proven its genuine concern for the well-being of the Arab people, and so could be counted on to prove a reliable friend in the future as well. Soviet support of the UN partition plan in the late 1940s was pointed to as proof that Moscow had the real interests of the Arabs at heart. (This argument was conveniently dropped in the 1950s, and examples of Soviet goodwill were sought in Moscow's support in the United Nations for the Arab cause (its support for the Jordanian position after Israel's raid against Nahhalin, for example).[82] From the mid-1950s on, following the Czech arms deal, the economic and military aid that the Soviet Union provided Egypt was summoned as unmistakable proof of the type of support Moscow was prepared to give the Arab nations.

It was thus beyond all dispute, the party believed, that the leaders of the Arab world owed it to their people to recognize their true interests, ally themselves with the Soviet Union, and identify with its goals. Such identification should extend to the Soviet Union's role not only in the Midde East but elsewhere in the world as well. Thus North Korea's struggle against the South should be viewed as a just war and its victories seen as being in some degree the victories of the Palestinian people too.[83] Such identification should be total the party argued and so took issue with two common and, it believed, ill-informed claims: that there existed a threat of "Communist infiltration" into the area, and that there existed an alternative of "neutrality" vis-à-vis the two international camps. The first claim the JCP dismissed simply as being without foundation: the Soviet Union, it pointed out, had demonstrated the sincerity of its intensions in the Middle East by helping Egypt rid itself of its imperialist masters in 1956, by its unwavering support for the Arabs at the United Nations, and by its other activities in the area.[84] The call for a policy of neutrality in the struggle between the two major camps was first aired in the press in the early 1950s by such statesmen as Maruf Dawalibi and Mustafa al-Sibai in Syria, and Hafiz Ramadan and Fikri Abaza in Egypt. The party rejected this argument out of hand, claiming that it was propounded by people associated with Arab imperialism—the same people who had supported the invasion of Palestine yet simultaneously opposed the call for a ban on nuclear weapons. It was simply a stratagem designed to divert the attention of the people away from their struggle for national liberation and away from the treachery of their leaders. Thus there was no need to adopt a neutral position between the two rival camps, the party insisted, as the Arab people *belonged* in the camp headed by the Soviets, which opposed western imperialism and worked for international peace.[85]

Socioeconomics

Rather surprisingly for a Communist party, socioeconomic matters did not figure prominently in the JCP's publications. *Al-Muqawama al-Shaabiya* often did not cover these matters at all, and the party's leaflets, when they did cover them, usually gave them only brief, superficial attention. In those issues of *Muqawama* that do deal with socioeconomics, the subject takes up no more than 10 to 15 percent of the total copy. Even in their election campaigns and parliamentary activities, the party's representatives gave only cursory treatment to the issue. When the party outlined its objectives at the end of 1949, the struggle for social equality was mentioned only in third place, after its internal and external political objectives. Only in the leaflets issued to commemorate May 1 did the party give prominence to socioeconomic matters. Then its political preoccupations were momentarily eclipsed by the call for workers' solidarity and the slogan "Bread and Liberty," its analysis of international events colored by a socioeconomic awareness, with the decadent West portrayed as suffering one economic crisis after another while the socialist countries were marking up impressive economic successes. In this context, the countries of the Middle East too (including Israel, Jordan, and Palestine) were seen as approaching the point of revolutionary crisis.[86] The party was aware of the importance of socioeconomic issues, but deliberately chose to relegate them to second place. It felt the need to defend its position,[87] and explained to the working masses that their situation would improve, in the Middle East as a whole and in Jordan in particular, only after "the nationalistic tide" had succeeded in sweeping aside their present regimes. In other words, the precedence accorded to nationalist demands was seen as an essential preliminary stage before the social and economic problems besetting the area could be adequately dealt with. In the meanwhile, however, it would be necessary to continue to press for an improvement in the conditions of workers by demanding, for example, an eight-hour working day and a six-day work week. Nevertheless, the workers had to realize that the national interest came before special interests, and they were asked to cooperate with "the local industrialists" in an effort to develop and revive that sector of the economy.

The party drew a clear distinction between the masses, as an amorphous body, and the traditional leadership class—"the claimants to leadership"—which it identified with "reaction," or "reactionary feudalism."[88] By "reactionaries," the party meant all those who were not laborers, farmers, working intellectuals, or petty merchants and small property owners—in other words, "the noble nationalists."[89] Apart from the "noble nationalists" whose common denominator was primarily political and somewhat vague, all the others were relatively clearly defined social groups considered to be the antithesis of the "reactionary" classes. Reaction was the source of all the political problems besetting Jordan, because of its close identification with imperialism, and it was also the source of all the country's social and economic evils. It was reaction that prompted the Palestinians to leave their homes "only briefly" in 1948, and that prevented the emergence of a genuine nationalist movement in Mandatory Palestine. The reactionary classes were also accused of having cooperated with the British in Palestine to prevent the establishment of an adequate educational system and a free press. And after the catastrophe of 1948, the reactionaries were accused of seeking to perpetuate the miseries of the refugees, as this would enable them to take over the deserted villages and acquire their lands cheaply. They were further accused of embezzling the aid designed for the refugees, seizing control of the West Bank's economy, and acquiring key positions in the Hashemite administration.[90] The solution to all Jordan's ills lay in the overthrow of this reactionary leadership and its replacement by leaders who would truly represent the people[91] set about carrying out the necessary reforms.

However, the reactionary classes continued to rule the country. It was hardly surprising, therefore, the party argued, that the country's social and economic situation steadily grew worse. The various administrations continued to spend the bulk of their revenues (some 75 percent, the Communists claimed) on building up the army. Only a very small portion of the budget went toward education, health services, and alleviating unemployment, the party charged. Jordan was economically backward—its people plagued by unemployment, its farmers barely eking out a subsistence, its traditional crafts dying out in the face of foreign imports—not because of any fundamental deficiency but because of the corruption and inefficiency of its rulers. The situation could be greatly improved by short-term measures: diverting a greater proportion of the budget away from the army and toward developing the economy; lowering taxes; and restricting imports of goods that could be produced locally (in March 1953, for example, the party argued that the import of shoes severely affected the local shoe industry in Nablus). These, however, could be no more than palliative measures; the real, long-term solution would come with the establishment of a regime that would be prepared to ally itself with the socialist countries, would develop the natural resources of the country, would introduce a progressive system of taxation (with luxuries being heavily taxed) and would implement a thorough agrarian reform.[92]

The party, apart from criticizing the general social and economic ills of the country, would also occasionally single out the problems facing those sectors it felt to be most severely victimized by the

67

existing system—farmers and urban workers, among others. It is interesting that, despite noting the difficult conditions of the laborers (at the phosphates plant in Rusayfa, for example) and white-collar workers (at the electricity corporation in Jerusalem), the party on no occasion called on them to strike. While it would voice its approval of any strike taken on the workers' own initiative (that of the stonemasons in Bethlehem, the teachers in Nablus, or merchants in various West Bank towns),[93] the party would go no further. It was concerned with these developments in so far as they served to bear out its general thesis—that the unrest of the workers was merely a symptom of the general bankruptcy of the existing order in Jordan. But the ultimate salvation of the workers lay, the party believed, not in isolated strikes in individual plants but in the overthrow of the reactionary regime.

The Orientation Issue: Workers or Intellectuals?

The debate concerning the party's basic orientation—toward the proletariat or toward the intellectuals—was one that embroiled not only the JCP, but also its brother Communist parties elsewhere in the Arab world (in the Egyptian Communist Party it was this issue that divided the MELN wing led by Henri Curiel and the ISKRA wing led by Hillel Schwartz).[94]

The line taken by the JCP following the debate between Fuad Nassar and Ridwan al-Hilu in the early 1950s,[95] in favor of building up its cadres from the country's intellectuals rather than its workers, was also that ultimately followed by most Communist parties in the Arab world.[96] While this policy conformed with the Leninist avant-garde concept, it ran counter to the subsequent position of the Communist movement, which favored working primarily among the proletarian classes and including a high proportion of workers in its ranks.[97] Nevertheless, Fuad Nassar's view was undoubtedly the most realistic, given existing conditions in the West Bank. With a small and politically unaware proletariat in the area, and a peasant population that was even less aware politically, it was only natural that the JCP should turn to the intellectuals and lower middle classes at least as a preliminary step in building up its cadres.

Because the position it had been forced to adopt ran counter to the official Communist doctrine, the JCP, like its brother parties in the Arab world, refrained from giving it ideological formulation. But in its day-to-day activities, the party was clearly firmly based on the intellectuals. In its official publications, however, workers and fellahin were virtually always mentioned first. This followed traditional Communist practice throughout the world, and the JCP could not easily abandon it, even though it did not reflect the actual situation. The various pamphlets put out by the party did, however, also address themselves to other groups—intellectuals, women, students—which they considered the more important. Most of these groups were usually organized in various "front" organizations, such as students' or women's associations and youth leagues. The JCP also frequently addressed itself to the "uprooted" (that is, the refugees). This was somewhat a departure from traditional Communist practice as the refugees did not constitute a socioeconomic "class" by accepted definition; but the policy could be justified as an attempt to influence a downtrodden and frustrated group to forward the party's aims. Even more unusual for a Communist party was the JCP's practice of appealing to the "petty merchant" class and professionals (as opposed to the "intellectuals," in the traditional vocabulary) and white-collar workers (mainly clerks).[98] Occasionally, the party also addressed itself to the "national industrialists," clearly in an effort to bring them into its ranks.[99] Such overtures are not to be confused with the party's appeals to the workers to cooperate with "national industry" as part of the struggle against imperialist penetration of the area. One was part of the party's drive for new members from among the industrialist class; the latter simply sought to effect a temporary alliance[100] between the workers and their masters in the common nationalist interest— a phenomenon frequently observed in Communist parties in the Third World.

The groups to which the party directed its appeals are apparent not only from the formal headings on its publications but also from the content: the groups addressed in both places often conformed. Just as the heading gave precedence to the traditional proletarian classes, so the text—whenever dealing with socioeconomic matters— first addressed the workers and the trade unions. The JCP waged a constant—though sporadic—battle for shorter working hours. It defended construction workers in Salt, strongly attacked the dismissal of workers in the phosphate industry, and repeatedly called for fair wages. It also supported the strikes called by various workers (the quarry workers, for example), but, as already mentioned, never actually instigated strikes.[101] Such attention—though limited in quantitative terms—to the problems of the proletariat was, of course, only natural for any Communist party. But the JCP also directed its attention to the problem facing other groups. In its local publications, the party gave considerable notice to the problems facing the fellahin—a practice not unknown in other Communist parties, but always secondary to the attention paid to the problems facing laborers. The Hashemite regime received constant scathing criticism: it failed to provide adequate veterinary services in the West Bank; it did nothing about the scandalous hiking of seed prices by rich merchants in Hebron; it ignored the rising cost of water; it was indifferent to the callous exploitation of the tobacco growers by the cigarette companies; and it exacted exorbitant taxes from the farmers.[102] The JCP called on the farmers to organize themselves in each of their villages and later to form a common front with the country's workers.[103] At least in one instance, members were specifically instructed to work among the fellahin and win them over to the side of the party.[104] (This, however, may have been an isolated attempt to expand the base of the party once it had already established itself among the urban intellectuals and workers.)

Even more unusual, however, was the attention which the party paid in its various publications to groups generally ignored or even despised by most other Communist parties. It strongly attacked the government's new taxation law in May 1955,[105] which, the party complained, struck at shopkeepers, artisans, and vendors. The party supported these decidedly "bourgeois" groups, just as it had supported the petty merchants in Bethlehem, Ramallah, and Jericho when they struck against the new tax.[106] And, as already mentioned, the JCP supported the clerks at the Jerusalem Electricity Corporation[107] and the teachers' strike in Nablus.[108] In the same way, after the Free Officers in Egypt turned to the Soviet Union in the mid-1950s, the JCP began to show an interest in the army officers in Jordan, revising its previous position that they were the sworn watchdogs of the reactionary Hashemite regime and seeing them anew as potential revolutionaries.[109] The JCP's attempts to bring these groups into its ranks was an unusual characteristic of the party.

The JCP's Self-image

The distinction between the general masses, which were largely reactionary, and the revolutionary avant-garde was constantly applied to the situation in Jordan. But the JCP made one further, important, distinction: between the Palestinians and the Transjordanians.

The Palestinians, unlike the other Arab nations, had not yet acquired the national self-determination to which they aspired and to which they were entitled under the United Nations partition plan. Instead, the area allocated to the Palestinians had been overrun by the Arab armies. The Jordanian prime minister, Tawfiq abu al-Huda, in an interview published in the Egyptian weekly *Rose al-Youssef* stated explicitly that in the area conquered by the Arab Legion there would be no Palestinian state. The party strongly attacked this and similar statements, which it saw as part of the Hashemite plan "to annihilate the Palestinian Arab entity." This entity was viewed as distinct from the Jordanians, having its own separate "homeland" (*watan*).[110] This attitude accounted for the party's fierce objection to Abdallah's "imperialistic" intention of annexing the West Bank to his kingdom ("the annexation of our homeland to the colony of his [Abdallah's] British masters"). The term "West Bank" is never mentioned in party literature, and even long after the annexation, the party made a clear territorial distinction between "Palestine" and "Transjordan."[111]

A recurring motif in the party's publications is the conflict of interests between the people and their rulers in Jordan. Abdallah is referred to as an "Imperialist dog," a term also applied to the British commander of the Arab Legion, Glubb Pasha. Many demonstrations which took place in the different towns of the West Bank are described as anti-imperialist—first, against the imperialist plot to annex the West Bank to Transjordan and, later, against the imperialist plan to bring Jordan into the Baghdad Pact. Abdallah's transfer of Jerusalem (though the historical truth of this event is contested), parts of the Hebron district, and the Arab "Triangle" to Ben Gurion are described as acts of treason;[112] the formal annexation of the West Bank was seen as an attempt to rule out finally the possibility of setting up an independent Palestinian state in the area. Thus it was not enough merely to change the Hashemite regime; the "criminal traitor Abdallah" had to die.[113] The so-called "democratic" institutions of Jordan were seen as having been designed for one purpose alone—to serve the class of exploiters who ruled the country. The party charged that the general elections were invariably accompanied by campaigns of terror and intimidation in the towns and villages of the West Bank, and that the results were always rigged, to assure that the ruling classes remained in power. Even so, the party claimed, the elected government failed to receive a popular mandate, with only a small portion of the population participating in the elections (the party placed the percentage poll in the 1950 elections, for example, at no more than 20 percent of the 200,000 eligible voters).[114] Despite its view of the Hashemite regime as being fundamentally anti-democratic, the JCP was prepared to judge that regime in the light of its policies. Thus the expulsion of Glubb Pasha by Husayn in 1956 and the shift in the king's previous positions earned him considerable praise both in the party's publications and from its members in the House of Representatives in Amman. But when Husayn returned to his previous policies, the JCP resumed its attack on him and his administration, once again stressing the deep rift that existed between the Jordanian people and their rulers, accusing the army of committing atrocities in the rural areas, and even hinting at concessions that the Hashemite regime was making to Israel.[115]

The Palestinians and the Transjordanians alike, the party claimed, were fully aware of just how evil their rulers were and expressed their opposition in numerous popular demonstrations. These demonstrations against the regime were supposedly inspired and led first by the National Liberation League and later by the Jordanian Communist Party. Since the Communist party was the "avant-garde of the struggling masses," the people should rally to its standard and take its lead from the party's leaders. In an effort to stress its revolutionary character, notwithstanding that this might cost it many potential members, the party gave wide publicity to the authorities' attempts to crack down on it and restrict its activities. The arrest and trials of such key party activists as Ridwan al-Hilu, Khaldun Abd al-Haqq, Rashid al-Habbab, and, above all, Fuad Nassar, were widely covered, with lengthy extracts from the proceedings and descriptions of the popular support throughout the Arab world for the defendants.[116] The identification of the masses with the aims of the party was seen as beyond all doubt—although few attempts were made to assess the actual numerical strength of the support enjoyed by the party. On the few occasions that the party did report actual numbers, the counts were reasonable (it claimed that some two hundred sympathizers signed a petition in Nablus in 1950 calling for the release of jailed party activists, a figure at most only moderately inflated).[117]

How, then, did the party consider that it should go about achieving its objectives? Realizing its limited numerical strength, the party tried, naturally, to attract members and supporters. From

1948 on, it adopted the name "Popular [or National] Front."[118] The Front was very broadly defined: it included the workers and farmers, democratic intellectuals, petty merchants, and small property owners. The solid foundation of the Front was to be provided by the workers and farmers, but these could be joined by members of any other class who identified with the national goals—first and foremost, the creation of an independent state in Palestine.[119] All parties were entitled—even *obliged*—to join this "Popular Front," including the Arab Nationalists, the Baath, and even the Muslim Brothers. The JCP was fully prepared to enter into an alliance with these parties, notwithstanding their political or even religious differences.[120] In 1954 the party spelled out quite openly the advantages that the "Popular Front" name had brought it, earning the support of the masses and even of nationalist leaders who did not share its political philosophy.[121] Later, however, the JCP rejected any possibility of an alliance with the Syrian Nationalists or with the Muslim Brothers, both of which it described as imperialist agents and the enemies of the people; but the call for national unity persisted. The establishment of the National Front in Nablus in the mid-1950s was seen by the party as a major achievement. When the Arab Nationalists broke away in 1956, leading to the Front's dissolution, the party made considerable efforts to persuade them to rejoin.[122] The importance of national unity to the party's strategy is illuminated by an open letter of mid-1956 from Fahmi al-Salfiti to King Husayn. Praising the king for his recent moves and expressing the hope that he would continue to fight imperialism in Jordan, al-Salfiti went on to ask the king to set up a government that would carry out a "nationalist, independent and democratic" policy, noting that the JCP would have no objection to being excluded from such a government, provided only that it were set up.[123] Al-Salfiti's public renouncement on behalf of the JCP of any claim to a share in ruling the country testifies to the party's awareness of how opposed to its ideas the public, and certainly the ruling establishment, in fact were—even at the height of pro-socialist sentiment in Jordan. At the same time, however, al-Salfiti's letter testifies to the degree of self-confidence the party possessed and to its realistic appreciation that this path afforded it the best chance of achieving its ultimate objective.

The Refugee Question and the UN Partition Plan

The party's demand that the United Nations partition plan be implemented to the letter and that the refugees be permitted to return to their homes, either in Israel or in the Palestinian state that was to be created alongside it, was pressed while the 1948 war was still in progress.[124] When the war ended and the situation in the area remained frozen, the party began to attack those whom it considered responsible for the refugees' plight. Applying the Marxist theory that capitalism needs a certain degree of unemployment in order to keep down wages, the party blamed "Jewish reaction and the imperialist Arab regimes" for seeking to perpetuate the refugee problem. This, they argued, would permit Arab feudal lords to exploit the refugees as a source of cheap labor; Arab capitalists would be able to take over the land they had abandoned; and the imperialist powers would be able to employ the refugees in implementing their aggressive plans in the area. Reactionaries on both sides were anxious to keep "racial hatred" alive between Jew and Arab, and the perpetuation of the refugee problem was one way of achieving this.[125] The JCP scornfully rejected the aid being offered to the refugees by the United Nations Relief and Works Agency (UNRWA). It called for the rejection of all attempts by that agency to settle the refugees in permanent homes, as well as of rehabilitation projects such as that initiated by Musa Alami, viewing them as part of the plot to prevent the "return" of the refugees and the settlement of the refugee problem.[126] Its attacks on the international organizations providing aid to the refugees did not deter the JCP from approaching these same bodies for financial help; the party saw itself as the natural and authentic voice of the refugees, and felt that aid to the refugees should be channeled through it.[127] As the refugees' representative, the party attacked the Red Cross, accusing it of corruption and inefficiency, yet at the same time demanded that it do something to improve housing and sanitary conditions in the camps. The party tried to organize the refugees in the camps, inciting them to reject the patronage that various dignitaries tried to impose on them.[128]

There can be little doubt that the JCP hoped at first that such grassroots organization would become one of its most important activities. The party's interest in the refugees would seem to indicate that it viewed them as an indispensable component of the amorphic mass awaiting the guidance and leadership of the revolutionary avant-garde. This view also dictated the party's attitude to the question of a Palestinian state. The JCP demanded that both Israel and the Arab states that had occupied the territory allotted to the Palestinians under the UN partition plan withdraw and enable the creation of an "independent and democratic" Palestinian-Arab state that would gather in its exiles.[129] This state, the Communists held, could come about only in the context of "solidarity with the peace-loving nations of the world," and as part of the struggle against imperialism. The label "democratic" hints at the nature of the state envisaged by the Communists: that is, one oriented toward the Soviet Union, while its political system was socialist or even Communist.[130] Only such a state in "the Arab part of Palestine" would be able to live in real peace with Israel, where the JCP expected a similar revolution to take place. The relationship between the brother Arab and Jewish states in Palestine would then be one of "cooperation and amity."[131]

The adoption of an uncompromising nationalist position vis-à-vis Israel in the mid-1950s indelibly affected the party's attitude on the Palestine question: it was now the Israeli leaders alone who were guilty of aggression against the Arab states and who were responsible for the plight of the refugees. Israel was pursuing this policy in the interests of imperialism, and with the connivance of Turkey, also the enemy of the Arab peoples. Thus the party's earlier dream of peaceful coexistence with Israel was abandoned. The party continued to press for the right of the refugees to return to their homes in Israel, but without implying, as it had in the past, that this would pave the way to peace with the Jewish state.[132]

The JCP's earlier demand for the establishment of an "independent, democratic Palestinian-Arab state" was gradually forgotten, and when it supported the demand for Israel's withdrawal from Sinai and the Gaza Strip following the 1956 Suez War, it called for the return of Gaza not to the Palestinians but to Egypt. Presumably, the JCP found it difficult at this stage to oppose the pro-Soviet Egyptian regime's return to the Gaza Strip. The implication is clearly that the JCP considered the major issue at this time to be the conflict between the "Socialist" camp (represented by Egypt) and the "Imperialist" camp (represented by Israel). The creation of a Palestinian state would have to wait: the main objective was to promote Soviet influence, through Egypt, in the area.

The Egyptian-inspired pan-Arab ideal which swept through the area in the mid-1950s undoubtedly contributed to the JCP's relegation of the Palestinian question to a position of secondary importance. The Palestine problem and the plight of the refugees were seen as part of the larger pan-Arab complex, and the wrong done to the Palestinians was presented as a crime perpetrated against the *entire* Arab nation. The question of Palestine's independence was no longer viewed as important as the fact that Palestine was, first and foremost, Arab.[133] The JCP accordingly paid increasingly less attention to Palestinian particularism and viewed itself increasingly more in the context of pan-Arabism.

Arab-Israeli Relations

The JCP radically shifted its position on the UN partition plan and the issues stemming from it—Israel's right to exist, the question of an independent Palestine, and the Arab invasion of Palestine in 1948. The shift was motivated by several political developments in the area, primarily the Soviet Union's revision of its policy in the Middle East.

The party's original position found expression in 1948–49. At this time, the Soviet Union stood behind Israel, providing the nascent state with considerable military and political support. Accordingly, the Communists in the West Bank directed their attacks against the Arab armies that had invaded Palestine, seeing Israel as the victim of these reactionary Arab states and imperialism. The establishment of an independent Palestinian state alongside Israel, in the area allotted to the Arabs under the partition plan, was then a central pillar of the party's platform.

The next phase, between 1950 and 1955, was marked by a steady deterioration in Israeli-Soviet relations. This was reflected in a parallel deterioration in the JCP's attitude toward Israel's leadership: the party began to attack the Ben Gurion administration, equating it with the reactionary Arab regimes in the area, but at the same time sympathizing with the citizens of the state.

The third phase, which began at the end of 1955 and continued until the early 1960s, coincided with the growing Soviet influence in Egypt and Syria, and the spread of Abd al-Nasser's concept of pan-Arabism. During this period, the JCP began to question Israel's very right to exist, and the idea of an independent Palestinian state in the area allotted under the UN partition plan receded still further into the background, replaced by a growing demand for the creation of an Arab state in the *whole* of Palestine.

The National Liberation League and its successor, the Jordanian Communist Party, had at first consistently supported the UN partition plan. This stand was primarily the result of Moscow's position on the subject, but was presented as part of the party's ideological commitment to the right of both the Jewish and the Palestinian-

Arab peoples to set up independent political entities of their own in Palestine. Not only did the two peoples have an equal right to such an entity but they shared a common interest in seeing that this right was fully realized; thus whoever opposed the implementation of the UN partition plan was acting against the desires and interests of the inhabitants of Palestine. The 1948 war was viewed accordingly as a British-American imperialist plot, instigated by petroleum interests, designed to deceive both the surrounding Arab states and the Palestinian Arabs. The imperialists used the Arab League, which was seen as an imperialist tool, to achieve their design. The Arab League's claim that it had intervened on behalf of the Arabs of Palestine was rejected as a blatant lie; the party pointed out that the Palestinian Arabs had neither desired nor requested the League's intervention. The Arab League's real motive, the party charged, was to forestall the creation of an independent Arab state in Palestine and to enable the annexation of the West Bank to Transjordan. Thus what occurred in May 1948, the Communists arued, was an "Arab invasion," an "aggressive war," which turned more than half a million Palestinian Arabs into homeless refugees. These views were akin to those expressed by Andrei Gromyko at the United Nations in May 1948. It is hardly surprising, therefore, that while the war was still raging the Communists in Palestine demanded that the *Arab leaders* withdraw their invading armies so the local Arabs could implement the partition resolution in direct cooperation with the Jews of the country.[134]

The signing of the armistice agreements with several Arab countries in 1949 was viewed by the party as officially confirming the Arab conquest of Palestine, and further proof of the treachery of the Arab leaders who had been prepared to forefeit in negotiations with Israel parts of "our [that is, Arab] Palestine." Even then the withdrawal of the Arab armies was presented as the Palestinian people's prime objective; a similar withdrawal of Israeli troops from those parts of Palestine allotted to the Arabs under the partition plan was presented as only the third of the Palestinians' three major objectives.[135] At this time no complaints were directed at the Jewish state or its leaders. Israel was seen as an innocent victim of the same imperialist plot that had deprived the Palestinians of their rights. What criticism existed was directed at those Jewish "reactionaries" who, in collusion with their fellow reactionaries in the Arab world and the imperialists, had brought catastrophe to Palestine. But these Jewish reactionaries were on no account to be

identified with the Israeli leadership; on the contrary, they constituted the right-wing opposition to the leadership in Israel. The Deir
Yassin massacre was seen as the symbol of this Jewish reaction:
the Communists charged that when the inhabitants of the village
refused to reach an understanding with the Jews as they had been
asked to by the Arab Council, they provided the Jewish underground minority group, the Irgun, with the opportunity to perpe-
trate the atrocity, which was publicly condemned by the nonreac-
tionary Jewish community in Palestine ("all the Jewish democratic
parties" and the Jewish Agency). This and other atrocities committed in Arab villages after they were captured caused distress not
only to the Arabs but also to the majority of Jews in Palestine, the
Communists argued.[136]

The second phase commenced in the second half of 1949 and
continued throughout 1950. The party began to draw a distinction
between the Jewish citizens of Israel and the Israeli leadership,
which was increasingly considered just as evil as the reactionary
Arab regimes of the area. The "reactionaries" in Israel now included
Ben Gurion and his administration in addition to the country's
right-wing opposition. The need to liberate the Arab part of Palestine from the armies of Ben Gurion, Faruq, and Abdallah was at
first all viewed as equally pressing. Later, however, the JCP revised
its view of the 1948 war: the Ben Gurion government was held
largely responsible for the war, which had expelled the refugees,
and was regarded as still persecuting the Arabs who remained under its control. The Israeli government was accused of hounding
Communists in Israel and of forging ever closer links with American imperialism—just as the reactionary Arab regimes were doing.
At the same time, the Arab regimes were accused of initiating
racial (anti-Jewish) hatred in the Arab world in an attempt to
divert the people's attention "from their own miserable plight"
and away from the regime's treacherous alliance with the imperialist powers. This racial hatred was exploited by the reactionary
government in Israel, which used it as an excuse to refuse to allow
the return of the refugees and to justify its harsh treatment of
Arabs in Israel. In this way the reactionary regimes in both Israel
and the Arab countries served each other's interests while giving
the impression of being enemies. The first step toward solving the
problems confronting both the Arab and the Jewish peoples and
settling the conflict between them, the Communists argued, would

be to get rid of Abdallah, Faruq, and the "criminal" Ben Gurion government.[137]

Later the JCP began to voice further reservations about Israel. By the beginning of 1953 the label "Zionist" was attached to the Israeli ruling establishment.[138] The JCP had before this avoided referring to Zionism, as the movement was frowned on not only by the Communist parties in the Arab countries but by the international Communist movement as well. Because it was not possible to reconcile Communist antipathy for Zionism with Moscow's de jure recognition of the Jewish state, the JCP chose to ignore that recognition. When the Soviet Union began to condemn Israel for its closening ties with the West, the JCP followed suit. The fact that Israel was a Zionist state need no longer be ignored, and the party began to attack Israel's Zionist identity more and more openly. There can be little doubt that the party's anti-Zionist pronouncements struck a responsive chord among the Arab population and greatly increased its popular appeal. But beyond its tactical or propagandistic significance, the new criticism of Zionism led the party to reevaluate the entire ideological basis of the Jewish state, which resulted in a growing hostility in its basic attitude to Israel.

The JCP's revised attitude also influenced its previous stand on peace (*sulh*) between Israel and the Arab states: henceforth, the party openly opposed such an eventuality. It justified this opposition by pointing out that such a peace would be "an imperialistic peace between the criminal Zionist Israeli government and the treacherous Arab governments," when the real objective should be "peace between the Jewish and Arab peoples." The kind of peace which the imperialist powers wished to impose on the area was designed to serve only their own interests: it would facilitate the cooperation of their agents in the Middle East and would lead to the creation of an aggressive military bloc directed against the Soviet Union. Such a peace was also undesirable as it would take no account of the refugee problem, and the right of the Palestinians to set up an independent state in the territory allotted to the Arabs under the 1947 partition plan.[139]

But while the JCP was becoming increasingly hostile toward Israel and its leadership, it continued to differentiate in most of its publications between the Zionist state and the Jewish inhabitants of that state. A large sector of the Jewish people in Palestine, the party argued, was acceptable as a legitimate part of the Third World.

The "Jewish people in Israel" were called upon, along with the peoples of Indonesia, Vietnam, Palestine and the rest of the Arab world, to see the light and throw off the yoke of imperialism in their countries, under the leadership of their workers. Thus Israel was accorded a measure of legitimacy insofar as, like the other countries of the Third World, it possessed "progressive," "democratic," and "popular" elements. These elements were represented primarily by the Israeli Communist Party, whose publications and pronouncements the JCP followed regularly with great interest. The party considered other sectors of the Israeli population, apart from the Communists, as also comprising "progressive" elements, and singled out for praise in its publications the criticism in the Knesset of the Nahhalin raid. These elements, the party believed, were on the ascendent and would eventually lead the masses in Israel (as would their counterparts in the Arab world) to the final victory.[140]

Until the mid-1950s, the JCP consistently demanded that the UN partition resolution be implemented. There could be no mistaking the party's view that an independent Palestinian state should be created *alongside* Israel, and not *instead of* it. Even its demand that the refugees be permitted to return to their homes in Israel was not presented as a tactic to undermine the integrity of the Jewish state. On the contrary, the intention was that the refugees should return and rebuild their homes "in a spirit of brotherhood and equality with the toiling Jewish masses."[141]

In conclusion, the 1950–55 period, despite a certain degree of ambiguity in the party's publications, was not marked by a change in the JCP's fundamental recognition of Israel's right to exist as the sovereign state of the Jewish people. However harsh its attacks on the country's leadership, the party was careful to balance these attacks with the expressions of support for the peace-loving Jewish masses in Israel, who were suffering under their present leaders and deserved better. Thus Israel was in effect regarded by the party as being no less legitimate than countries like Morocco, Iraq, Turkey —or even Jordan.

The third and final phase in the JCP's changing attitude toward Israel began in the mid-1950s. The party continued to attack the Israeli leadership, but from about 1954 on, it placed less stress on the positive and peace-loving nature of the Jewish people in Israel. References to the "progressive," "democratic," and "popular" forces in Israel disappeared from the party's publications, and only "the ruling clique" was mentioned.[142] Henceforth, Israel was no longer considered as belonging to that group of "normal" states in the Third World ruled by reactionary anti-Soviet rulers against their own will. In the party's attacks on Israel, the state and its people appeared to be wholly identified with its reactionary leadership. Nationalist slogans current among the Palestinians began to infiltrate the party's vocabulary. This process was particularly noticeable in 1956, starting first in the regional publications and gradually spreading to the party's official organ. Israel was now described as having been from its very inception an aggressive state. The "criminal Zionists" (no longer merely "the Zionist government") were imperialist lackeys, and were "digging their own graves" in the area;[143] Israel was an imperialist base;[144] it was wholly the creation of the Anglo-American imperialists whom the "criminal Zionists" continued to serve;[145] Israel was a "criminal state," all pressures from the imperialists to come to terms with it should be resisted; it should be fought "till the final victory." It was quite apparent by this time that, whereas the JCP had in the past rejected the prospect of an imperialist-imposed peace with Isreal, it now opposed peace with the Jewish state under any circumstances.[146] The party continued to press for the return to their homes in Israel, but, unlike in the past, no reference was made to the prospect of the Arab and Jewish peoples in Palestine living in peace and friendship. Khrushchev was quoted as saying that "Israel will not succeed in building an independent political entity on a [Jewish] sectarian base, just as it [Judaism] has failed to do so throughout its history." As a final nationalist aim, the party now presented "the Arabization of Palestine."[147] Whether or not Khrushchev was quoted accurately, there could be little doubt in the mind of the Arab reader that the Jews were no more than a religious community and so had no right to a state of their own. Palestine (by which the party apparently meant the whole of Palestine) was to become an Arab country. Israel, if it were to survive at all, would have to abandon its narrow sectarian basis.

A final indication of the JCP's retreat from its former unambiguous endorsement of Israel's right to exist was the almost total absence in its publications of any reference to the UN partition plan from about the mid-1950s on. The Soviet Union's role in the creation of Israel was ignored and the Jewish state was depicted as entirely the creation of the imperialist powers whose interests it continued to serve. The infiltration of the nationalist slogans into the party's literature resulted in the growing sense of Israel as an "evil" entity, confronting a united and fundamentally "positive" Arab nation. "The Arab position has always been one of self-defense," the party now maintained, and it is Israel alone that has to mend its ways.[148] This view represented a retreat not only from the party's former distinction between the Jewish masses in Palestine and the Israeli leadership but also from the traditional Communist distinction between "progressive" and "reactionary" forces in the Arab world.

Nevertheless, at no point did the JCP *explicitly* reject Israel's right to exist or renege on its former commitment to the UN partition plan. Not even the Soviet Union was prepared to make such a volte-face, so one could hardly have expected it of the JCP. There was, however, an unmistakable change in the party's formerly positive attitude toward the Jewish state, which stemmed from the growing rift between the Soviet Union and Israel and the concomitant rapprochement between the Soviets and the Arab nationalists following the Czech arms deal with Egypt in 1955. This undoubtedly paved the way for closer links between Communists and nationalists in the Arab world. The anti-imperialist nationalist slogans of the Baath and the Nasserite movements accorded well with the Soviet line, and so made them much more acceptable to the ideologues of the JCP. This also facilitated the party's adoption of other nationalist positions, not least of which was the traditional Arab nationalist hostility toward Israel. The attack on the Jewish state was given ideological justification as an attack on Zionism, the handmaiden of American imperialism.

Thus in a single decade a full cycle was completed. At first, the JCP fully supported the creation and existence of Israel, which was regarded as the Soviet Union's first potential foothold in the Middle East. Its support for Israel isolated the Communists and alienated the bulk of the Palestinian population, to whom acceptance of the Jewish state's existence was an unforgivable heresy. The party was prepared to suffer the consequences of this unpopular position, both because it had been dictated by Moscow and because it served as a test of its unshakable conviction in the rightness of its path, despite the antipathy of the unenlightened masses and the persecution of its members by the reactionary authorities. The decade ended with the JCP all but rejecting the right of the Jewish state to exist, and closing ranks with the Arab nationalist forces on this and several other issues.

The Arab Countries

The JCP's interest in the internal developments taking place in the neighboring Arab countries was present, to a greater or lesser degree, throughout the 1949-67 period. But the party's concern with the Arab world was always secondary to its interest in Arab-Israeli relations and the great power rivalry in the Middle East. This was especially true of the party's attitude to developments in Jordan itself, in which it displayed only sporadic and superficial interest.

The party, for most of the period under review, viewed the Arab world as being divided not only into separate states, but also into separate, vaguely defined "Arab nations."[149] These nations were ruled by reactionary feudal leaders who neither represented their peoples' aspirations, nor fought for their interests. In many cases, there was little difference between the policies pursued by these leaders and those pursued by the reactionary government in Israel. It was the Arab leaders who had initiated the conquest of different parts of Palestine, resulting in the Palestinian nation's humiliation and loss of independence. It was they who had created the refugee problem and who wished to perpetuate it, as it served their capitalist economic interests—despite the fact that it meant striking directly at the Palestinian Arabs. The Arab armies of occupation were seen as acting no differently from the Israeli occupying forces: they harassed the fellahin and levied heavy taxes and various other imposts designed to prop up the emergency regimes in their own countries.[150] Even declaration of hostility toward Israel by the various Arab governments, and their vows to work for its annihilation, were dismissed by the party as empty gestures, intended to divert the attention of their own peoples from their own miserable lot and cover the fact that their leaders were in collusion with their counterparts in the Jewish state, under the aegis of imperialism. King Saud was referred to as "American imperialism's leading pimp," while Husni Zaim was called "Imperialism's dog" for selling out Syria to the British as part of his attempt to pawn the entire "Arab East" to colonialism and imperialism.[151] The signatories to the Baghdad Pact were stigmatized as traitors to the Arab cause, not only for strengthening ties with the hated imperialists but also for forging an alliance with Turkey—the traditional enemy of the Arab people whose most recent act of aggression had been the annexation of Arab Alexandretta. With the overthrow of Nuri al-Said, the party revised its former hostility to Iraq as a British lackey state and threw its full support behind the new republic, expressing the hope that a similar change of regime would take place in Jordan and Lebanon.[152]

Of all the Arab countries, Egypt most interested the JCP, particularly following the Free Officers' coup (*inqilab*) in 1952. Before the July Revolution, the party recognized a dichotomy between the reactionary king, Faruq, and the courageous Egyptian people who were fighting the British imperialists in the Suez Canal zone. As early as February 1952, the party prophesized a popular revolution in Egypt.[153] While the party's official organ made no reference to the revolution in Egypt in any of its July and August issues, a leaflet put out by the party at the end of July presented the party's official line vis-à-vis the aims and aspirations of the Free Officers. The imperialists, the party held, viewed the Middle East as a potential base for aggression against the Soviet Union, and tried in various ways to establish a military influence in the area. When they failed to do this through an alliance with the existing regimes, they tried another method—forging links with disgruntled politicians and especially with army officers who had been trained by their military delegations. Their purpose was to "impose open military dictatorships" on the peoples of the Middle East and to prepare them to fight in the service of imperialist interests. The rise of Shishakli in Syria, for instance, was cited as an example of this stratagem, as was the Free Officers' coup in Egypt. The coup, the party charged, was planned in London by the American, British, and French foreign ministers a month before it took place. The actual implementation of their plan in Egypt was entrusted to their fascist agent Ali Maher, Muhammed Neguib (the nominal leader of the coup), and a handful of Neguib's fellow "adventurers" in the Egyptian army. The coup was portrayed as a desperate preemptive action, designed to forestall the genuine popular revolution (*thawra*) of the Egyptian people. It was hardly surprising, in the party's view, that America and Britain came out in support of the coup as a welcome internal Egyptian development, discouraging any outside intervention. The rebel officers, for their part, reciprocated by promising to safeguard imperialist interests in Egypt and to endorse the imperialists' occupation of the Suez Canal zone. According to the party, a similar community of interests existed between the new regime and the country's feudal and capitalist elements, and promises of reform were no more than a ruse to deceive the Egyptian people. The conclusion drawn by the party was that the Egyptian people, who had waged a painful struggle to get rid of Faruq and his entourage, would not be daunted and would continue to fight the new military dictatorship, undeceived by its claim to be "defending the constitution."[154]

The party's open hostility to the Egyptian Revolution persisted throughout 1952. Egypt was grouped together with Iraq and Jordan, countries whose people were struggling for their freedom. The party's attacks on "Neguib's fascist dictatorship" became even more hostile during 1953. The disbanding of all political parties in Egypt, the dissolution of the parliament, the imprisonment and execution of scores of workers were presented as clear proof of the vast gulf which separated the ruling junta and the Egyptian masses. Not even Neguib's eclipse and the rise of Abd al-Nasser satisfied the party, and Nasser's threat to leave the Arab League if Iraq joined the Baghdad Pact was dismissed as an imperialist tactic to split the League into two blocs, northern and southern, and thereby facilitate the creation of anti-Soviet alliances in the area.[155] Nevertheless, the first signs of a change in the party's attitude toward Egypt were beginning to appear, as the party slowly came to accept that Egypt's opposition to the Baghdad Pact—which the JCP automatically rejected—was quite genuine. The fact that Egypt was still seen as pressing to turn the Mutual Defense Pact into a military alliance with the imperialist powers continued, however, to arouse considerable criticism in the JCP.[156]

The real shift in the JCP's position came following the Czech arms deal. From this time on, the Egyptian regime was considered no longer aligned with the imperialists. The arms deal proved that Egypt was determined to protect its independence and defend itself against Israeli aggression and, at the same time, served to demonstrate the Soviet Union's support for "the Arab people and their governments." Egypt's motive in concluding the arms deal was purely one of national defense: after it began to follow a more independent foreign policy, opposing the Baghdad Pact, the imperialist powers had incited Israel to attack Egypt and had refused to sell arms to Egypt without unacceptable strings attached. Thus, Egypt had been left with little choice but to turn to the Czechs for their arms requirements. The JCP interpreted this shift in Egyptian policy as having been inspired by the purest ideological motives and felt it should thus serve as an example to the other Arab countries.[157] Henceforth, Egypt (together with Syria) was presented as the champion of Arab nationalism and liberation. It was referred to in the party's publications as "sister Egypt," with whom Jordan should cooperate and seek to ally itself.

The JCP's attitude cooled somewhat following Egypt's rift with Iraq. At first Egypt was warned not to forge links with the United States, which was arming Israel and abetting its aggressive designs against its Arab neighbors. American aid to Egypt was no more than a ruse designed to lull the Arabs, to woo them away from the Soviet Union, and to bring about the fall of Kassem's administration in Iraq on the pretext that it was based on the Communist Party. "Whose interests is Egypt serving by attacking the Communists?" *al-Muquwama al-Shaabiya* asked, noting that Abd al-Nasser had "disappointed" the Arab nationalists by declaring a "truce" with the imperialists. It was not long before the Egyptian regime was once again reviled, as conducting "a reign of terror" at home and attempting to extend its control over the other Arab countries (mainly Syria and Iraq).[158]

Nationalism and Pan-Arabism

From their inception, Communist parties in the Arab world were faced with a dilemma which although it was mainly ideological also had serious practical political implications—how to relate to the question of Arab nationalism. Ideologically, the Communist parties displayed a natural inclination to wage their struggle within the framework of the existing countries rather than encourage the unification of the Arab world under the banner of a nationalist pan-Arabism. Arab unity was seen as a wasteful diversion of energy from the more important, in Communist terms, struggle for international proletarian solidarity. Thus when they were first confronted with the dilemma of either opting for identification with the class struggle or working for the realization of the pan-Arab ideal, there was little doubt that they would opt for the former. But the parties were not in a position to make their choice on purely ideological grounds and could not ignore the fact that pan-Arabism was a powerful and growing force among the masses in the Middle East in the 1930s and 1940s: to oppose this force would be to court political isolation and alienation from the masses. In the late 1930s, Syria's most prominent communist leader, Khalid Bakdash, could still permit himself to state categorically that the Arabs were not in fact a distinctive nation because they possessed only one of the five attributes of genuine nationhood specified by Stalin—a common language.[159] While the Communists did not change this stance in the 1940s and the early 1950s, they grew increasingly wary of declaring it openly, preferring to remain silent on the subject. They did not present Arab unity as one of their political goals, and when outlining their position on the relationship that should exist between the various Arab states, envisaged a situation of somewhat loose ties between separate sovereign entities—in other words, more or less a continuation of the status quo. They would speak of "economic ties" and "cultural cooperation," or more generally of "solidarity" and "cooperation," while at the same time, stressing the particularist nature of each Arab country.[160]

This was more or less the position taken by the JCP. Like its sister parties in the rest of the Arab world, it expressed its reservations about pan-Arabism either by ignoring it or by stressing the party's commitment to the idea of separate Arab nations each living in their own sovereign state—but never by openly attacking the movement. In its pamphlets, the party went no further than calling for "solidarity between the sister Arab nations," a relatively innocuous and non-controversial rallying cry. Sometimes it would extend its call for solidarity to all the "nations of the Middle East," including by implication Turkey and Iran as well. This solidarity was not seen as a nationalist aim in itself, but rather as a means toward fighting the Western-oriented military alliances in the region.[161]

The translation of a Russian article was printed in *al-Muqawama al-Shaabiya* in December 1953, stressing the patriotism inherent in Communism—obviously part of the party's effort to counter the argument that its commitment to the idea of internationalism constituted an act of treason against the Arab nation. No attempt was made to portray the Arab proletariat or the Communist Party as being Arab nationalists (*qawmiyun*), a term regarded as "bourgeois." The proletariat was simply described as being composed of "nationalists" (*wataniyun*), *not* "Arab Nationalists," the implication being quite clear: the national loyalty of the proletariat in each individual Arab state was due to that state alone. A similar view emerges from one of the editorials in *al-Muqawama al-Shaabiya*, in which the patriots in Morocco and Tunisia are equated with patriots in China or Kenya. When the JCP spoke of unity, and used such terms as *"wahda"* or *"ittihad,"* they were referring to the unity of laborers and fellahin, or the progressive forces, within the particularist framework of the Jordanian nation (*shaab*).[162]

The Communist movements in the Arab world underwent a fundamental change in 1955, which became unmistakable in the course of the following year. In an address to the Syrian parliament in October 1955, veteran Communist leader Khalid Bakdash noted that "all the attributes of a nation...as defined by scientific socialism [that is, Stalin] are to be found among the Arabs, and this is clear as daylight." When it came to the actual political application of the pan-Arab ideal—the political unification of the Arab countries—the change in the attitude of the Communists was somewhat less obvious but quite apparent nevertheless. At first the Syrian Communist Party began to acknowledge the fact that the aspiration of the Arab states to unite was not a passing phenomenon or the aim of individual parties or interest groups but the "result of an objective historical development" and a "realistic need." The conditions were not yet ripe for such a development, the party believed, but stressed that it should work to create the conditions conducive to "total Arab unity."[163] When Syria and Egypt united to form the United Arab Republic in 1958, the Arab Communist parties gave the merger their whole-hearted blessing, despite the reservations they had expressed about the idea before it became a reality. The Egyptian Communist Party even proclaimed that the masses throughout the Arab world were moving ineluctably toward union (*wahda*) and that it was only the machinations of imperialism that were preventing the realization of their goal. Everything possible should be done to assure the success of the merger between Syria and Egypt, the party urged—even if this meant that the party should voluntarily disband itself. Following the Kassem coup in Iraq, the Egyptian Communists invited the new regime to bring Iraq into the camp of the "liberated Arab nations" (that is, Syria and Egypt), which was moving rapidly toward total Arab unity.[164]

The JCP lagged behind most of the other Communist parties in the Arab world, which had endorsed the pan-Arab ideal in the latter part of 1955, and in the spring of 1956 was still calling for "solidarity" among the Arab nations without singling out unity as one of the fundamental aspirations of the Arab masses (which were "liberty, national sovereignty, and dignity"). The party paid little attention to the question of nationalism; when nationalism was mentioned in party literature, it was not related to the issue of Arab unity.[165] The first signs of a change in this attitude appeared

in the June 1956 issue of *Nidal al-Shaab* (one of the party's regional publications), which called for the forging of closer links between
Jordan, Egypt, and Syria and praised the recently signed Jordanian-
Syrian pact as an important step on the way to union (*ittihad*).[166]
The journal detailed the visit of Shukri al-Quwatli to Ramallah,
where he was greeted by students bearing placards inscribed with
such slogans as "We want a national (*qawmiya*) government!,"
"Long live Arab unity!" It commented favorably on these slogans,
and described the courage and glory of the Arab nation. The JCP's
central committee came out, somewhat more guardedly, in favor
of the pan-Arab ideal at the end of 1956. While it reflected little
of the heady enthusiasm expressed in *Nidal al-Shaab* at the time of
al-Quwatli's visit, the central committee in November 1956 added
to its familiar call for "solidarity" the Arab nations' obligation to
fight Zionism and imperialism in order to realize their goals of independence, dignity, liberty—and *unity*.[167]

During 1957–58, the JCP's support of the aims of pan-Arabism
grew increasingly enthusiastic and open (it was expressed quite un-
ambiguously in the campaign leaflets put out by Dr. Yaqub Ziyadin
and by Fayiq Warrad at the beginning of 1957, and in other leaflets
published and signed by the party during this period).[168] Thus by
late 1956 the JCP had come to accept without reservation the line
that had emerged first in Syria and afterward in Egypt and Iraq.
This implied abandoning, or at least relegating to secondary importance, the doctrinaire Communist position it had taken hitherto
in favor of important elements of the nationalist doctrine espoused
by the Baathists and the Nasserites in the Arab world.

Once the revolutionary regime in Iraq had established itself, the
nationalist fervor that had permeated the Communist movements
in the Arab countries began to cool a little. The disillusion that set
in stemmed largely from political developments in the area rather
than from any ideological reappraisal of their position. In Syria
the Communist Party, which had refused to disband itself voluntarily after the merger in Egypt, fell out of favor with the new
regime and was forced to go underground. Abd al-Nasser's administrations, both in Egypt and in Syria, began severe repression of
the Communists in the end of 1958. This alone would have been
sufficient cause for the Communist parties in both countries to reappraise their former enthusiasm for the merger. The Communist
Party in Iraq, which enjoyed a position of unprecedented importance and influence during the first year following Kassem's coup,

began to have misgivings about Iraq's joining the UAR for fear that it too would suffer the fate of its brother parties in Syria and Egypt. Thus in September 1958 the party in Iraq published a statement expressing the fear that Iraq's joining the UAR would adversely affect the country's Kurdish population, its army officers, and its economy. To deflect accusation that it was trying to split the Arab nation and subvert its nationalist aspirations, the party tried to draw a distinction between the Nasserite and Baathist concept of merger (*wahda*) and their own much looser concept of union (*ittihad*), which it felt implied some form of federation between the different Arab countries. At about the same time or perhaps even a little earlier the Communist parties in Syria and Egypt began to refrain from expressing any actual political support for the idea of merger. Accordingly, they dropped their earlier call for Iraq to join the UAR and began to press fairly explicitly for its dissolution. In their publications they would still occasionally nod to the ideas of Arab nationalism and Arab unity, but with nothing like their former enthusiasm or commitment. When Bakdash spoke of "unity," he now used the term almost completely devoid of its original pan-Arab and nationalist connotations. Clearly, then, by this time, when the Communists in the Arab countries spoke of "unity," they meant no more than some form of loose federation between the Arab states—and eventually they retreated from even this position.[169]

Here again the JCP lagged behind the Communist parties in the neighboring Arab countries. In September 1958 their official organ was still calling for elections that would enable the people to give expression to their wish for a merger (*wahda*) "between Jordan and its sisters, the liberated Arab states"—meaning Syria and Egypt.[170] No mere rhetoric, the statement expressed a genuine practical political aspiration at a time when the other Arab Communist parties had clearly abandoned such sentiments. The JCP's continuing commitment to the pan-Arab ideal was particularly apparent in *Nidal al-Shaab*, the regional publication from Jerusalem, which was the first to come out in favor of Arab nationalism and Arab unity and which continued consistently to express its support for these ideas.[171] In January 1959, when the Communist parties in all the Arab countries as well as the Kassem regime in Iraq and the Soviet Union itself had ranged themselves against the Nasserite pan-Arab camp, *Nidal al-Shaab* struck a dissenting chord. While it vigorously attacked the Baath and the reactionary press in Egypt, the journal was very careful not to offend the sensibilities of the nationalists on two key issues. It refrained from attacking Abd al-Nasser or the UAR (on the contrary, the UAR was represented as fundamentally anti-imperialistic, it being only the *press* in Egypt that was reactionary in that it failed to warn the masses of the dangers of American imperialism); and it went out of its way to praise "Arab nationalism" and Arab unity, stressing that the Communist parties and the Soviet Union were the most faithful champions of these causes (the Baath and other reactionary elements in the Arab world—excluding Abd al-Nasser—were reviled for exploiting these two sacred slogans to deceive the Arab masses). While *Nidal* failed to make any distinction between the terms merger (*wahda*) and union (*ittihad*), as the Communist Party in Iraq had done, it did speak of "a genuine Arab merger," or "a free and democratic Arab merger," which would seem to imply some reservation for the Nasserite concept. Nevertheless, there can be no mistaking the Jerusalem journal's markedly "nationalistic" tone, at a time when it was conspicuously absent among Communists elsewhere in the Arab world.

The JCP's continuing commitment to pan-Arab ideas long after they had become passé in other Communist circles was apparent also in the circulars sent out by the regional committee in Nablus to party activists in the area.[172] After the al-Shawwaf revolt was successfully suppressed in northern Iraq in March 1959, there was a burst of reaction and Communist parties in all the Arab countries came out violently against Abd al-Nasser and the Baath, decrying them as criminals, traitors, imperialist agents, and lackeys. The Nablus committee's circulars did reprimand Abd al-Nasser for turning the religious establishment against the Communists (at one point the committee even denied that religion should have any political role at all), but it carefully refrained from injuring the nationalist sensibilities of the bulk of the population in the area. While Communist parties throughout the Arab world were by this time openly expressing the view that Arab unity was a goal that could not be achieved in the foreseeable future,[173] these circulars carefully avoided this highly sensitive issue completely.

The JCP, then, followed for the most part even if sometimes belatedly the political line taken by its brother Communist parties in the neighboring Arab countries. But ideologically the JCP somewhat differed, having been permeated by nationalist ideas to a significantly greater degree than had these other Communist parties. There are a number of possible reasons for this. First, the JCP's situation in Jordan was different from that of the Communist parties in Iraq, Syria, and Egypt. In Iraq, the Communist Party's opposition to the Nasserite concept of Arab unity was perfectly acceptable to the country's rulers, while two important sectors of the Iraqi population—the Kurds and the Shiites—had good reason to fear Arab nationalism. Accordingly, the party ran little danger, on this issue at least, of falling into disfavor with the authorities or alienating itself from the local population. The Communist parties in Egypt and Syria, on the other hand, had nothing to lose by coming out against nationalism and very little to gain from supporting it. The majority of the population in both countries was fervently behind the pan-Arabism of the Nasserites, and the parties could have little hope of weaning them away by playing up to their nationalist sentiments. Forced underground, the parties depended entirely on their cadres and had no need to curry the favor either of the authorities or of the populace. There was little chance that they would alienate their own members by returning to the traditional position that had preceded their brief flirtation with pan-Arabism. Furthermore, the Communist parties in Syria and Egypt (particularly the former) could only gain from the dissolution of the UAR, and thus saw no practical purpose in helping to perpetuate it.

The situation in Jordan, and especially on the West Bank, was very different. Here the JCP and the nationalist parties alike were outlawed. They were thus locked into a fierce rivalry for the allegiance of the large Palestinian population which had not come to terms with the Hashemite regime. Accordingly, the JCP simply couldn't afford to ignore the obvious nationalist sensibilities of the bulk of the West Bank population and cede its support, by default, to its nationalist rivals. By coming out against the notions of pan-Arabism and Arab unity, the party would risk alienating large sections of the population which would otherwise support the anti-Western, anti-Zionist, and anti-Hashemite stand taken by the JCP and its various front organizations. The party leaders were clearly not blind to the fact that the 1956–58 period, when the JCP's membership grew appreciably, was precisely the time when the party had expressed its support for Arab unity (*wahda*) and nationalism (*qawmiya*). Tactically, this led the party to continue to press for the creation of a "national front." It should also be stressed that, ever since the 1948 war, most of the population in the West Bank felt themselves to be second-class citizens in the Hashemite kingdom, and many were convinced that the final solution to the

Palestine problem lay in the realization of the pan-Arab ideal (this was especially true of the refugees, who were convinced that this was the only way in which they would ever return to their homes). Accordingly, pan-Arab sentiments were, from an early date, considerably more prevalent in the West Bank, than they were in most other parts of the Arab world.[174] Finally, as will be discussed further below, there was a considerable blurring of the boundaries between the various political parties in the West Bank. (The division between the Communist Party and the Baath in Iraq, for example, was much sharper and more pronounced than between the two parties in the West Bank.)

3. Al-Qawmiyun al-Arab

ACTIVITIES

General

The Arab Nationalists Movement (Harakat al-Qawmiyun al- Arab, or simply Al-Qawmiyun al- Arab) was founded in Beirut, shortly after the defeat of the Arab armies in 1948. For some years before this, however, students in the Lebanese capital had been holding meetings at a club called The Firm Bond (Al- Urwa al-Wuthqa), where they discussed at length how the aims of Arab nationalism could best be achieved. After 1948 Arab intellectuals—both Muslims and Christians—established the core of the movement at the American University of Beirut (AUB), Lebanon. At first they met once a year at the annual AUB graduates' reunion, but gradually some of them became active in several other Arab countries. One such meeting took place in Jerusalem, to discuss the Johnston Jordan waters plan, and this, it seems, provided the main impetus for the founding of the Qawmiyun in Jordan.

The Arab Nationalists Movement was founded in Jordan at the end of 1952 or the beginning of 1953. A number of accounts describe how it came to be established there. According to one of them, George Habash and Wadi Haddad arrived in Amman from Beirut in 1952, made contact with a group of Palestinian notables ("The Amman Congress"—Mutamar Amman), and operated openly until the end of 1954 within the framework of the Arab Cultural Club (Al-Nadi al-Adabi al- Arabi).[1] According to another account, Habash and Haddad arrived in Amman only at the beginning of 1953, and were active at first in a front organization called "The Committee for the Struggle against Peace with Israel."[2] The initiators of the Qawmiyun in the West Bank were two physicians,

This chapter draws on the Hebrew version of 1972 prepared by Gideon Braude and Ella Landau; pages 94–115, specifically, are revisions of the former's work.

Dr. Salah Anbatawi of Nablus and Dr. Subhi Ghosha of Jerusalem. Its first members were mainly intellectuals (physicians, lawyers, and so forth). Initially membership in the movement was dependent on family ties with an existing member, and outsiders could join only on the recommendation of one of the latter. Its major period of development was in the late 1950s and early 1960s, when popularity of the Baath and Communist parties was low and Abd al-Nasser's prestige in the Arab world was at its height. At the beginning of the 1960s, the Qawmiyun had several hundred members in Jordan, more than half of them in the West Bank.

From the mid-1950s, the Qawmiyun displayed a blind loyalty to Abd al-Nasser, whom it saw as the undisputed champion of Arab nationalism and the man who would realize its most sacred objective—Arab unity. Many people joined the movement simply because they idolized the Egyptian leader, often without understanding what he stood for.

In the mid-1960s the movement was dealt several crippling blows which all but ended its activities in Jordan. Many of its leaders and members were either arrested or kept under close surveillance by the security services. A certain disillusion with Abd al-Nasser also began to set in, following his conduct of the war in Yemen and developments in Egypt itself. The nationalists in Jordan began to have misgivings about his ability to lead the Arab world toward unity or to solve the Palestine problem. The monarchy in Jordan, which the Qawmiyun wished to see fall, proved itself to be well entrenched—the assassination of the king or any other central figure in the Hashemite establishment would not be sufficient to topple it. The movement was plagued by internal dissension, with many members being expelled or deciding to leave its ranks. And finally, a new generation of leaders, weaned on more radical revolutionary ideas, began to emerge, replacing the veteran leadership, and turning the political movement into an active terrorist organization.

The Qawmiyun's Activities

In its early stages, when the Qawmiyun had only a few dozen members, its activities were limited.[3] In the mid-1950s, by which time it had managed to overcome its early organizational difficulties, the movement became an active pro-Nasserite force in Jordan, setting as its immediate aims the overthrow of the Hashemite monarchy and the unification of the Arab world under the leadership of Gamal Abd al-Nasser. Its final objective was to avenge the defeat of 1948 and restore Palestine to its rightful owners. Jordan had a strategic role in attaining this objective: "Jordan stretches along the entire length of Israel.... The West Bank of Jordan constitutes the largest part of Palestine still in Arab hands. More than one million Palestinians live in Jordan. That being the case, this group and this country have the major role in the Arab nationalists' struggle against the Zionist invaders and against imperialism.... It is thus imperative that Jordan prepare itself at every level to serve as the advance base in the liberation of Palestine."[4] Accordingly, the first task of the Arab Nationalists was to remove the reactionary Hashemite regime, the prime enemy of Arab unity in Jordan.

In the course of 1954, the Qawmiyun waged a vigorous campaign, mainly in its weekly newspaper, *al-Rai*, against the Baghdad Pact and other Western-inspired alliances, against British influence in Jordan, and in favor of Glubb Pasha's dismissal. At the end of 1954, the authorities reacted by closing down *al-Rai* and outlawing the party, which continued to operate underground until the Nabulsi government took office in October 1956. Several key members were arrested during this period, including George Habash. After his release, the Qawmiyun began to support the line taken by Nabulsi, which called for a reduction of British influence in Jordan and the forging of a military alliance with the radical Arab states, Syria and Egypt (Saudi Arabia, while hardly a "radical" state, was to be included in the alliance). The Qawmiyun participated openly in the election campaign at the end of 1956 and the beginning of 1957. Its rallying cries were Arab unity, expulsion of the Jews from Palestine, elimination of all Western influence, complete neutrality in international affairs, and social reform at home. It performed abysmally, however, in the 1957 elections, and failed to have a single candidate elected to the House of Representatives. It immediately claimed that the elections had been rigged, a claim not totally without foundation.

With the resignation of the Nabulsi government in April 1957, the Qawmiyun once again went underground. At first it actively opposed the regime, along with the other parties in Jordan, by organizing demonstrations and strikes, and by carrying out acts of sabotage in public buildings and against foreign institutions. But following a series of crippling arrests, the Qawmiyun decided to change its tactics. While there is little information in the files of the security services concerning the party's activities at this time, Qazziha writes that in late 1957 and early 1958, apparently under the leadership of Wadi Haddad, it bombed a number of carefully selected targets in Amman. These included government buildings and the homes of government ministers. The saboteurs were subsequently arrested and sentenced to long terms in jail. Haddad himself was released in 1960, and he moved to Damascus.[5] Reports at the end of 1958 indicated that one of the Qawmiyun's leaders in Beirut, Samir Abu Jawda, was engaged in directing members to Jordan for the purpose of carrying out acts of sabotage. One such saboteur, captured while crossing the border with Syria in 1959, told his interrogators that the authorities in the Syrian region of the UAR were making preparations to arm the Qawmiyun in Jordan and that Syrian Intelligence was in regular contact with the party. Other reports indicated that members of the party were receiving training in the use of explosives in Syria, and that arms were being smuggled in from Lebanon. From 1963 on, with the rise of the Baath to power in Syria, the reports of arms-running from both Syria and Lebanon multiplied, the arms being brought into the country concealed in consignments of Syrian cotton or in special hidden compartments built into cars and trucks crossing the border.

There were a number of reports concerning the Qawmiyun's ties with Egypt, mainly through Egyptian envoys and military liaison officers stationed in Syria and Lebanon. Egyptian Intelligence was even reported to be trying to recruit mercenaries in Lebanese refugee camps, train them in the use of arms and explosives, and send them into Jordan to carry out acts of sabotage on behalf of the Qawmiyun. Jordanians working in Kuwait regularly called on the Egyptian Embassy there, to provide information and to receive instructions. The Egyptians would even send representatives to attend the movement's meetings.[6] In an attempt to prevent the Qawmiyun from contacting the Egyptians, the Jordanian authorities would sometimes ban travel abroad by known or suspected members of the party. At the same time, they would keep a close watch on their activists in Jordan itself. In one raid, on the house of a school teacher who was known to be a member of the Qawmiyun, the security authorities discovered a diary containing the following description: "I have never in my life seen so powerful a demonstration as that which took place today. Students, workers, and citizens all took part. The army intervened, using batons and firearms. The people seized control of the government offices and the radio studio. The battle lasted an hour and a half, during which 11 people were killed, 150 were injured and 300 were arrested.... The masses in Nablus declared an insurrection.... Nablus announced: 'This is the capital of the Jordanian Republic.' The number of persons killed in the disturbances came to 300.''[7] The teacher claimed he had received his information from Cairo's "Voice of the Arabs" broadcasts, and was fully aware that the reports were, in fact, entirely false. Still, this was a clear indication of the party's intention to incite as many people as possible in Jordan to rise against the Hashemite regime. It is hardly surprising, therefore, that throughout the 1960s the authorities hounded the Qawmiyun incessantly, sentencing members they caught to long terms in prison. Nevertheless, the conflict between the Qawmiyun and the security services was somewhat less severe than that between the authorities and the JCP and the Baath, which were both regarded as more powerful than the Qawmiyun and hence more of a threat to the regime.

Despite the fact that all the opposition parties were locked in bitter conflict with the Hashemite regime, they did not generally join forces or cooperate with each other. The fierce rivalry between them was, in fact, considerably exploited by the security services. There was, however, a fairly long period of cooperation between the Qawmiyun and the Baath. When all political parties were outlawed in 1957, the National Front was created to encompass the Baath and the Qawmiyun—as well as the Communists and the National Socialist Party. The Qawmiyun, like the Muslim Brothers, continued to function as a separate party even after the creation of the Front. Following the coup in Iraq, relations between the Baath and the Qawmiyun, on the one hand, and the JCP on the other resulted in the expulsion of the JCP from the Front. The reason for this was the close ties between the Communists and the Qassem regime, which the JCP supported in its struggle against the Baath and the Nasserites, coming out openly against the idea of Arab unity. There were reports at one time that the Qawmiyun and the Baath planned to publish an underground monthly called the "Political Office of the Arab League." There were even rumors that the Qawmiyun and the Baath were jointly planning the assassination of government leaders in Jordan, and that arms were being smuggled in from Syria and Lebanon for that purpose (a number of such consignments were in fact seized). In any case, after the Baath came to power in Syria and Iraq in 1963 and began to crack down on the Qawmiyun for their past support of the Abd al-Nasser, the National Front finally broke up in Jordan.

Propaganda

The Qawmiyun's aspiration to attract wide support for its ideas, sow the seeds of nationalist consciousness, and become a broad-based "movement of the masses" obliged it to engage in extensive propaganda. In order to reach the population at every level, it organized public meetings, distributed leaflets, and instigated debates. While it made an effort to reach a wide range of groups—intellectuals, workers, fellahin, and petty traders—it achieved its greatest success among the students, whom it found especially receptive to its ideas (as did the other parties opposed to the regime in Jordan).[8] One of the schools where the Qawmiyun was particularly successful was al-Najah college in Nablus.

At first the Qawmiyun distributed simple leaflets containing catchy slogans designed to arouse nationalist sentiments among the public at large. Then the simple catch-phrases disappeared and were replaced by lengthy ideological tracts; the heady emotional style of the earlier leaflets gave way to simpler, more rational language.

In the years 1956–58, the party published a series of special leaflets dealing with a specific current event which it wished to comment on (such as the war in Algeria or the crisis over Suez Canal). Each pamphlet opened with a brief resumé of the subject under discussion, which would be followed by a detailed exposition, liberally interspersed with such interjections and rallying cries as "O you sons of the Arab nation!," "O you stubborn Arab people!" At the bottom of the page there would usually appear one or two slogans, in a distinctive script: "Long live the struggle of our eternally united Arab nation!" or "Long live our struggle, O people, for unity, liberation and revenge!" Each newssheet concluded with the date and the inscription "Al-Qawmiyun al- Arab."

A newssheet called *al-Shaab Aqwa* ("The People Are Stronger") was put out, in an amateurish way, on a simple duplicating machine. It was published regularly once a month. Each issue was dated and numbered and bore the legend "Arab Nationalist Bulletin published on behalf of the Pioneers of the National Struggle." It comprised two or three pages, and contained a number of regular columns. The first would usually deal with a current political issue, for example, the events in Lebanon in 1958 or the latest act of treason perpetrated by the Jordanian regime, or would discuss topics such as the 1947 partition of Palestine. Another, headed "Did You Know?," presented a purported exposé of one or another dramatic political scandal (for example, "Did you know that Egyptian Intelligence has acquired sensitive documents from the Jordanian Embassy in Beirut, and that these documents reveal the treachery of Jordan's rulers who have conspired with Henderson, the envoy of American imperialism, to attack Arab Syria and impose Western domination there?"). Another feature, called "News the Papers Don't Print," reported alleged acts of sabotage and terrorism in Jordan, in an attempt to convince its readers that the Hashemite regime was locked in armed conflict with the popular masses who were struggling to overthrow it.

Al-Wahda ("Unity") was another publication put out by the Qawmiyun in the early 1960s. Consisting of between three and six duplicated pages, the pamphlet provided in-depth analysis of major events in the Arab world, with special emphasis on the way these affected the question of Arab unity. There were also several other publications distributed by the party, including pamphlets such as "The Socialist Unity—Unity, Socialism, and Liberty" or *Al-Hurriya* ("Liberty").

The simplest of the Qawmiyan's publications were the hand-written leaflets, which were passed from hand to hand. The students' associations put out their own newssheets, such as *Al-Talib al Arabi al-Thawri* ("The Revolutionary Arab Student) and *Nida al-Talib* ("The Student's Cry"). These newssheets generally called on the country's students to engage in revolutionary activities against the regime. One put out by the Students' Association in May 1963 contained the following appeal: "In the name of God the Compassionate the Merciful! O ye brothers in the struggle! We call on you to boycott your final examinations in protest against the government's refusal to acquiesce to the demands of the students and the people of Jordan for complete Arab unity."[9]

The Qawmiyun's publications were usually intended for its own members rather than for outsiders. Their purpose was to formulate the party's ideology, strengthen the beliefs of its members, and keep them up-to-date with its latest thinking. They were passed from hand to hand and eventually destroyed after they had been read (an instruction to this effect was often printed at the end of each one). On more than one occasion, the security services were forced to photograph the party's pamphlets as their informer was usually obliged either to return it to the person from whom he had received it or to pass it on to another member. Newssheets were often put out before or after one of the movement's conferences, committing to writing what was discussed at them. Occasionally members would receive publications by mail. Certain of the Qawmiyun's leaflets were intended for the general public, to bring the message of the Qawmiyun to the attention of the masses; these were usually simply left on doorsteps, in the markets, outside schools, or placed in mailboxes.

The authorities waged a vigorous campaign against the distribution of leaflets, viewing the practice as a serious security threat. The leaflets were described as "Destructive," and those who distributed them as "sick minds." Strict instructions were issued to collect and destroy all leaflets before they reached the general public and to arrest anyone found distributing them.

The police carried out frequent searches for the Qawmiyun's printing equipment, usually in the homes of suspected members. Typewriters belonging to various institutions were carefully examined, to see if their type matched that of the party's publications. Printing firms were also inspected to make certain that their presses were not being used by the Qawmiyun, and a close watch was kept on the duplicating machines in the country's schools and government offices. The police also closely surveyed and regularly searched vehicles they suspected may have been used to distribute the Qawmiyun's publications. Often the publications could be anticipated, before a significant anniversary (July 23 or May 15) or following some major political event in Jordan or the Arab world. Following the rise of the Baath to power in Syria in March 1963, for example, members anxiously awaited clarification of the Qawmiyun's position in the light of this new development. The police too expected the party to put out some form of publication outlining its position, and were instructed to keep a sharp lookout in the hope that they would be able to trace its printing press or at least arrest those who were distributing the publication. In May 1964, following the Palestinian National Congress in Jerusalem, Jordanian Intelligence reported that the Qawmiyun were dissatisfied with the outcome of the Congress and could be expected to put out leaflets expressing its feeling.

During 1954 the Qawmiyun's official newspaper, *al-Rai*, published in Amman, was distributed in the West Bank. Members of the party who could afford it contributed toward the cost of publishing the newspaper, which was distributed free of charge to the public. The paper was closed down at the end of 1954 and reopened in Damascus at the beginning of 1955. The Jordanian authorities lifted the ban on the paper in July 1955, when publication was permitted to resume in Jordan.[10] But it is not known how long it continued to be published there.

Another method of disseminating antigovernment slogans was painting on walls. Examples of the slogans that appeared from time to time in various towns in the West Bank are: "Fall, Hussein and His Zionist Government!," "Long Live the Jordanian Republic, Its Army and People United in One Rank!"[11]

Jordanian members of the Qawmiyun who went to work in other Arab countries continued to disseminate anti-Hashemite propaganda in those countries. Teachers, clerks, and other workers employed in Kuwait, for example, disseminated anti-Hasmemite and pro-Nasserite ideas both in the form of leaflets and orally.

One final way of spreading the party's ideas and gaining new supporters, many of whom eventually became members, was through the Arab clubs which had sprung up in several of the larger urban centers in the West Bank (Tulkarm, Nablus, Ramallah, and Jerusalem). The Qawmiyun's ideas were often well received by many of those participating in the political and ideological discussions that took place at these clubs. Occasionally George Habash himself was invited to address these meetings. The Arab clubs were closed down after the Qawmiyun was outlawed, and when they reopened had become purely sports clubs, no longer the forum for political discussion.

STRUCTURE AND MEMBERSHIP

Structure

In its early years, the structure of the Qawmiyun was fairly amorphous. Only later, particularly after it went underground and stepped up its activities against the regime, did the party begin to evolve a clearly defined infrastructure. Its aspiration to transform itself from a "vanguard" movement to a popular "mass" movement, working for the overthrow of the reactionary regimes throughout the Arab world and preparing the ground for the unification of all the Arab countries, obliged the Qawmiyun to pay greater attention to its organizational framework. The importance of "the weapon of organization," in addition to "the weapon of [nationalist] awareness," was frequently stressed in its publications, which pointed out that the two aspects were interdependent. Its desire to become a mass movement, and the need to protect itself against infiltration by government provocateurs, led the party to elaborate a structure that would serve both aims.

The Qawmiyun described its mode of organization as "flexible centralism," which, according to one of the party's leaders in Jordan, Hamid al-Farhan, reflected the practice of the Communist parties in the Soviet Union and China. From 1957, the Qawmiyun even began to use the Leninist term "democratic centralization"[12] to describe this practice. But most of the party's rank-and-file members, and even some of its leaders, were unaware that its structure had in any way been modeled on that of the Communists.

The structure of the party was pyramidal. At the base were the groups *(halaqa)*. Then came the cells *(khaliya)*, the associations *(rabita)*, the branches *(shuba)* and, at the apex, the regional (or national) command *(qiyada iqlimiya)*. This last term empahsized the Qawmiyun's fundamental belief in the unity of the Arab world, with each individual country no more than a "province" of a unified Arab homeland. Each level was subordinate to the one above it, and was controlled by a member from the immediately superior level. Thus group leaders were themselves members of cells, cell leaders were members of an association, and so on.

Communication between levels was in two directions: instructions were passed down from the apex to the base, and regular reports in turn were passed upward. The leaders on each level held regular meetings (cell leaders met once a week, for example) to discuss current issues, to pass on instructions, to transmit information, and to solve various problems affecting their particular level. Reports of their meetings, queries, and requests for instructions were communicated to the immediately superior level. The most important reports were, of course, those prepared at the two highest levels, the branches and the district committee. These were prepared every few months and were later combined to form annual reports comprising some sixty pages.

As in the Communist Party, communication was vertical, between the levels, and not horizontal, within each level. Thus, for example, a group could not on its own initiative establish contact

103

with another group; any such contact had to be, in this case, through the cell. This procedure eliminated the danger of the entire party network being uncovered should one or another of the groups be infiltrated by the authorities. According to members of the Qawmiyun, the "compartmentalization" procedure was strictly adhered to in practice[13]—a claim that appears to be largely substantiated by the fact that the security services found it very difficult to "crack" the organization even if they were able to infiltrate individual groups.

Although the groups were the simplest and lowest-ranked elements in the party's hierarchy, they were of very considerable importance. For it was at this level that new members were inducted into the Qawmiyun, where they received their first instruction, and where they were carefully evaluated. The groups thus constituted the "entrance" to the party, and it was only after proving themselves at this level that suitable candidates could advance to the higher levels. The groups were also the most vulnerable element in the party's structure, as it was through them that the security services tried to infiltrate their agents.

Each group comprised between three and seven members, usually five or six. Each cell was composed of five members, each in charge of his own group. The associations were made up of five cell leaders, and the branches, of six association leaders.

The party was organized on a numerical rather than geographic basis. Thus the lower levels, the group and the cell, were not necessarily confined to villages, or the higher levels, the association and branch, to the towns and cities. A village that had only a few members would be organized into a cell that was subordinate to the association in a neighboring town or village, while villages with a larger number of members were divided into several cells which were subordinate to an association in the village itself. Some cells were organized in factories as well, taking in members who were not necessarily all from the same town or village. Nevertheless in practice the associations usually covered a large village (or factory), the branches a town (Nablus, Jerusalem, Ramallah), and the regional command the whole of Jordan (including the West Bank).

Advancement within the party was from the base to the apex. A member would progress on the basis of an assessment by his superiors of his talents, enthusiasm, and loyalty. In theory the party was democratic, and much was written about the "equal opportunities" for advancement that existed regardless of the member's social standing or past history. Leaders of each level were meant to be democratically elected by the members themselves. In practice, however, this was not the case, and the heads of cells and associations were usually appointed from above. It is possible that this was true of the branch leaders as well. Even the regional command, at least in part, was appointed by the party's executive committee, its overall controling body.

The Qawmiyun rejected in principle the concept of personal leadership, and individual leaders were never singled out for mention in its publications. The stress was clearly on a collective leadership. There can be little doubt, however, that the party in the West Bank was effectively controlled by one man—George Habash, who by virtue of his very considerable charisma and authority was able to impose his views on his fellow leaders.

Congresses

The National (Pan-Arab) Congress was usually held once a year. It reviewed the party's activities over the previous year, planned activities for the future, elected a new chairman and executive committee, and discussed financial matters. Occasionally the Congress would be called into extraordinary session to discuss some important development in the area—such as the Baathist takeovers in Syria and Iraq in 1963. In between each National Congress, the Qawmiyun's activities were controled by the executive committee.[14]

Congresses theoretically were also supposed to take place on a regional-national level in each individual country. In practice, however, they were held in the "Lebanese Region." The party's leaders claimed that the regional congresses were not held because of security problems, arguing that it would be foolhardy to bring members together in a forum in countries where the Qawmiyun was outlawed and thereby enable the authorities to wipe out the party in one blow. Within the lower levels, however, complaints were made that the leadership was unwilling to expose itself to some of the embarrassing questions that might be raised at such meetings. There were also suggestions that the party's leaders had little respect for the intellectual level of many of their subordinates and considered the regional congresses a waste of time. In any case, no regional congress was ever held in Jordan.[15]

Obligations and Duties of Members

The Qawmiyun encouraged its members to be critical of their colleagues as well as to engage in constant self-appraisal and self-criticism. This was expected not only of the rank and file but of the party's leaders as well. Each member was entitled to criticize any other member regardless of his status. Such criticisms or complaints were not transmitted directly to the leadership but through the vertical channels of communication linking the lower and higher levels. Thus a situation could arise in which a member would find himself having to pass on to the next level a criticism directed against himself. If he attempted to smother the complaint and failed to pass it on for fear of incurring disciplinary action, he was liable to expulsion from the party. In the case of a serious complaint, a special Commission of Inquiry would be convened to investigate and pass judgment. If the offense was found to be relatively mild, the member usually had his membership suspended for a short time; if the offense was more serious, the member would be expelled. Members could make complaints about their fellows only within the framework of the movement itself: it was absolutely forbidden for a member to go to the authorities, even if a criminal or civil offense were involved. This was not only the result of the party's strong sense of solidarity, but also because it did not recognize the legitimacy of the authorities. The matter had first to be brought before the party's leadership; only after the alleged offender had been judged, found guilty, and expelled could a complaint be made to the police.

Members paid subscription dues in proportion to their means. According to interviewees, the dues ranged from 6 percent of a member's salary (if he earned less than 10 dinars a month) to as much as 90 percent (if he earned more than 150 dinars a month). But it is most unlikely that this scale was actually followed in practice. Students, heads of large families, and members with very low incomes did not have to pay dues, but were free to contribute whatever they wanted. Any member could make a special contribution in addition to paying his regular dues. It was common practice after a meeting to request contributions for some specific purpose, such as the purchase of printing equipment. In any event, the party appeared to raise most of its funds from among its own members, primarily through dues. Despite all the information we have of Egyptian moral and political support for the party there is no indication that the Qawmiyun received financial aid from Egypt. Nevertheless, such a possibility cannot be ruled out.

Absolute secrecy was one of the strictest demands made of the party's members. Special meetings were called to discuss ways of ensuring secrecy which was recognized as one of the party's most effective weapons against the Jordanian Security Services. Details about the upper echelons of the party and the identity of its leading activists were kept secret from the rank-and-file membership. As mentioned earlier, informers planted by the security services were generally able to penetrate the party at the lowest level only, so their effectiveness was greatly restricted. All sources appear to confirm the impression that the Qawmiyun adhered to an extremely strict code of secrecy, and managed to conceal from the Jordanian Security Services most of the facts about their party's organization and activities.

Recruitment

The question of recruitment was naturally a subject of primary importance for an underground organization that wished to attract a mass following. The party's strict code of secrecy made recruitment an extremely sensitive issue, for in trying to attract new members, the party inevitably left itself open to exposure, at least at the lower levels. Another danger was penetration either by informers planted by the security services or by provocateurs infiltrated by rival movements. A great deal of attention, therefore, was devoted to this subject.

Special pamphlets were put out by the party which outlined recruiting procedures and the precautionary measures to be followed. Recruitment was carried out in the following way. The recruiting officer would make a survey of a certain village and single out the most suitable potential recruits. After receiving the go-ahead from the party's leadership, he would then set the recruiting process into motion. The first step would be to establish contact with the candidate's family and acquaintances, in an effort to glean information about his political views. All this would be done without the recruiting officer making his intentions known. After making a preliminary assessment of the candidate's suitability, the recruiting officer would then report to his superiors who would make the final decision whether or not the recruiting process should continue. The next step would be to approach the candidate himself and sound out his political ideas. These would have to be consistent with those of the party (for example, he would have to be convinced not only of the need for Arab unity but also of the steps necessary to realize this aim). If this proved to be the case, the candidate would then be given a selection of the party's literature—leaflets, newspapers and other publications—without being told whose ideas were represented. The purpose was to enter into a discussion with him, on the basis of the literature, in order to ascertain whether or not the candidate was sufficiently mature ideologically and aware enough politically to join the party. The final step (when sanctioned by the party's leadership) would be actually to recruit the candidate. During the swearing-in ceremony the candidate would usually take an oath in the name of God and on his own personal honor, to be a loyal member of the party and to work for it and for the Arab nation in whatever way he was asked to. In certain cases, particularly in the later stages of the party's development, this swearing-in ceremony was dropped.

The new recruit was initially considered to be an "associate member" of the party. He was attached to a group, along with a number of other recruits who had joined the party at about the same time. For the first few months he was on probation and could not be elected to any official position. Neither was he made privy to any of the party's secrets. He did, however, attend the regular meetings of the group, listening to lectures and taking part in political discussions. After this probationary period was over, the most promising of the new recruits was attached to a cell, at which point he was considered to be a full-fledged member. Like the group, the cell met about once a week, usually in the home of one of its members. A lecture on a topical subject was delivered, either by the cell leader or a member, followed by a debate. The meetings also discussed organizational and operational matters, studied the instructions that had been transmitted from the upper echelons, and aired various complaints and criticisms. At the end of each meeting, the date and place of the cell's next meeting would be set.

Social Characteristics of the Membership

One of the factors that enabled the Qawmiyun to gain support in various sectors of the population was the large number of doctors among its leading activists. These doctors were widely known in the community for the free medical care and sometimes even medicines they provided to the needy. Despite the fact that they were well off financially and belonged to the social elite, they performed this service out of a strong sense of public commitment. As a result they earned considerable goodwill among the population, not only for themselves but also for the party as a whole, which went a long way toward enabling the party to project a positive image. Members of the Qawmiyun and their families received medical treatment for free or at reduced rates.

The party did not restrict its activities to a specific social class or occupational group. Clerks, teachers, students, merchants, lawyers, laborers, engineers, drivers, restaurant and cafe owners, technicians, and artisans were all considered potential members or sympathizers. The party placed great emphasis on having highly motivated, charismatic people in key positions at the highest levels of leadership—men one party member called "the beautiful people."

In the mid-1950s, members holding Marxist views became increasingly prominent in the party and started criticizing the lifestyle of some of their more affluent comrades. The conflict between the bourgeois and the working classes was increasingly discussed in the party's various forums. This new focus offended many veteran members, some of whom preferred to leave the party, seriously damaging it in the long run.

In a retrospective view of the Qawmiyun's activities in Jordan, George Habash concluded that the party's strongest influence had been among the refugees, in both the West Bank and the East Bank, and among the students and workers. This seems to be, however, clearly a romanticized notion and, except for the reference to students, finds little support in our sources. Like the Baath and the Communist Party, students did play a major role in the Qawmiyun's activities. High school students displayed a marked willingness to accept radical ideas, and to participate in demonstrations. The party strived to organize student associations or even a student's movement which it hoped to control. In this field, however, the Qawmiyun had to vie with the similar efforts of other opposition parties. Students were not inducted into the Qawmiyun in the usual way, through the groups, both for security reasons and because it was felt desirable that they should not be removed from their "natural" framework. Thus attempts were made to establish separate organizations for them. The students were clearly enthusiastic when it came to participating in demonstrations and protests, but there was always the fear that this youthful enthusiasm would pass, and the party was careful not to reveal to them more about itself than was absolutely necessary—and certainly none of its secrets. The student associations (which included girls as well as boys) were established and run by teachers, former students, or even by more mature students themselves, with the help and encouragement of the party's activists. Certain members were specifically charged with the task of maintaining liaison with the student associations.[16]

The student associations were structured on about the same lines as the parent party, with members organized into "student cells." The associations devised a strict set of rules and regulations, which was copied and distributed among their members. The Students Liberation Movement (al-Haraka al-Tullabiya al-Tahririya), for example, carefully set out its procedures for recruitment (in the first stage, only students were to be recruited; later workers, fellahin, clerks, and merchants would be brought in), its view of the economic and political evils plaguing Jordan, its hierarchy, the subscription dues to be paid by each member, and the main tenets of its ideology. Students were primarily demonstrators and helped distribute leaflets. But above and beyond their immediate usefulness, the students constituted a source of the party's future cadres and even of some of its most active leaders. A striking example is Khalil Sufyan, who first became involved in the Qawmiyun as a member of one of the student associations in Jerusalem and rose to the highest levels of its leadership.

The student associations were known by a variety of names: Union of Revolutionary Arab Youth (Ittihad al-Talaba al- Arabi al-Thawri), The Rebel Student's Front (Jabhat al-Talib al-Thair), Revolutionary Arab Students Front (Jabhat al-Talaba al- Arabiya al-Thawriya). These impressive names were chosen for their aura of strength and power when often they referred to no more than a handful of youthful pupils at a single school. Occasionally an association would include students from a number of schools in the same town, but there is no evidence of organized student activity within a single body on a national level.

IDEOLOGY

Ideological Flexibility

The Qawmiyun in Jordan did not have a well formulated ideology as did the Communist Party or the Baath. When it first came into being, the party comprised a few dozen members who shared little more than a strong sense of nationalist consciousness. Outraged by the humiliating defeat of the Arab armies in Palestine, they rallied behind the slogan "Unity, Liberation, Revenge." Their goals were the unification of the Arab nation, liberation from the imperialists and their Arab allies, and revenge for their humiliation in Palestine. The means through which these three goals were to be attained were summed up under another stirring slogan "Blood, Iron, Fire." But neither of these slogans arose from any kind of comprehensive political ideology; both represented no more than the crystallization of a powerful emotional sense of wounded nationalist pride and an urgent need to seek redress. Their formulation owed something to the thought of Sati al-Husari, one of the most active proponents of Arab nationalism, but al-Husari could by no means be considered the party's "spiritual father," as, for example, Michel Aflaq was the Baath's.

The Qawmiyun's ideology began to evolve in the late 1950s, and became more coherent in the early 1960s. This process was precipitated largely by the emergence of a more clearly defined Nasserite ideology in the Arab world. Abd al-Nasser was widely regarded as the one Arab leader who could unify the Arab nation, a belief shared by the Qawmiyun, whose members became some of his most ardent disciples. The breakup of the UAR dealt a severe blow to the Qawmiyun's faith in the Egyptian leader, and after it they adopted an ideological position that sought to synthesize elements of neo-Baathist and Nasserite thought. They did not speak in terms of an "ideology," but rather of a "philosophy"—taking the cue from Abd al-Nasser's seminal essay "Philosophy of the Revolution." Even when there were clearly defined trends in the thinking of the Qawmiyun, they did not really represent ideological principles guiding the party's actions. Many ideological questions were not resolved, and most often when they were, the explanations given were not the product of original thought but rather the recapitulation of ideas adopted from others. This ideological flexibility became a principle in the party's philosophy: in order to attain its objectives, W. Qamhawi stated, the Qawmiyun should be prepared to adopt any ideas that would help further its aims. Such flexibility, he argued would enable the party constantly to revise its positions to conform with an ever-changing reality, would prevent the emergence of ideological schisms, and would allow the party to ignore certain questions which, if raised, were likely to be detrimental. Ideas should never become sacred ends in themselves and should be seen as no more than the means to a much more important end. Ideas should be revised as realities changed and should never be allowed to atrophy.[17]

The Qawmiyun's adherence to the principle of ideological flexibility, and the pragmatism it advocated in dealing with events as they arose, account for the many radical changes in direction the party took in its thinking over the years. The same right-wing party thirsting for revenge (it had even been described by one of its critics as "fascist"[18]) became in the course of a few short years a largely left-wing movement, concerned with far-reaching social reform. Its members ultimately became self-professed "Marxist-leninists" and looked to China, Cuba, and Vietnam for their models.

Judaism, Israel, and Imperialism

The Qawmiyun did take occasionally a somewhat original approach to the question of Judaism, Israel, and imperialism. The traditional Arab view was that Zionism and Israel blindly followed the instructions and served the interest of the imperialists in the Middle East. This view was occasionally reflected in the thinking of the Qawmiyun in the West Bank,[19] but was clearly overshadowed by the party's own belief that Zionism was not subservient to imperialism but an equal ally of the imperialists in the area. In other words, the Zionists were not the vassals of imperialist masters but free agents whose objectives coincided with those of imperialism.[20] By stressing Israel's fundamental independence from the imperialist powers the Qawmiyun sought to dispel what it considered to be the illusionary hope that by allying themselves with the Western powers, the Arabs would be able to bring about the liquidation of the Zionist state—or, conversely, by evicting the Western powers from the area, the same end could be attained. Israel would not disappear, they argued, simply by breaking the bond between it and the imperialist West. What was needed was a direct confrontation, a concerted Arab effort to uproot the independent Zionist entity that had planted itself in their midst.

The Qawmiyun were extremely anxious to make certain that the Palestinian refugees were not forgotten and that the Arab states did not enter into a separate peace agreement with Israel.[21] Thus, in addition to stressing Israel's existence as an entity independent of the imperialist powers, the party constantly sought to depict the Jewish state as an aggressive body possessing a military might out of all proportion to its size,[22] bent on conquering not only the whole of Palestine but the entire Arab world. In the face of such an expansionist state, no Arab country could afford not to be involved in the fray, for that would be against its *own* long-term interests. The Arab world must stand united and locked in battle with Israel until the final victory.

Israel derived its strength, the Qawmiyun argued, from its close ties to world Jewry, no distinction could be drawn between Jews, on the one hand, and Zionists, on the other. This idea was formulated by the party's leadership in Beirut, and was reflected in its publications in the West Bank. Two of the Qawmiyun's most prominent leaders in Beirut asserted that Ben Gurion, Mikunis (a Communist leader), Alfred Lilienthal, and Elmer Berger—men of markedly divergent political views—were party to the Zionist plot: "All of them are Jews having the same clear and definite aims, styles and patterns which to others may seem contradictory and different."[23] While this line is not explicitly spelled out in the literature the Qawmiyun put out in the West Bank, a similar view is clearly implicit, and Israel is almost invariably referred to not by name but as "the State of the Jews." The danger that Israel represented to the Arabs was "the Jewish peril," while Zionism was referred to as "the Jewish idea," and so on. The real enemy of the Arabs was not just Isreal or Zionism, but the Jews themselves, and the three concepts—Isreal, Judaism, and Zionism—were, in their eyes, inextricably intertwined.[24] World Jewry, the Qawmiyun argued, possessed huge resources on which it could draw in fulfilling its aim to subjugate the Arabs. And above and beyond these resources, it also wielded formidable influence, which it had brought to bear in the past on the Ottoman Empire and which it was now bringing to bear on the United States, Britain, and the Western world in general.[25] Moreover, world Jewry not only influenced the Western nations but actually controlled them.[26]

In addition to its essential independence and great military power, the Jewish state was accredited by the Qawmiyun with a series of evil designs against the Arabs. After planting their first seed in the land of Palestine, the Zionists were now carefully nurturing the sapling that had sprung forth. Their purpose, so the argument went, was for this sapling to grow into a huge tree whose roots would in time strangle the entire Arab world. The Jewish "tree" would flourish and grow strong on the ruins of the Arab people and on their shattered right to live on their own land. Thus the duty of the Arabs was clear: they were locked in a life-or-death struggle with the Jewish state. The question was; "Who shall survive—we or they:" for the Jews were intent on the total destruction of the entire Arab nation.[27]

The Qawmiyun in the West Bank, Lebanon, and Egypt shared the same view on the question of Israel, Zionism, and Judaism. The only differences were nuance and formulation. While the Qawmiyun in Lebanon tended to phrase its ideas on this issue in relatively erudite and impassionate terms, its counterpart in the West Bank used much cruder, inflammatory language. Part of the difference could be attributed to the nature of the type of publication the party put out in Beirut as opposed to the West Bank. The language used in leaflets designed to incite the masses in the West Bank was naturally more volatile than that used in the various books and articles appearing on the subject in Beirut. But even more relevant, perhaps, was the relative isolation of the West Bank population from the rest of the Arab world, in contrast with what seemed to them as the imminence and proximity of the Israeli threat, and their constant fear that the other Arab countries might disengage from the conflict and leave them alone to face the Zionist enemy. Hence the insistence that the danger Isreal presented was not to the Palestinians in the West Bank alone but to the Arab world at large.

For all its preoccupation with the Jews and their evil designs, the Qawmiyun did not entirely ignore the threat posed by Western imperialism and, on occasion, by international Communism. Like many Arab nationalists, the Qawmiyun tended to blur the distinction between medieval Christian Europe and present-day Western Europe, which was portrayed as the traditional enemy of the Arabs from time immemorial, the "Jewish National Home" in Palestine being simply the most recent of a long line of European designs on the Arab world. The unholy alliance between the British imperialists and the Zionist colonialists was consecrated in the Balfour Declaration. Western imperialism, represented in the Middle East at the beginning of the Twentieth century by Great Britain, saw in the introduction of "foreign invaders" into the area the surest way of perpetuating the backwardness and division of the Arab nation. They accorded the Jewish invaders unlimited privileges while turning the native population into "oppressed slaves," depriving them of their property and their rights.[28] After the British left the area, the privileged position of the Jews and the oppression of the Palestinians was institutionalized in the 1947 United Nations partition plan, which represented "a plot devised by imperialism and the forces of evil against our homeland . . . with the support of the . . . western countries, which are controlled by the Zionists, and by the Eastern Bloc, led by Russia." It is interesting to note that this "traditional" attack on imperialism included the Soviet Union. At the time it was written, the end of 1957, the Soviet Union was already supplying massive aid to Abd al-Nasser, the Arab leader most highly esteemed by the Qawmiyun, and also to Syria. This could be taken as an indication either of the party's ideological consistency, in that it clung to a position undeterred by the dictates of "Realpolitic," or of the Qawmiyun's blind and fanatical adherence to an outmoded principle, naively ignoring or misinterpreting events in the area.[29] The party's attacks on the United Nations were vicious and uncompromising: the world body's partition resolution was the first "knife in the back of Arab rights. We do not recognize such base resolutions or their legitimacy, and will oppose them to the end."[30]

Despite the gravity of the "Jewish peril" and the might of the imperialists, the Qawmiyun refused to be intimidated and rejected any thought of compromise. Despite all the attempts of the imperialists to get the Arabs to come to terms with the Jewish state, "we must stick by our resolution that there is no solution to our problems in Palestine short of total revenge." The Qawmiyun believed that "the day is not far off when national fervor will take the place of religious fervor." Members of the Jewish religion throughout the world will assimilate and become part of the gentile world. Israel, an atavistic religious state out of step with modern history, will lose its supporters and disappear.[31] The Qawmiyun did not, however, advocate sitting still while history did its work for it. On the contrary, the party laid great stress on the need to mobilize the Arabs for a fierce and relentless struggle against the Jewish state. It was comforting nevertheless, to believe that history was on its side and that the ultimate victory would definitely be the Arab nation's.[32]

Revenge

The urge for blood revenge was a major leitmotif in the Qawmiyun's ideology, and throughout its publications. Not only had the imperialists and the Zionists robbed and enslaved the Arabs, they had shattered their pride. They "have robbed us of at least one precious jewel: our honor. It is our feeling that this precious jewel has been stolen from us that makes us feel humiliated and vengeful, so long as the influence of imperialism is present in our country."[33] The historic wrong done to the Arabs could be amended and their pride restored only after the last traces of imperialism—including Israel—had been removed from the area.

The Qawmiyun's view on the subject of revenge is well-represented in the following excerpts from a pamphlet put out by the party: "The Arab nation is determined to uproot the Jewish presence from the Arab homeland. It will not settle for compromises or partial solutions . . . no peace and no partition . . . . Our national duty obliges us to fight any plot to make peace with the Jews, . . . to work for the realization of our unity, . . . and prepare ourselves for the approaching day of honor, our day of revenge."[34] The slogans "Unity, Liberation, Revenge" (occasionally: "Unity, Revenge, Liberation"),[35] and "Blood, Iron, Fire"[36] summed up the centricity of the urge for revenge in the Qawmiyun's ideology. Even the rank and file members, who make no pretense to understanding the finer points of the party's philosophy, were well versed in these stirring phrases. Toward the end of the 1950s, stung by accusations of fascism, the ideologues in Beirut began gradually to drop the slogans from the party's literature, replacing the call for revenge with one for "the return of Palestine."[37] This was not the case, however, among the local leadership in the West Bank, who stuck by the old slogans. Nevertheless, a change did occur even at this level, and while the terminology remained the same, the call for revenge became perceptibly less prominent in the late 1950s than it had been earlier in the decade. One reason, perhaps, was that with the passage of time revenge may have lost some of its earlier emotional appeal and urgency. Other issues, rising out of the more immediate political conditions, began to fire the imagination of the masses. One was the question of "the Palestinian entity"and how to incorporate this into the pan-Arab ideal. Another was the dissolution of the UAR and how to prevent such breakups in the future. By the early 1960s, issues such as this last had clearly replaced the question of revenge for the 1948 defeat as a major subject of discussion among members of the Qawmiyun.

The notion of revenge continued to appear in the party's leaflets, not so much in the actual body of the text as in the slogans that invariably followed it, beside such slogans as "the Restoration of Palestine," "the Return of Palestine," and "the Annihilation of Israel."[38] In other words, the motif became to a certain extent "ritualized" in the party's publications—but not, according to one member, among the rank and file, for whom the idea of revenge was still very emotional and for whom the urge to avenge the Arab humiliation in Palestine was no less powerful in the early 1960s than it had been a decade earlier. Perhaps the most compelling of the Qawmiyun's aims in the early years, revenge never lost its hold on the imagination of the masses, at least in the West Bank.

It is possible that this loyalty toward a concept inspired by the Arabs' tribal past and by elements of European fascism derived from the nature of the party in the West Bank, which differed considerably from that of the party in Beirut. In Beirut, the party's ideologues came into regular contact with liberal or "westernized" circles. Its publications, which were aimed at a cosmopolitan audience, had to adapt their style to the needs of the time. The Qawmiyun in the West Bank, on the other hand, were not subject to these pressures. Far more important than this, however, was the fact that from the hilly uplands of the West Bank the inhabitants of the area could actually see the fertile coastal strip which was now part of Israel, so revenge was not so much an abstract ideological formula as a deep emotional urge that constantly demanded an outlet. Any party that aspired to attract a mass following would have to take into account the proclivities of the local population and certainly could not afford to ignore the tremendous emotional appeal the idea of revenge had for the population of the West Bank.

As we have seen, the Qawmiyun arrived at a generalization on the Judaism-Zionism question which struck an extremely responsive chord among the largely unsophisticated population of the West Bank. They succeeded in presenting to the population the image of a clearly defined enemy, not only in terms of the contemporary situation in the Middle East, but also in terms of Islamic religious tradition. This argumentation was not unknown in modern Arab thought: even more sophisticated ideologues in other parts of the Arab world tended to confuse the two terms from time to time. It should not be assumed, then, that the actual leadership in the West Bank was any less sophisticated than the party's leaders in Beirut, simply because it had failed to acquiesce to the ideas that had caused Beirut's party to play down the concept of "revenge" as reeking too much of fascism. The party's leaders, including George Habash himself, paid frequent visits to the West

117

Bank, and literature printed in Beirut also found its way into the area.[39] Moreover, the ideas and positions expounded by West Bank leaders were sometimes published in Beirut, where it is reasonable to assume they evoked some response.[40] The West Bank leaders, then were by no means isolated from the mainstream of the party of cut off from the ideas being expounded in Beirut of Damascus. They refused, however, to follow blindly the party policy, realizing that the particular line they were taking in the West Bank was probably better suited to the needs and desires of the local population.

Arab Unity

The Significance of the Concept

The aspiration for Arab unity was the most prominent element in the party's thinking from the very beginning. The call for unity generally took precedence over its other two major objectives—liberation and revenge—and featured in every leaflet or pamphlet that the Qawmiyun published. While the Qamiyun presented the achievement of Arab unity as an end in its own right, they considered it also the means to an even more important end: the liberation of Palestine from its Jewish usurpers and revenge for the humiliation of 1948. A publication of January 1957 succinctly reveals this idea: "This nation will attain....the day of total unity...from which it will derive its great strength,...which will sweep away the Jewish presence from the heart of our homeland and will restore to us our beloved Palestine."[41]

These designs for Arab unity did not change even when the great Pan-Arab ideal was about to be realized: on the eve of the merger between Egypt and Syria in 1958, the Qawmiyun distributed a special pamphlet to mark the event, in which it described the creation of the UAR as the first step in the unification of the entire Arab world. But the final objective was not forgotten, and the pamphlet went on to point out that the end result of this Arab unity would be the liberation of Palestine: "Go forward to unity on your way to glory, to the restoration of the great homeland and to your homes on the shores of Palestine."[42] Four years later the same view was still prevalent. Commemorating the anniversary of the Free Officers' coup in Egypt, the Qawmiyun defined the objective of Arab nationalism (which, they believed, the revolution in Egypt had served to advance) as "the sacred nationalist progress" toward the liberation of Palestine. The pamphlet then dealt with the question of the Palestinian entity in the following terms: "The path to Palestine is the path of the organized Arab nation, struggling...to establish a single state that will include Jordan, Iraq, Syria, and the southern area, [a state] whose army, behind which would stand the entire Arab nation, will burst forward in a drive that will obliterate the shame of the disaster... in 1948. The struggle of our nation to liberate itself...will build the firm and secure bridge over which we will advance to Palestine."[43] The liberation of Palestine was to be the *final* objective, but occasionally a secondary objective was mentioned: unity would enable the Arab nation to liberate itself from "foreign influence" and from imperialism.[44]

Here too, then, the Qawmiyun gave their final objective a concrete form that was clear to all, unlike the somewhat sophisticated abstract objectives set out by parties with a fully evolved political doctrine, such as the Baath. As a result, the party was far more accessible to the masses in the West Bank and much easier for them to identify with.

In the mid-1960s a new attitude began to emerge. Following the dissolution of the UAR and the failure of the tripartite unity talks in the spring of 1963, it became apparent that Arab unity was not likely in the immediate future. This led the Qawmiyun to have second thoughts about the speedy liberation of Palestine. Egypt's revised stand on the Palestine question undoubtedly had a considerable effect on the Qawmiyun. Toward the end of 1963, Abd al-Nasser began to speak increasingly of a "Palestinian entity," and this too induced the Qawmiyun to separate the hitherto intertwined issues of Arab unity and the liberation of Palestine. While the link between the two issues was never finally broken, the party began to view it as considerably less strong than it had been in the past. Arab unity ceased to be a prior condition for the liberation of Palestine, and the latter came to be seen as the more immediate objective. Accordingly, the Qawmiyun, taking their cue from Abd al-Nasser began to speak of the need for a closely defined Palestinian entity.[45] The concept of Arab unity and its significance as a precondition for the liberation of Palestine was so deeply rooted, however, that it could not be jettisoned, and the idea continued important in the party's thinking—but now as an end in itself.

The first signs of this shift in emphasis began to emerge even before the final breakup of the UAR. Influenced by the Baath and the gradually crystallizing Nasserite ideology, the Qawmiyun began to consider Arab unity the solution to a far wider range of problems besetting the Arab world than merely that of the Palestinians. First, they began to see unity as a way of achieving "socialist liberation"—which is why, they argued, the concept was so fiercely opposed by the reactionary Arab regimes and by the enemies of the Arab nation alike. Beyond this, unity was seen as the key to achieving the Arabs' most important nationalist goals. The link between Arab unity and the Palestine question was referred to only in passing, as a secondary issue. Moreover, at the end of some leaflets, slogans appeared calling for the success of the UAR and Arab nationalism, with no mention whatever of Palestine.[46]

In the years that followed, 1963–64, the Qawmiyun continued to keep the two issues separate. Palestine was an issue that demanded immediate action, which should be spearheaded by the Palestinians themselves. The question of unity was discussed as a separate long-term issue, far less superficially than it had been in the past, with a clear awareness that it concerned the entire Arab people and involved the ultimate success of Arab nationalism.[47]

In a pamphlet put out to mark the publication of the proposed tripartite unity plan in the spring of 1963, the Qawmiyun stipulated that Arab unity must be associated with a number of socialist principles, including those of social progress and revolution.[48] Even when discussing the proposed union between Iraq and Egypt in 1964, the Qawmiyun stressed the social implications of unity. It was this socialist element inherent in unity that would enable the Arab nation to realize its full potential. Socialist unity would enable the Arab nation to safeguard the achievements that had already been made in the advanced Arab countries—Algeria, Yemen, Iraq, and Egypt—and it was socialist unity that would "open the way for Arab thought to participate in the building of human civilization."[49] From being merely a means to advance the liberation of Palestine, then, Arab unity had become an ideological goal in its own right. A consideration of the nature of this unity thus becomes important.

The Nature of Arab Unity

The Qawmiyun viewed Arab unity as a historic imperative. While its ultimate achievement was inevitable, much was needed to be done to hasten the process. According to the party's theory unity was the aspiration of the Arab masses and no power on earth could deny its realization. The idea of unity was imprinted on the soul of every true Arab, and the desire to realize it was an organic part of his very being. Despite the vicissitudes of history, despite the machinations of the Arabs' enemies, their present divisions and weaknesses, Arab unity remained an eternal truth.[50] This view was largely inspired by Sati al-Husari's assertion that Arab unity was "a natural idea...which stemmed from the very nature of society."[51] The Qawmiyun saw it as the party's function to arouse this dormant idea among the Arab masses.[52] It was aware that this would not be easy to do, with only a small minority of the Arab people aware of the inner command calling them to rally for nationalism. The majority was captive to its cruder emotions, its awareness was circumscribed and atrophied, and to some extent it was even hostile to the idea of unity.[53]

The Qawmiyun's publications were strongly silent on the subject of what features characterized a nation. But we can assume that the party would have accepted al-Husari's view that the Islamic religion alone was not sufficient to define nationhood, and that the Arab nation would have to be characterized by its "Arabness," not by its Islamic features.[54] Nowhere in the party's publications was there the slightest hint that Islam had any relevance as a basis for political identity: the call was for *Arab*, not Islamic, unity. Beyond this, however, the Qawmiyun made no attempt in its publications to clearly define the nature and characteristics of this Arab nationhood. At the same time, the party gave no indication of rejecting al-Husari's thesis that it was their common language and their common history that made the Arabs a nation. The impression that emerges from the publication is that, like al-Husari, the party viewed the basis of Arab nationhood as being not a common religion, economic integration, geographic contiguity, or race, but its "Arabness"—a linguistic-cultural entity which had evolved in a context of historic continuity.[55]

The Need for Unity and the Path to Its Realization

From its inception until the mid-1960s, and perhaps even later, the Qawmiyun incessantly discussed the lessons to be learned from the defeat of the Arab armies in 1948. This discussion crested every year with the approach of May 15, the day Israel was declared a state. Because the need for Arab unity was the primary (and almost only) lesson the Qawmiyun took from the 1948 defeat, whenever some form of Arab union appeared imminent, the party would draw attention to the tragedy in Palestine to justify the move and call for further steps toward total unity. With the dissolution of the UAR in September 1961, the Qawmiyun began to deal with the Palestine tragedy and with the breakup as a single issue. Both disasters, it argued, stemmed from the same causes. By dealing with these causes, therefore, both objectives—the return to Palestine and the realization of Arab unity—would be achieved at the same time. In the 1960s, however, when the Qawmiyun tended to separate the two objectives, they were discussed jointly only on the appropriate occasions—such as the moves toward unity in March 1963 and mid-1964, and again when these moves ran aground.

Lessons of the Palestine Tragedy. The defeat of the Arab armies in Palestine in 1948 was not only a great military and political disaster for the Arabs, but also a staggering blow to their pride and the cause of their deep sense of humiliation. The events in Palestine were thus referred to as the "tragedy," or "disaster." In retrospect, however, the Qawmiyun did not see the defeat as a freak incident, but rather the outcome of the situation in which the Arabs had found themselves for a long time prior to 1948, "the expression of the crises affecting the Arab world."[56] The analysis of these crises and how to go about overcoming them preoccupied the Qawmiyun in its leaflets and other publications. Unlike many other analyses of the tragedy, the Qawmiyun's did not attempt to place the blame for what happened in Palestine exclusively on outside forces and their corrupt agents in the area, even though it recognized that these had undoubtedly played a part. Rather, the party sought the cause in the Arab world itself, fixing the blame on the Arab leadership, the nature of the Arab society, and even on the character of the Arab individual.[57]

In the 1950s, even though a great deal of space was given in the Qawmiyun's publications to the Palestine tragedy and its lessons, much of the analysis was relatively superficial, going no further than attaching the blame for the disaster on the divided nature of the Arab world and the selfish corruption of its leaders.[58] Unity was to be the panacea for all these ills. Unity was the answer to the question of how the potential strength of the Arabs could be realized as quickly and effectively as possible. "The bitterness of the tragedy obliges us to be in a genuine state of war, and obliges those responsible to mobilize all the might of the nation and direct this toward the usurped homeland....Let May 15 be the motivat-

ing force that will drive us...along the way of might and power...
toward unity and liberation."[59] It is hardly surprising, therefore,
that the Qawmiyun placed great hopes on the first tentative steps
leading to the merger between Syria and Egypt, and urged the
Arab leaders to step up their efforts to overcome the deficiencies
preventing the Arab world from uniting, those deficiencies that
had led to the defeat in 1948. On June 27, 1956, the Syrian prime
minister, Sabri al-Asali, declared that he would work toward
bringing his country into a union with Egypt. A short time later he
met with Abd al-Nasser and the two leaders issued a communiqué
announcing that negotiations would start on the unification of
their countries. The Qawmiyun received the news enthusiastically:
"May the merger [*ittihad*] between Syria and Egypt be the first
step, to be quickly followed by...the union [*tawhid*] between
Jordan, Lebanon, Iraq, the [Arabian] peninsular, and the Arab
Maghreb."[60] Only unity would enable the Arab nation to realize
its aspirations, and give it the strength to "obliterate its humiliation, its weakness, and foreign influence...and restore the usurped
parts of your homes." Only unity would "remove the hated artificial barriers...that are rending our homeland...and the weak and
divided entities will fall."[61] In a similar spirit of enthusiasm and
anticipation that the divisions that had led to the 1948 Arab
defeat would somehow magically disappear, the Qawmiyun received
Jordan's decision at the beginning of 1957 to accept Arab economic aid in place of the aid Britain had provided.[62]

The only difference in tone which made itself felt after the
merger between Egypt and Syria was a renewed hostility to the
Jordanian regime: "Let us...take upon ourselves a firm...commit-
ment...to work together fearlessly for the abolition of all the
artificial entities along with all the monarchies."[63]

It would appear, then, that until the creation of the UAR, the
Qawmiyun viewed the Palestine tragedy in a one-dimensional,
simplified way: the failure of the Arab armies in 1948 was the
direct result of the political divisions in the Arab world, and
the unification of the Arab states would generate the strength
necessary to obliterate the humiliation. Little systematic thought
was given to how unity was to be achieved, and the Qawmiyun's
views on this question, insofar as they can be deduced from the
party's literature, are self-contradictory. On the one hand, leaflets
distributed in the 1950s called on the entire nation to unite. This
was reflected in the name the party gave its official organ in those

years—"The People Are Stronger." Slogans like "the duty of the people" and "it is our duty to continue the struggle so that through our fight we will bring about...unity," which were very common in the leaflets of the 1950s, were invariably addressed to "the sons of the Arab Nation." Superficially, then, there can be little doubt that the party's approach was a popular one, and that unity was to evolve from the masses, whom it was the Qawmiyun's duty to enlighten and educate to a full awareness of their innate desire for unity.[64] On the other hand, however, the Qawmiyun pursued their political activities on an entirely different plane. Whenever it appeared that two or more Arab states were moving toward some form of meaningful cooperation, the Qawmiyun would become charged with enthusiasm and call for an extension and deepening of whatever ties were being contemplated. This was even the case when the Hashemite regime in Jordan happened to be involved—as it was when Sulayman Nabulsi was prime minister—notwithstanding the party's deep-seated antipathy for that regime. In other words, the Qawmiyun were not prepared to wait indefinitely for the enlightenment of the masses, and were not averse to pressing for a form of Arab unity imposed by the existing regimes, provided only that this led to the abrogation of the hated borders that divided the Arab world and prevented it from mobilizing its full strength to redeem Palestine and throw off the yoke of Western imperialism.

In a pamphlet put out by the party to mark the creation of the UAR, the dissonance between these two approaches—of unity generated by the masses or imposed by the existing regimes— emerges quite clearly: "In February 1958, the trend toward unity which is deeply rooted in the Syrian Arab people combined with the creative leadership associated with the people in Egypt and representing it...and, in conformity with the wish of both peoples, the Egyptian and the Syrian, the United Arab Republic was created."[65] Elsewhere the following appeared: "The merger did not suddenly come about as the result of the wish of the Egyptian and Syrian leaders alone, but is the true expression...of the wish of the Arab nation in every Arab land."[66] It was apparently possible for the Qawmiyun to resolve the contradiction between these two views. Pragmatism was the keynote of the party's thinking in the West Bank. The primary goal was to achieve unity in order that Palestine might be liberated: all other considerations were secondary. While the Qawmiyun genuinely sought to enlighten the masses, it at no time expressed the opinion that Arab unity was dependent on the completion of this process of enlightenment.[67] The task of the masses, the party believed, was to bring pressure to bear on their governments to unite, and not necessarily to bring about Arab unity through their own direct efforts, from below. Unity would come about, then, in the name of the Arab people, not necessarily directly through them. The steps taken by those regimes which the Qawmiyun quite arbitrarily deemed to be "creative regimes" (such as that of Egypt) represented the implementation of the people's wishes, and should thus be seen as constituting a movement toward a genuine and comprehensive Arab unity.[68]

Lessons of the Breakup of the UAR. In the 1960s the Qawmiyun's approach to the causes of the tragedy of Palestine took on a new dimension. The merger between Egypt and Syria was enthusiastically supported by the party, which began to show signs in its publications of socialist influences derived from the Nasserite ideology. The most significant change in approach, however, was precipitated by the breakup of the UAR in September 1961. The blow the breakup dealt to the Qawmiyun (who for several years had held the implicit belief that the Egyptian-Syrian merger represented the start of the irrepressible move toward total Arab unity) was no less shattering than that dealt by the defeat of the Arab armies in Palestine in 1948, and led to a great deal of soul-searching and reappraisal. The debate on the question of Arab unity and the redemption of Palestine was renewed on a higher level of abstraction than it had been in the past, but it followed much the same lines. The faults were sought among the Arabs themselves, rather than placing the blame on outside forces. Because the tragedy of division in the Arab world was the direct cause of the disaster in Palestine, the two issues were viewed as interrelated: "The Arab nation once again finds itself confronting a great national trial.... In the face of this heavy blow, it is essential that we undertake a thorough reappraisal of ourselves in order to analyze the lessons to be learned from the event."[69]

Shortly before the dissolution of the UAR, a new trend of thought emerged in the Qawmiyun's publications. Under the influence of Michel Aflaq the party began to talk of the "spiritual revolution" that the Arabs would have to undergo, as individuals and as a nation. This represented an implicit criticism of the position the party had taken in the past: "The reactionary rulers will not cease...to work against the Palestine problem and...the division [of the Arab world]...if we don't carry out a revolution of our spirits, a revolution against our reality...a collective revolution in which each one of us will take part."[70] After the breakup of the UAR, the debate on the need for this spiritual revolution became even more intensive, and dwelt also on the notion of the "revolutionary vanguard." Each individual, the party said, must undergo this spiritual revolution in order to make him a "good citizen" of the Arab homeland: "On the rememberance day marking May 15, we are duty-bound to adopt an alert, conscious, and revolutionary stance...that will be reflected in every citizen and will make him a responsible, committed, and active individual."[71] The role of the Qawmiyun was to revitalize the emotional, apathetic individual who evaded all responsibility for his fate and pinned his hope on miracles. This "new man" would be balanced, aware, and able to confront reality and work to change it. He would be prepared to accept responsibility, and to "place the good of society and the homeland before his own personal well-being."[72]

After the failure of the tripartite union between Egypt, Syria, and Iraq in the spring of 1963, the Qawmiyun took one step in their quest to account for the shattering blows that had struck their vision of Arab unity. They developed from their concept of "the good citizen" a new image—that of the "revolutionary vanguard." Every member of the party was to serve as a prototype of the "new man" of the future, in spirit, in his way of life, and in his every action. In this way he would become the living embodiment of the type of change that every Arab individual would have to undergo. Four chief characteristics marked the revolutionary vanguard: identification with the suffering of the people, awareness of the need for change, willingness for personal sacrifice in order to help bring about this change, and the ability to act with determination and initiative. The image of the ideal member of the revolutionary vanguard was articulated in the eulogy published in honor of a member of the party, a native of Jerusalem, who was assassinated by the Baathists in Iraq at the end of 1963: "In your way of life you served as an example of how the Arab citizen should live. You lived in constant revolt....You realized your [own] revolution in the framework of organized activity to wipe out the failures of your Arab homeland....And you prepared yourself to bear even greater [burdens]."[73] Qamhawi enumerates other attributes of the vanguard: a practical and realistic approach to planning activities, a capacity for uncompromising self-appraisal, and an ability to withstand long periods of loneliness and sometimes even social ostracism. This latter quality was particularly important, as was the ability to withstand an almost complete alienation from one's surroundings. The value of a member of the revolutionary vanguard was not as an individual but as a component of the avant-garde group, whose sole function was to translate the ideals of the party into action and to inculcate these ideals in the Arab public at large.

The debate on this topic began immediately after the dissolution of the UAR, with severe criticism being directed not only at the path the party had taken in the past, but also at the Arab leader the Qawmiyun most admired—Abd al-Nasser. The party viewed the breakup of the UAR as "a defeat for the idea of unity...a blow to the faith of those who believed in it and a victory for those who claimed that it was an unrealistic figment of the imagination."[74] But at the same time, the breakup was not seen as a final blow to the idea of Arab unity. It was undoubtedly a setback, and demanded serious analysis in order to determine what had gone wrong and how this might be corrected: "The fundamental weakness of the situation of the Arab nation" was "the lack of popular organization," which would provide the impetus for the Arab's spiritual revolution. In what was clearly an indication of how the party believed the merger between Syria and Egypt to have come about, with an implicit criticism of its own stand at the time of the merger, the Qawmiyun concluded: "Arab reaction will continue to guide the path of this people, imperialism will continue to control the fate of our nation.... and feudalism and capitalism will continue to control a large part...of our nation as long as it fails to organize itself on a popular basis, [a form of organization] derived from the people and not imposed on it."[75]

Later, the Qawmiyun separated its new approach to the question of Arab unity into a number of distinct elements, which they analyzed one by one. First, unity must have a popular base. Second, the masses should be armed with "the weapon of awareness." Revolutionary-national awareness was the foundation on which all action was based.[76] Third, an organizational framework should be created, to educate the masses and make them intp a cohesive group capable of concerted action. These were to be the three fundamental attributes of what the Qawmiyun called "a popular ideological organized movement." Only such a movement, it held, would bring the masses to the point where they would be able to "carry out their historic function."[77] Such a movement, incorporating the ideals outlined above, would constitute "the revolutionary vanguard in the Arab homeland."[78]

"The United Arab Movement"

In the National Covenant which he presented before the Egyptian people after the dissolution of the UAR, Abd al-Nasser suggested a new approach: before the political unification of the Arab world, socialist regimes would need to be established in each individual Arab country through a program of subversive activity controlled, or at least directed, by Egypt.[79]

The Qawmiyun adopted the Nasserite approach, at least in its broad outlines.[80] Concerning the ultimate objective of the Arab nation, they had no reservations. The Qawmiyun fully agreed that unity could not be based on a superficial constitutional agreement between a group of states. Unity would have to come about as the result of a series of "popular-patriotic revolutions that would evolve into a socialist revolution of unification." The party also accepted that the struggle for a unified Arab state, based on socialist principles, would have to be led by "the Arab revolutionary command in Cairo." Influenced by Abd al-Nasser's new approach to the question of Arab unity, the Qawmiyun also reviewed their concept of the time involved. "Constitutional unity," which they had striven for in the 1950s, was now seen as only a pale reflection of the genuine socialist unity, which would take much longer to realize.[81] Having adopted the Nasserite approach, the Qawmiyun set about formulating the path to be taken in realizing its final objective—the path of "unified revolutionary action."

In their analysis of this path, the Qawmiyun ideologues displayed a considerable degree of independence and originality. The Arab masses would not be able to spark off the revolutionary "explosion" that would result in a progressive form of Arab unity, as they were currently in a state of crisis. Instead of being fused and working in concert, the various popular movements were split up, each working independently in its own section of the divided Arab world. In the absence of any form of consolidated organization or coherent ideology, each of these separate movements was captive to the outworn ideologies current in its own particular region. How could the masses break out of this paralyzing stranglehold? The Qawmiyun tried to come to grips with the problem by devising a plan which, it believed, would lead ultimately to the unification of the Arab world on a socialist-revolutionary basis. In each Arab country, a consolidated popular movement should be created out of the various popular-patriotic organizations that at the moment were functioning independently of each other. At the same time, the activities of each national movement should be coordinated. In other words, the process of consolidation within each individual country should be accompanied by a similar consolidation of popular mass movements on the pan-Arab level. This was to constitute a single process, which the Qawmiyun called "the regional-national path" (*tariq qutri-qawmi*) to Arab unity. The fusion of the two processes was intended to overcome the artificial barriers dividing the Arab world, which were dissipating the revolutionary strength of the Arab people, and to prevent the movements when they were in the process of formation in each individual country from losing contact with the overall Egyptian leadership of the concerted revolutionary struggle in its initial stage.

On the pan-Arab level, the revolutionary movement would go through two phases. The first would be the preliminary revolutionary phase, in which certain ideological inconsistencies associated with a blurring of class boundaries would be tolerated. This was inevitable as a result of existing conditions in the Arab world. During this phase, the first tentative steps would be taken toward coordinating the activities of the movements in each individual country. These movements would by nature still be largely popular-patriotic rather than socialist; only at a later stage would they be "fused" into a unified socialist movement which would bring about the consolidation of all the Arab countries in a single socialist revolution.

All the movements would be striving toward unification on both the regional and pan-Arab levels, and would constitute avant-garde movements that would ultimately bring about the total unification of the Arab world.[82] The Qawmiyun saw itself as one of these avant-garde movements. Others were the National Union in Egypt, The Algerian Liberation Front, and the Baath (this was before the Baathists came to power in Syria and Iraq). While each of these latter movements would have to purge themselves of certain "inappropriate elements,"[83] their final objectives were identical with the Qawmiyun's: Arab unity, a socialist society, and liberation of the Arab homeland.

In formulating this program, the Qawmiyun displayed a good deal of flexibility. It is true that the party's final objective was considerably more far-reaching than the type of unity it had postulated in the 1950s. But it acknowledged the fact that there was more than one way to achieve this objective, and was prepared to endorse any course of action that would further its ultimate aim. In this respect, the party exhibited an admirable sense of realism. In the short term, before the creation of the "unified Arab movement," the Qawmiyun was prepared to place its movement under the direct control of Abd al-Nasser in order to advance, even if slowly and hesitantly, the course of the popular-socialist revolution in the Arab world.[84] While this represented a significant departure from its former position, the Qawmiyun did not let it become a deterrent. Its main objective during this phase was simply to improvise, taking its cue from the revolutionary leadership in Egypt. This willingness to forge links with other movements in the Arab world was a measure of the realism displayed by the Qawmiyun's leadership. The long-term objective was, of course, the complete fusion of the various movements and of the various Arab countries. But in the meantime, the Qawmiyun set itself the less ambitious objective of "providing the opportunity for the establishment of serious ideological and organizational links between the various socialist elements [in the Arab world] and the revolutionary leadership represented by...Abd al-Nasser," paving the way toward "complete ideological and organizational fusion."[85] But at the same time, the Qawmiyun was opposed to revealing the details of its infrastructure or the names of its members to its brother movements—not even to the Egyptians. It was George Habash who insisted on retaining this secrecy, as he strongly suspected that the Egyptians' desire for unity was somewhat frivolous and was not willing to rely on them completely—despite their ideological commitment to the revolution and their trust in the Egyptian president.[86]

Democracy[87]

In its discussions on the question of democracy, the Qawmiyun closely echoed the thinking of Abd al-Nasser in the National Covenant. The party accepted the Egyptian leader's definitions of socialism as "economic justice," and democracy as "political justice." It was the function of socialism to raise the level of popular consciousness, while democracy was intended to provide the ruling regime with its popular basis. The unified Arab state of the future would have to combine what was positive in the Communist world (social justice) with whatever was positive in the West (political justice and individual liberty). Western democracy, the Qawmiyun believed, had ignored what it called "economic justice" in allowing capitalists to use their money to influence the political system in pursuit of their own selfish interests. Abd al-Nasser's Covenant spoke of the way in which the capitalists and feudalists had exploited their position in Egypt, stressing their control of the press. The Qawmiyun singled out as its example the United States, where, it claimed, the capitalists influenced both the legislature and the executive (and sometimes even the judiciary) despite the country's democratic tradition. The power and the privileges that their great wealth accorded the capitalists in the West made a mockery of the principles of social justice, liberty, popular government, and the rule of law.

The Qawmiyun did not go into detail concerning the actual shape democracy was to take in practice (it did not, for example, mention the role of political parties in its future democratic Arab state), but the impression that emerges from the party's publications is that it would be essentially that of the West, purged of its undesirable capitalistic elements. This impression is strengthened by the party's description of the form the future Arab state's institutions were to take. At the same time, the Qawmiyun also espoused a doctrine of "popular democracy" (see above), which was completely alien to the Western democratic tradition. The contradiction between the two concepts did not appear to trouble the Qawmiyun, and the party made no attempt to resolve it.

Thus far, the approach of the Qawmiyun was essentially that of Abd al-Nasser in the National Covenant. The party did, however, differ somewhat in its view of the history of democracy in the Arab world, and the obstacles that stood in the way of its evolution in the area. Displaying an admirable degree of intellectual candor, the Qawmiyun admitted that democracy was a concept imported from the West. In the party's view, the idea had entered the area at the beginning of the century, when the first Arab nationalists were fighting "the tyranny of Ottoman imperialism" and demanding Arab autonomy and various individual liberties, such as freedom of expression. Democracy was, therefore, "one of the most prominent demands of the Arab awakening" and had been put forward by numerous nationalist organizations ever since.[88]

Between the two World Wars, the struggle against Western imperialism was portrayed as a struggle for the democratic principles of national liberation and individual freedoms. After the tragedy in Palestine, the Arabs began to perceive the defects in Western democracy, so the argument went, and evolved the purified form of socialist democracy, where democracy and socialism were fused, as the correct path to genuine freedom.

The Qawmiyun acknowledged that true democracy demanded a high level of "popular, national, political, and social awareness." Democracy was not merely a question of rights, but also one of obligations and responsibilities. The Arabs had not yet attained this level, the Qawmiyun admitted, and it would be a long time before they did. Accordingly, during the interim period while the masses were being prepared, there would have to be some form of political regime that was less than democratic—provided that this regime were committed to preparing the ground for the ultimate realization of true democracy.

Socialism

In the 1950s, the Qawmiyun paid little or no attention to social issues. The unmistakable populist tendencies the party displayed even in those years, accompanied by a distinct distaste for the current Arab regimes, were not the result of any firm ideological commitment to the oppressed masses or any other comprehensive social philosophy. Disillusion with the Arab leadership stemmed rather from its failure in Palestine, its failure to unite the Arab world, and its failure to devote itself to the real interests of the Arab nation. In other words, the Qawmiyun was at this time prepared to come to terms with the social status quo, regarding any attempt at social reform to be an unnecessary diversion of energy from the main objectives of the Arab nation—the liberation of Palestine and the unification of the Arab countries. In this respect, the Qawmiyun in the West Bank did not differ from its leadership in Beirut.[89]

Following the merger between Syria and Egypt in 1958, the Qawmiyun gradually started to adopt elements of the Egyptian brand of socialism. In the years 1958–61, the influence of this doctrine on the Qawmiyun was slight. The subject was not discussed in any of its publications, and even the term "socialism" appeared only very rarely.[90] After the breakup of the UAR in 1961, the term was used more frequently, along with associated concepts such as "popular socialism" and "progress." This reflected the Qawmiyun's growing ideological affinity with Nasserite ideology, but the party still refrained from discussing the subject in any great depth, or from drawing any conclusions concerning its relevance to the party's view of Arab nationalism.[91] The term appeared regularly in connection with Abd al-Nasser's campaign against Syrian "reactionism," which he blamed for the breakup of the UAR. The Qawmiyun in the West Bank accepted Abd al-Nasser's view of the interrelated nature of Arab unity and socialist principles, but as yet went no further than formally echoing his views without making any real effort to analyze or appraise them for itself.

During this period, the Qawmiyun elsewhere in the Arab world, particularly in Beirut and in Iraq, went considerably further in relating socialist doctrine to its concept of Arab unity. The Qawmiyun in Iraq entered into a sharp confrontation with the regime and with the Communists as a result of its support for Abd al-Nasser and his call for union between Iraq and the UAR. In the course of this confrontation, the Qawmiyun decided to fight the Communists on their own terms, and began to woo the "workers, fellahin, and the masses" by purporting to have at heart, in addition to their nationalist interests, their everyday material needs: it was fighting not only for Arab unity but also for every Arab's right to his daily bread.[92]

On May 1, 1960, one of the party's leading ideologues in Beirut published an article in which he argued that there existed an organic link between "the political-national question," on the one hand, and the "question of the workers" and the "question of the farmers," on the other. "The Arab question today involves an overall revolutionary approach that will serve to fuse the national, political, economic, and social aspirations of the progressive Arab masses."[93] This represented a significant departure from the Qawmiyun's previous pronouncements on the question of socialism, as it raised social issues from the status of attractive catch-phrases to an integral part of the party's ideology. The group that put out the party's paper *al-Hurriya* adopted an increasingly radical approach to the question of socialism, and a few months before the publication of Abd al-Nasser's National Covenant, they already called openly for the annihilation not only of the "feudalists" and the "capitalists," but also the "bourgeoisie" and the "allies" of the upper classes. The National Covenant, however, numbered the so-called bourgeoisie among the five working "forces" in Egypt, and while acknowledging that many of them did in fact cooperate with the propertied classes, did not hold them responsible for the cooperation.

The growing gulf between the approach of the Qawmiyun in Beirut and that of the Nasserites did not influence the party in the West Bank. Loyal to the "traditional" approach, it did not overstress the significance of social issues, and until the middle of 1962, appeared to lag slightly behind the Nasserites on these matters.

When the National Covenant was made public, in May 1962, the Qawmiyun endorsed it wholeheartedly, describing it as "an ideological event of historic proportions, which the UAR and the Arab world had awaited for many years." The Covenant represented "an extraordinary ideological leap forward," a serious attempt to formulate an ideology in an original, analytic manner. It was "mature, deep, and comprehensive."[94]

Although not explicitly, the Qawmiyun accepted Abd al-Nasser's view of his doctrine in its entirety. The Covenant, the party stated, was not a static collection of ideals but an expression of independent thinking, "the living summation of the revolutionary experience undergone in Egypt."[95] Like Abd al-Nasser, the party firmly believed that theories should be shaped by reality—a pragmatic approach that had traditionally informed its position on social issues.

For all its enthusiasm, the Qawmiyun wrote, it did not feel that Nasserism was the only legitimate revolutionary force in the Arab world. The Covenant was not to be seen as the end of the road, but simply an important milestone along the way—for Egypt and the Arab world alike. This milestone was seen primarily as the beginning of a significant surge forward in Arab nationalist thinking: "Every Arab movement...and every Arab thinker, must...carefully study the Covenant,...to encourage the flourishing of new ideas." In this way the Covenant would undoubtedly help Arab thought to "extricate itself from the complexities that had paralyzed it" in the past, and make possible fruitful "ideological debate."[96]

The ambivalence that characterized the Qawmiyun's attitude to the National Covenant in the early 1960s made it easier for the party to absorb the socialist ideals it contained without exaggerating their immediate significance. This enabled it to adopt Abd al-Nasser's

"Arab Socialism" in its entirety, simply as another means to the final nationalist end, unity.

In the mid-1960s, the *al-Hurriya* group in Beirut took another step in the direction of Marxism. While purporting to be a staunch Nasserite, Muhsin Ibrahim began to criticize the nationalist leaders who had sprung up throughout the Arab world in the 1950s from the ranks of the army and from the middle classes. He accused them of being captive to their petit bourgeoisie mentalities, which left them with a "complex" concerning "classical Marxism and socialist thought."[97] Members of the group even criticized their own party, accusing it of having served the interests of the middle and upper classes in the 1950s. The Qawmiyun in the West Bank, however, remained loyal to the party's veteran leadership: George Habash, Wadi Haddad, Hani al-Hindi, and others, who rejected the new radical ideas that had taken hold in Beirut under the inspiration of men like Muhsin Ibrahim and Naif Hawatma.[98] Nevertheless, in one of its pamphlets published in 1963, the Qawmiyun in the West Bank did include what appeared to be a fairly radical interpretation of Egyptian "Arab Socialism." The pamphlet spoke of "the oppressed masses" who were duty-bound to bring about a social revolution that would liberate them from the "exploitative class system" and make them master of their own affairs. It was essential, the pamphlet continued, to bring about "a radical change" in the distribution of power so that the oppressed masses could attain "the revolutionary leadership of the socialist revolution." What Abd al-Nasser called "the union of popular working forces," the Qawmiyun called "the union of the masses" or the "popular front" (*al-Jabha al-shaabiya*)—the first hint of the names given to the organizations that emerged in the late 1960s. According to Abd al-Nasser, these "popular working forces" were the fellahin, workers, middle classes, soldiers, and intellectuals; according to the Qawmiyun, they were "the fellahin, workers, middle classes, and revolutionary intellectuals."

The Qawmiyun believed that the Arab revolution should also base itself on "an alliance of the popular ideological organizations and the trade unions." While the National Charter spoke of the "participation" of the workers in the control of production, the Qawmiyun spoke of "transferring" the means of production to the masses after a period of preparation.[99] This would seem to indicate an identification of the Qawmiyun with the socialist principles of the Charter, albeit with a certain degree of originality and a clear tendency in the direction of the leftist wing of the Nasserite camp.[100]

Concerning the democratization of production, the Qawmiyun held that nationalization alone was not sufficient, and the process should also include the establishment of "workers' councils" which would elect a "management council" to work alongside the government-appointed manager. This was, of course, seen as an interim arrangement pending the final socialist revolution. It conformed with the principles laid out in the National Charter, but, interestingly, the Qawmiyun looked not to Egypt but to Algeria for its example of how the arrangement should work in practice.[101]

The Qawmiyun, which had at first been considerably more conservative than the Free Officers regime in Egypt in its stand on social issues, underwent a gradual process of radicalization which took it beyond the position of the Nasserites. By the mid-1960s, the socialism advocated by the party in the West Bank was thus somewhat to the left of that advocated by the Nasserites, and was to some extent influenced by neo-Baathist ideas. Nevertheless, the Qawmiyun in the West Bank refrained from openly opposing the Nasserite line, as did their comrades in Beirut.[102]

Just as the party tried to preserve a considerable degree of organizational autonomy, so too did it display considerable ideological independence vis-à-vis the Nasserites in Egypt. While its basic outlook did not differ substantially from that of the latter, various differences of emphasis and nuance did emerge over the years. It was in the field of social issues that these differences were most pronounced, but even here the Qawmiyun in the West Bank were a good deal more orthodoxly "Nasserite" than their comrades elsewhere in the Arab world.

The Palestinian Entity

The call for a "Palestinian Revolution" was first raised in 1958, by the recently founded al-Fath organization. The following year the idea of a "Palestinian entity" began to gain currency in the Arab world, and developed during the 1960s. The Qawmiyun had very good reason to welcome the idea, as it served the party's fundamental aim of assuring that the Palestinian problem was never forgotten or neglected. Nevertheless, the party was less than enthusiastic about the notion of the Palestinians constituting a separate "entity," as it had always maintained that the road to redemption for the Palestinians lay in the final attainment of the pan-Arab ideal. To stress the idea of Palestinian particularism could only serve to weaken the drive toward this ideal. This view prevailed in the late 1950s, when the merger between Egypt and Syria was seen as the first important step toward the redemption of Palestine.

Writing in 1961, Qamhawi expressed the reservations of the Qawmiyun on this question: "There is no agreed definition of this entity, or of its goal."[103] The Palestinian entity had no value as a body comprising a few individuals whose objective would be to represent the Arabs of Palestine, or even as a formal government, as long as the Palestinian Arabs remained without their natural rights as citizens. Neither would there be any value in an army composed of Palestinian Arabs, whose objective would be to restore Palestine to its owners, "as this would mean no more than the creation of another Arab command" instead of the much needed "unification of [the existing] military commands and the creation of a single army."

If the intention was to make the Arabs of Palestine responsible for a military solution to their problem, it was unrealistic, both because Israel was too powerful and because the creation of the Jewish state had been no more the responsibility of the Palestinian than it had been that of any other Arab. If the intention was the creation of an Arab state in the unconquered part of Palestine (that is, the West Bank), it would accord legitimacy to the 1949 armistice lines, would imply the tacit recognition of Israel, and might even lead to negotiations with the Jewish state. If the intention was that this state should take upon itself the restoration of the whole of Palestine, it would be too great a burden for the state. And finally, "the establishment of a new Palestinian Arab statelet would mean the dismembering of the Jordanian entity, and whoever believed in [Arab] unity should not contemplate division, even if this were only the means to another end."[104]

The grave doubts the Qawmiyun had about transferring the full responsibility for the Palestinian problem from the Arabs in general to the Palestinians themselves were expressed in many of its leaflets of 1962. One of the party's main objections was that the notion of a Palestinian entity had been initiated by Arab leaders who were not to be trusted, so that the notion was, of itself, suspect. Jordan, the Qawmiyun claimed, had offered to set up a Palestinian army that would be deployed along the border with Israel, ostensibly posed for the liberation of the conquered territory. The party argued that in actual fact, however, Jordan was "the last Arab state that could speak [of the liberation of Palestine] honestly or seriously." Husayn was seen as the symbol of Arab reaction and the ally of imperialism, which was the guardian of Israel. Saudi Arabia was another reactionary state that had come out in favor of the idea of a separate Palestinian entity. Saudi Arabia, the Qawmiyun held, was an "immoral" state; King Saud used the vast oil wealth of his country to satisfy his own personal avarice and cooperated with the Shah of Iran. The idea of a Palestinian entity was also supported by Qassem "who was keeping the Iraqi people prisoner." All three of these leaders were seen as having ulterior motives in calling for the creation of a Palestinian entity. Their open hostility to the popular Abd al-Nasser made it necessary for them to woo the masses away from the Egyptian leader, and their support for the Palestinian entity was one way of doing this. They were further accused of cooperating with the imperialists and the Zionists. Finally, the notion of a Palestinian entity was designed to neutralize the Palestinians and remove them from the struggle against the reactionary regimes in the Arab world, by making the entity conditional on "the noninterference of the Palestinians in the affairs of the Arab countries in which they lived."[105]

The Qawmiyun's great fear that the Arabs would attempt to absolve themselves of the responsibility to liberate Palestine and shift this onto the Palestinians themselves, led the party to reject any attempt to compare the Palestinian problem with the liberation struggle in Algeria. The path taken by the liberation movement in Algeria should not be emulated in Palestine; this very concept could be disastrous for the Palestinians.[106] In the first place, while some eight million Arabs remained on their own land in Algeria, no more than a quarter of a million Palestinians remained in conquered Palestine. Moreover, these quarter of a million Arabs were subject to continued harassment and surveillance, which made the prospect of an "internal revolution" almost impossible. The second major difference lay in the size and nature of the territories involved. Algeria was a huge, rugged country, ideally suited for guerrilla warfare, while Palestine was much smaller, with only the Galilee sufficiently rugged for this type of fighting. Finally, the arms and equipment that the Algerian revolution had at its disposal were infinitely greater than those at the disposal of the Palestinians. If there was any prospect at all of a revolution taking place inside Palestine, it would have to be provided with outside Arab resources at least equaling those that had been available to the Algerians. These had not been provided because of imperialism and the "reactionary regimes" in Syria, Jordan, and Lebanon—and "for various strategic reasons, such as in the case of the Gaza Strip, which is narrow and isolated from the UAR."[107]

Having demonstrated the differences between the two liberation struggles and having rejected the possibility of any effective guerrilla activity in Palestine under the existing conditions, the Qawmiyun did nevertheless accept the argument that the Palestinians would have to be prepared to make greater sacrifices than their Arab brothers, and would have to take their place in the "progressive Arab vanguard." The practical implications of this attitude were that while some form of guerrilla activity against Israel should be encouraged, it should be on a relatively small scale and be designed primarily to harass and inconvenience the enemy—on no account should it be seen as constituting part of an "armed revolution." Furthermore, the Arab countries should be prepared to retaliate in force for any reprisals such actions might provoke on the part of the Israelis, and protect the Palestinians from falling victim to an Israeli military attack: "Any logic based on divisiveness [that is, the creation of a separate Palestinian entity supported by isolationist forces] and which does not demand the creation of a single Arab state encircling Israel will only lead to another disaster."[108]

This position changed suddenly in 1963. In its May issue that year, devoted to the Palestine tragedy, *al-Wahda* analyzed the feasibility of Arab unity in the immediate future, and in the light of this analysis drew conclusions regarding the liberation of Palestine. In the new circumstances, greater emphasis should be given to the Palestinian element in the Arab-Israeli conflict: "The preparation plan for the Palestine campaign should run along two inseparable lines: the one placing the Palestine problem in the long-range nationalist context, as part of the struggle for liberation and unity; and the other, designed to prompt the liberated Arab countries to harness their potential...and to crystallize the burning hatred of the Palestinians in a revolutionary movement of their own, which will enable them to fulfill their vanguard role on the road to Jaffa, Haifa, and the [Palestine] coast."[109]

The Palestinian organization is here viewed as having an exclusive vanguard role, and is no longer seen as simply forming part of the general Arab vanguard movement. What is more, the Palestinians are viewed, for the first time, as the equals of the rest of the Arab nation in the struggle for a solution to the Palestine question. Another important innovation is the distinction made between the long-range struggle for Arab unity and the immediate goal of mobilizing the Palestinians for the liberation of their homeland. The Qawmiyun attempted to blur this distinction somewhat, by stressing that the two goals were inextricably intertwined. But it is quite clear that the party had radically revised its former view of the Palestinians limiting their guerrilla activities to merely harassing the enemy, and now saw them as standing in the forefront of the battle to liberate Palestine. Finally, there appears an ideological innovation that was to reach its full realization only after the 1967 war: while in its earlier years the party viewed Arab unity as merely a means to a more important end—the liberation of Palestine— the liberation of Palestine now came to be viewed as the means and Arab unity as the end. This volte-face was apparently inspired by the Qawmiyun's desire not to be misrepresented as being primarily concerned with its own selfish goal of liberating Palestine and being less than wholly committed to the general Arab goal of unity. This was spelled out even more clearly the following year (1964): "We believe that the Palestine problem is the problem of the entire Arab nation, and that our struggle for Palestine is at the very heart of our struggle for the realization of its [the Arab nation's] objectives: unity, liberation, socialism, and the redemption of Palestine."[110]

In 1964 the Qawmiyun shifted its position somewhat, and now saw this new approach as being justified not only on pragmatic grounds but also for deep ideological reasons. Following the first Arab summit in Cairo, where Nasser called for the creation of a Palestinian "entity," the Qawmiyun wrote: "At this stage, following the [Cairo] summit, where the Palestine problem was presented in a new light, the field has been opened for the first time to the Palestinian[111] Arab people to bear responsibility for their problem, through [the creation of] the proposed Palestinian entity."[112] This entity was "the first serious step in the direction of the proper solution"; it was the first practical move to be taken, a far cry from the empty declarations and false tears shed by Arab leaders in the past.[113] The goal should be the creation of "a revolutionary organization belonging to the Palestinian people, which would be able to bear the battle standard...[and which would be] the fulcrum for the redemption of Palestine and the erasing of the shame of the [Palestine] disaster."[114]

The Qawmiyun remained somewhat suspicious of the idea of a Palestinian entity, and it still was at pains to stress the form it believed the Palestinian entity should take. So it presented a number of conditions which it claimed must be met if the entity were not to be stillborn. Only if these were met would the party agree to cooperate with and support the new Palestinian organization. One of these conditions was that the new organization should include in its ranks genuine representatives of the Palestinian people, who would work for the realization of the Palestinian's hopes and aspirations. This would be possible only if such representatives were freely elected by the Palestinians themselves, and were not appointed by elements "outside the scope of the Palestinian people's will."[115] The entity should be made up of "the organized revolutionary toiling forces of the people." Only this would assure that the Palestinian movement would take the "revolutionary path," the path of armed struggle, and would reject any attempt at compromise. Another condition was that the Palestinian entity should have "the right to represent the Palestinian nation and speak in its name...in all Arab and international forums." Regarding the aid to be provided by the Arab countries, the Qawmiyun set the following condition: in order that the Palestinian organization be able to prepare the Palestinian people for the struggle, it must be provided with all the necessary support—"arms, finances, and training." This latter demand reflects the Qawmiyun's new view of the primary role the Palestinians themselves were not to play in the liberation of their homeland. It was stressed, however, that the liberation army to be set up by the new entity would operate "within the framework of a united Arab command." The Qawmiyun's persistent doubts about the intentions of the Arab states were clearly reflected in the condition that the Palestinian organization enjoy total "administrative, financial, and political" independence. Elsewhere, the party demanded that the organization be accorded "immunity." It would seem that the Qawmiyun's concern for the independence of the Palestinian entity stemmed from its fear that the entity might be forced into making compromises with the enemy to serve the interests of the other Arab states. In fact, the Qawmiyun demanded that the Palestinian organization be responsible for the day-to-day affairs of the refugees in all the Arab countries. It also demanded that the Palestinian organization be allowed to participate in political events affecting the Arab world as a whole. Taken together, these last two demands represented an attempt on the part of the Qawmiyun to secure for the Palestinians far-reaching rights to participate in the political affairs of the host countries.[116]

In May 1964, the first Palestinian National Council met in Jerusalem. The way in which it was constituted and the appointment of Ahmad Shuqayri to lead it were bitterly opposed by the Qawmiyun. In a leaflet put out after the meeting,[117] the party claimed that the Cairo conference, which had proposed the establishment of the Palestinian entity, had not performed its duty properly. It "had failed to lay down how the proposed entity was to come into being. As a result, the field had been left open to reactionary and opportunistic elements." Shuqayri's preparatory tour of the Arab countries, the Qawmiyun charged, had served the interests not of the Palestinian people but of King Husayn. Instead of engaging in rational debate with the Palestinian masses, Shuqayri had opted for theatrical oratory. The preparatory committees that had paved the way for the meeting had been arbitrarily constituted in such a way that "opportunistic elements" in the Arab countries would be able to impose their will on the Palestine Liberation Organization (PLO) and purge it of any "revolutionary" tendency. The council itself had met in a totally inappropriate venue and atmosphere, the Qawmiyun charged. The venue was the Intercontinental Hotel on the Mount of Olives—"far from the masses and under the watchful eye of the [Hashemite] intelligence services and government officials."[118] The Qawmiyun summed up its view of the council meeting in Jerusalem as follows: the meeting "raises the possibility of a return to the miserable manner in which the Supreme Arab Council had conducted the struggle of the Palestinian people before the disaster."

In criticizing the Cairo summit, the Qawmiyun did not so much as mention the fact that Abd al-Nasser had been the guiding spirit behind the meeting, and bore much of the responsibility for its outcome. It would seem that the Qawmiyun in the West Bank refrained from criticizing Abd al-Nasser openly, knowing the great esteem in which he was held by the masses in the area.

The 1963–64 period, then, was marked by a fundamental change in the Qawmiyun's attitude to the notion of a Palestinian entity, from one of outright rejection to one of enthusiastic endorsement. The demands the party made for the new Palestinian organization in no way detracted from its support for the essence of the concept, while its sharp attack on the leadership of the PLO following the Jerusalem meeting was probably due to the fact that the Qaw-miyun found itself in the minority.[119] The party made no attempt to explain its volte-face on the Palestinian entity question, but it would seem that it was due to the failure of the attempts at Arab unity in the early 1960s (the breakup of the UAR and the abortive tripartite union in the spring of 1963). The ideological vacuum left as the prospects of the Arab unity receded made it relatively easy for the Qawmiyun to adopt the new concept of a Palestinian entity, especially as such a concept appeared to present an acceptable alternative that would lead ultimately to the same goal. At the same time, particularly in the West Bank, the Qawmiyun continued to see Abd al-Nasser as the paramount Arab nationalist leader. Even though some of the party's leaders may have had reservations about some of them, by and large the Egyptian leader's pronouncements were taken with considerable seriousness and weighed heavily in the Qawmiyun's ideological debates. Abd al-Nasser's public support for the concept of a Palestinian entity undoubtedly played a major part in making the idea acceptable to the Qawmiyun, and it became a central element in the party's ideology in the years that followed.

4. The Moslem Brothers

HISTORY, STRUCTURE, AND MEMBERSHIP

History in the West Bank

A strong Egyptian initiative lay behind the emergence of the Moslem Brothers movement in the West Bank. Emissaries were sent from Egypt to preach the movement's ideas and to help set up branches in the area. The first branch in the West Bank for which clear evidence exists was set up under the British Mandate in May 1946, in Jerusalem[1] The fact that Jamal al-Husayni—vice-president of the Supreme Muslim Council and its acting president while Hajj Amin was in exile—took an active part in the establishment of the branch and was registered as one of its first members is indicative of its importance. It immediately embarked upon an extensive public relations campaign, holding mass meetings and launching a highly effective fund-raising drive (in a very short time, the branch managed to raise some six thousand Palestinian pounds—then a very considerable sum—for the construction of its headquarters in Jerusalem). Other branches were established later that year, in Jaffa, Lydda, Haifa (where two existing Muslim associations, Ansar al-Fadil and al-Itisam, joined the movement), Nablus, and Tulkarm. Branches were also set up in Transjordan, where the movement received king Abdallah's (somewhat qualified) blessing: he expressed his confidence that the Moslem Brothers would "devote themselves completely and absolutely to God." In October 1946 the movement's activities in the West Bank received official endorsement at a Moslem Brothers conference attended by delegates from Lebanon, Jordan, and Palestine. The conference came out in support of Arab aims in Palestine, in addition to backing Egypt in its demand that Britain evacuate the Nile Valley.[2]

During the 1948 war members of the movement, fighting with

This chapter draws on the Hebrew version of 1972 prepared by Rachel Simon.

144

the Egyptian expeditionary force in Palestine, reached Hebron. It was apparently their presence in the area that led to the establishment of a Brothers branch in the town toward the end of 1949. That same year a branch was also established in Bethlehem, giving the movement a firm foothold in the south.[3]

Following the war several of the movement's branches were closed in those towns that had fallen under Israeli control. But several new branches began to spring up in the towns and villages of the West Bank (Jenin, Qalqilya, Anabta, Dura, Surif, Sur Bahir, Tubas, Kufr Burqa, Jericho), as well as in several refugee camps (including Aqabat Jabr, near Jericho, and al-Arrub, near Bethlehem).[4] New branches were also established on the East Bank, in Amman, Salt, Karak, and Irbid. At first the branches functioned independently, with very little cooperation or coordination between them.

Abd al-Latif Abu Qura, who was closely watched by the authorities because of his extreme anti-Western views, headed the movement in Jordan until 1953, when he was superseded as general supervisor (al-Muraqib al-Amm)[5] by Abd ar-Rahman Khalifa.[6] Under Khalifa's leadership, the movement's activities began to be organized on a national level, with increasing coordination and cooperation between the various local branches.[7] The next general supervisor (known also as the general guide and the head of the Brothers Association), was Said Ramadan, who replaced Khalifa in the spring of 1954. He was expelled from Jordan the following year, however, to reemerge as head of the movement a decade later, at the beginning of 1965.

From 1954 to the mid-1960s, Khalifa was the undisputed leader of the movement in Jordan, and he alone was referred to as the general supervisor. In mid-1963, however, the title was also applied to Yusuf al-Azm,[8] who had been a leading activist in the movement since its inception in Jordan. It would seem that, by this time, Khalifa no longer played an active role in the movement's affairs, and was regarded as a sort of "honorary" leader. But there can be little doubt that Khalifa was by far the most important figure during the first fifteen years of the Moslem Brothers' existence in Jordan, and that he more than any other individual left his personal mark on the movement. Branch leaders used to make what amounted to pilgrimages to Amman, simply to consult with him; and his presence at a branch meeting or party conference was always assiduously sought.

145

Relations with the Authorities

Unlike most other political parties in the West Bank under Hashemite rule, the Moslem Brothers were officially recognized as a legal organization. They operated openly, often with the encouragement and support of the authorities. The movement was, however, required to clear all its activities with the authorities. If, for example, it wished to establish a new branch, it would have first to seek official permission. It went out of its way to present its aims and aspirations as entirely compatible with those of the Hashemite regime, or, in any case, was always careful to present them in such a way that could not possibly incur the outright disapproval of the regime. Thus, for example, after the West Bank was annexed to Jordan and the movement sought permission to establish a branch in Jerusalem, it laid great stress on the fact that its prime objective was to serve the interests of the king and the state.[9] Likewise, when it requested permission to set up the Bethlehem branch, it stated that its purpose was simply to serve the will of God and his Prophet, and to work for the realization of the Islamic ideal. And when it applied for permission to establish a branch in Jericho, stress was laid on the fact that the movement was bent on propagating the teachings of Islam and advancing the ultimate creation of an Islamic state, based on the Koran.[10] The movement had also to apply to the authorities on purely technical matters, such as to seek permission to build or lease a new building. The authorities generally approved these applications, further establishing the legal status of the movement and the legitimacy of its goals.[11]

The nature of the movement's activities also differed markedly from that of other parties in the West Bank, largely because, unlike most of its rivals, it was a legal association. Its meetings were held openly, and were often attended by official government representatives, military officers, and prominent religious leaders. Youth activities (which included even paramilitary training), sports competitions, and fund-raising campaigns were carried out openly, often with the support of the authorities.[12]

This symbiosis between the Moslem Brothers and the regime in Jordan was most apparent in the parliamentary elections. The movement regularly contested these elections, with campaigns being conducted openly by each local branch. In 1951 it did not contest the general elections as a party, apparently fearing that it was not yet sufficiently established to make a good showing, but it did allow its members to run as individuals. In the 1954 elections, the

Jenin branch carried out an intensive campaign on behalf of its candidate, who was a relative of the local chairman. The Qalqilya branch that year supported the Liberation Party candidate, Ahmad al-Daur, and did not put up its own candidate—but it made it quite clear that this was a purely tactical move, and did not mean that it would not be contesting future elections under its own name. In the 1956 elections, the Nablus branch organized a vigorous campaign including public meetings and excursions in support of its candidate, Dr. Hafiz Abd al-Nabi Natshe, who headed a four-man electoral bloc. The Brothers appointed their own men to supervise the elections, and were satisfied that they had indeed been fair. The 1956 election was, in fact, widely held to have been the fairest ever held under the Hashemite regime, and Dr. Natshe was duly elected to the House of Representatives in Amman. The movement participated in several elections in the early 1960s.[13] It contested the 1962 elections, even though these were boycotted by both the left-wing and the nationalist parties. It was hardly surprising, in these circumstances, that the Brothers fared well, and in Nablus, for example, their candidate, Shaykh Mashhur al-Damin, polled the largest number of votes. By virtue of their participation in the various elections, the Moslem Brothers lent their implicit support to the government and recognized its legitimacy in the West Bank. The government in turn provided the movement with its backing and assistance.

Considering the enormous encouragement the Brothers received from the government, their performance at the polls was not particularly impressive. This would appear to testify to their limited appeal to the bulk of the electorate. Only in those constituencies where economic power combined with strong clan ties (as was the case in Hebron) did the movement have any significant success. Elsewhere the Brothers were viewed as too closely allied with the largely unpopular Hashemite regime and as such enjoyed little popular confidence.

This is not, however, the whole story. The Brothers, by virtue of their highly radical ideology, clearly posed a serious threat to the Hashemite regime. Although they paid lip service to the aims and aspirations of that regime and avoided any form of open confrontation with it, a fundamental conflict of interests existed from the start. It was impossible that a movement which had a deep-seated hatred of the West and believed that the *sharia* was the only legitimate basis for the state should be able to make common cause indefinitely with the very pro-Western Hashemite regime. Moreover, the Brothers in the West Bank were closely affiliated with the movement in Egypt, which had a highly activist political tradition. The Hashemites' latent distrust of the movement was apparent from the start, and expressed itself in the regime's refusal to allow the Brothers to set up a branch in Hebron immediately after the 1948 war. Because this branch was organized at a time when authority in the town was jointly shared with the Egyptian expeditionary force that had taken part in the 1948 hostilities, the Hashemite regime feared that the movement supported the Mufti Hajj Amin al-Husayni, a deadly enemy of the Hashemites who lived in exile in Egypt. In later years too the regime sometimes withheld permission to establish new branches, ostensibly on "technical" grounds. Even though the initial suspicion that the Brothers were closely allied with the Mufti and his Egyptian patrons later turned out to be groundless (especially after the Free Officers' coup in Egypt, when the regime turned against the Moslem Brothers in that country), it was abundantly clear that the movement was closely involved in highly controversial political issues, and was, accordingly, to be closely watched at all times.[14]

The Brothers in the West Bank did, in fact, openly criticize the Hashemite regime from time to time, particularly for what they felt were deviations from the pure ethical values of Islam. While the movement did exhort the masses in sermons and at public gatherings to support the king against various subversive elements (such as the Communists or the Baath), particularly at times of crisis, it was at the same time often highly critical of the government's policies. Preachers and religious teachers consistently urged that the state reform itself along pure Islamic lines, and they frequently took the government to task for not acting in this spirit. Among the prime targets of the movement's criticism were moral laxity (the consumption of alcohol, the importing of dancers and other forms of entertainment, and the deterioration of the school curricula by laying too much stress on Western values) and the ruthlessness and corruption of the leadership in the Muslim world (including, it would seem, the Jordanian leadership, which appears to have sparked their call for a commercial strike in Jenin). In one case at least, the Brothers went so far as to call for the resignation of two ministers.[15]

The Brothers also criticized the Hashemite regime for its close ties with the West, particularly with Britain. In 1954 they demonstrated against the presence of British officers in the army and demanded their removal. Until they were removed, the demonstrators demanded, the officers should not be permitted to enter the army camps. The movement in Jordan was, from its inception, virulently anti-Western (its first general supervisor was in fact arrested several times on this count in the early 1950s), and was very outspoken in its attacks on imperialism and the imperialist powers. This sometimes led the Brothers to support Abd al-Nasser and what were seen as his anti-Western policies. But they did not follow the Egyptian leader blindly, and were quick to react when they themselves came under fire from him.

Nevertheless the movement's sporadic support for the Nasserites in Egypt, coupled with their open attacks on certain of the Hashemite regime's policies, was sufficient to periodically antagonize the authorities in the West Bank.[16]

The movement was highly suspicious of the Hashemite regime and very early on set up a clandestine apparatus to keep a close watch on its various moves and inclinations.[17] The authorities, for their part, were no less suspicious of the Brothers. This mutual suspicion was particularly marked during times of crisis in the area— such as in 1955, when King Husayn's openly pro-Western stance and his flirtation with the idea of joining the Western-sponsored Baghdad Pact led the regime to tighten its secret surveillance of the movement.

In April 1955 the Jordanian Chief of Staff put out a report calling for up-to-date information on the various "destructive organizations" operating in the country. Although he specifically excluded the Moslem Brothers from this category, he stressed that the movement should be closely watched to make certain that the ideas it was disseminating did not, in fact, run counter to the interests and policies of the state. Earlier that year, the authorities began to monitor the preaching of the Friday sermon at the mosque in Nablus, and also the speeches of the movement's leader in the town, al-Damin. During the course of the year, as part of their campaign to clamp down on other movements in the West Bank, the authorities placed a ban on the Brothers' weekly lectures and even kept certain key members of the movement under personal surveillance. As we have already mentioned, the first general supervisor was arrested on several occasions in the early 1950s. His successor, Abd al-Rahman Khalifa, also had trouble with the authorities from time to time, and in 1955 he was forced to flee to Damascus to escape an arrest order that had been issued against him. His supporters in Jordan intervened on his behalf, however, and the order was repealed, enabling him to return to Amman after a brief exile. There were other occasions too when the general supervisor clashed with the authorities (at the end of 1955, for example, when he was arrested for a short time).[18]

The fluctuations that occurred in the Moslem Brothers' attitude to the Hashemite regime were influenced by a combination of factors, involving both domestic and foreign policy issues, and the movement's position at various times did not always appear consistent—at least not on the surface. At the end of 1956, following the ouster of Glubb Pasha from the command of the Arab Legion and Jordan's abrupt shift from almost total reliance on the West to greater military and economic dependence on its fellow Arab states, the movement praised the king for "advancing the causes of Islamic and Arab unity, and for [helping to] free the Arab world from the yoke of imperialism." This show of support became even stronger following the 1956 Suez war, when Jordan, in principle at least, stood behind Egypt.[19] At the beginning of 1957, with the announcement of the Eisenhower Doctrine, the Brothers once again shifted their position, and their forthright attacks on that doctrine caused considerable embarrassment to the Hashemite regime.[20] Later that year, however, when the king entered into a dangerous confrontation with his opponents in Jordan, the Brothers came out solidly behind the monarchy. This had considerable impact in the West Bank, where passions were running very high at this time. It appears that the movement actually increased its following during this period, when most other political parties were outlawed. It held a number of mass rallies in support of the king, praising his stand on behalf of Islam and attacking the misguided and deceptive position taken by the Nabulsi government.[21] Even though it was quite clear that Jordan was in the process of reorientating itself toward the West, the Brothers chose to ignore this in the interest of turning the tables on their rival parties in the West Bank, the Qawmiyun and the Communists.

The pendulum swung back at the end of 1957 and reached its low point by mid-1958. Following Jordan's rapprochement with the West and the suppression of the Nasserite movements in that country, the other Arab states withheld the aid they had promised a year earlier. The United States was quick to fill the vacuum, and this prompted a violent attack from the Brothers. Their general supervisor was taken into custody, which resulted in mass protest demonstrations in Nablus. These in turn led the authorities to place several members of the movement under close surveillance.[22] For the time being, apart from stepping up its vigilance, the Hashemite regime took no further action against the Brothers.

In the summer of 1959, however, relations between the authorities and the movement deteriorated still further. Several newspapers and pamphlets put out by the movement were impounded, and persons caught distributing them were arrested. Among their other attacks on the regime, these publications strongly condemned what was described as Jordan's imperialist-inspired attempt "to postpone [the solution of] the Palestine problem." In autumn that year, the general supervisor was again arrested, and the movement set about systematically destroying all its papers in case the authorities decided to embark upon a large-scale crackdown on its activities in the West Bank.[23]

From the mid-1950s on, the Moslem Brothers exploited their representatives in parliament to protest against certain aspects of the government's policy, particularly its failure to implement the principles of Islamic law in the running of the state. The movement's representatives supported a vote of nonconfidence in the government in the autumn of 1957 and voted against al-Majali's new government in May 1959, disseminating pamphlets in the Hebron area explaining their position. In January 1963, the Brothers' representatives (Mashhur al-Damin of Nablus, Yusuf al-Azm of Maan, and Abd al-Majid al-Sharida of Irbid) expressed a vote of nonconfidence in al-Tall's government for failing to do enough to apply the laws of Islam and propagate its moral values in the country—as well as for failing to keep Jordan out of the Western sphere of influence and for doing nothing to advance the *jihad* against Israel. These same representatives spoke out in parliament a few months later against the performance and policies of al-Rifai's government.[24]

In the 1960s the Moslem Brothers were on more than one occasion the cause of considerable concern to the authorities. During this period, however, their attacks were mostly confined to aspects of the government's domestic policy. In the summer of 1960 the Brothers protested against what they saw as the government's laxity in moral matters, and were especially incensed by its decision to allow a foreign ice-ballet company to perform in Jordan. Several members of the movement, including the general supervisor, were arrested during the latter part of that year. In 1965 there were reports of several arrests among the Brothers, for allegedly planning to strike at cinemas and other places of entertainment, as their counterparts in Egypt had done that year and again in 1966.[25] It would seem that the authorities' suspicions on that occasion were unfounded; but the incident did reveal just how little trust the regime placed in the movement. Despite the legal status enjoyed by the Brothers in Jordan, and despite their very considerable cooperation with the regime, there was clearly a great deal of mutual distrust and suspicion. At times of crisis this expressed itself in overt opposition to the regime on the part of the Brothers, and in suppressive measures against the movement on the part of the authorities. Nevertheless, these measures were never as harsh or as farreaching as those taken against the Communists or the Baath.

There was a certain similarity between the position of the Moslem Brothers in Jordan in the 1950s and 1960s and that of the movement in Egypt throughout the 1940s and early 1950s. Until they were outlawed in 1954, the Brothers in Egypt had operated quite openly and on a considerably larger scale than their counterparts in Jordan. In both countries the movement maintained close ties with the king and his court and came out in support of the regime when it clashed with its nationalistic internal opponents. In Egypt the Brothers supported the king in his struggle against the Wafd and the Communists, while in Jordan they supported the king against the Nasserites, the Baath, and the Communists.[26] In both countries the Moslem Brothers were clearly political parties in every sense—although in Egypt they insisted on referring to themselves as an "association" and did not participate in parliamentary elections, while in Jordan, as we have seen, they regularly took part in elections and participated fully in the parliamentary life of the country.

But in the West Bank as in Egypt the Moslem Brothers were clearly on a collision course with the established regime. The gulf between the ultimate goal that the Brothers had set themselves (and the means by which they sought to achieve it) and the political realities of the modern Islamic state, which functioned according to entirely different criteria from those espoused by the movement, was too vast to be bridged by any long-term interest. In Jordan the differences between the Brothers and the regime centered mainly on the question of the latter's close economic and military ties with the West, and on the openness of the regime to a wide range of Western cultural and social influences. The situation in Egypt was somewhat similar until 1954; after that, however, with the reorientation of the Free Officers regime away from the West, the movement concentrated its efforts on the propagation of Islamic values inside the country, postponing its political struggle to some future date.[27]

There was, however, one respect in which the Moslem Brothers' relationship with the regime in the respective countries differed very significantly. The political violence that characterized the movement's activities in Egypt was entirely absent in Jordan. Although the Brothers in Jordan did take part occasionally in various protest demonstrations, they invariably displayed a great deal of self-restraint. This fundamental difference in approach expressed itself also in the way the movement organized itself in each of the two countries. In Jordan, for example, the youth movement organized by the Brothers engaged exclusively in scouting activities and in sport, and had none of the secret paramilitary overtones of its counterpart in Egypt.[28] It is entirely understandable, therefore, that the attitude of the authorities in the two countries to the movement should have been markedly different. There is no comparison between the harsh measures taken against the Brothers in Egypt (in 1948, 1954, and 1966) and the cautious, restrained measures taken against the movement from time to time in the West Bank.

The fact that the British presence was, on the face of it, relatively less provocative in Jordan in the early 1950s than it had been in Egypt a few years earlier, undoubtedly accounted, in part at least, for the difference in the movement's political image in each of the two countries. There can also be little doubt that the brutal repressive measures taken against the Brothers in Egypt left their mark on the movement in Jordan. For all that, it should be stressed that the element of violence which characterized the movement in Egypt was fundamental to its thinking and should not be seen as a passing phenomenon dictated by tactical considerations. The element of violence and aggressiveness of the Brothers in Egypt was primarily due to the fact that the movement drew its support mainly from the middle- and lower-class population in the cities—that is, those classes who retained strong religious sentiments while undergoing a certain degree of westernization, in the process of which they felt themselves becoming increasingly alienated in a society that was going through a rapid modernization over which they felt they had little or no control.[29] The situation in Jordan was quite different. Jordanian society was extremely traditional and conservative, much more so than Egyptian society. Egypt's urban population had for decades undergone a very rapid process of modernization, which had left it with a deep sense of alienation and frustration. This was not the case in Jordan, where modernization had come much later and had proceeded at a slower pace. Jordanian society had also preserved its fundamentally traditional Islamic character and had avoided the type of open moral permissiveness that had come to typify Egyptian society. Jordan was still to a considerable degree a tribal country; the king himself was strongly aware both of his very recent tribal origins and of his more distant kinship to the Prophet, factors that clearly helped to shape his own world outlook and, in consequence, the character of the Jordanian state, Unlike the case in monarchic (and even revolutionary) Egypt, the Jordanian king did not antagonize this movement; social conflict was also, relatively speaking, largely absent (or dormant) in Jordan,[30] and all of this enabled the Hashemite regime to ally itself with the Moslem Brothers—a movement that had originally emerged to protest the status quo and fight for radical change.

Organizational Structure

Since the Moslem Brothers in Jordan were, from the very beginning, a legal organization and were never forced to go underground to avoid the authorities, they did not evolve the type of sophisticated clandestine machinery that characterized the Communists, the Baath, or the Qawmiyun. The basic organizational unit of the movement, the only one that was clearly defined and functioned on a regular basis, was the branch (*shuba*). Unlike their counterparts in Egypt, the Brothers in Jordan did not organize themselves into cells, known in Egypt as "families." Each branch was headed by an administrative committee, which, in turn, was headed by a chairman or president (*naib*). In Egypt, the branch chairman was appointed by the movement's national executive,[31] but it was not clear just how this position was filled in the West Bank. It seems almost certain, however, that the chairman was invariably a local member and not brought in from some other locality. Neither in Egypt nor in Jordan is there any indication that the chairman was required to serve a prescribed period of time, and it would seem that the matter was left to the discretion of the movement's leadership. In the West Bank, branch chairmen tended to serve very long terms. In Nablus, for example, Shaykh Mashhur al-Damin was chairman of the local branch from its establishment in 1946 until the early 1960s, while in Jenin, Tawfiq Jarrar served as chairman from 1952 until 1960. In other branches, chairmen were replaced rather more frequently but even then usually only after serving for several years. In the smaller branches there was no mention of a branch chairman or president, and the longest-serving official appears to have been the branch secretary.[32]

Next in rank after the chairman was his deputy, the vice-chairman. Unlike in Egypt, where each branch had two vice-chairmen, branches in the West Bank had only one (and in some cases the position did not exist at all). The posts of secretary and treasurer in Egypt were filled every second year by secret ballot in each local branch.[33] While there is no information on how these posts were filled in the West Bank in practice, the principle of an annual secret ballot was included in the charter that the movement had drawn up in Hebron in 1949. And, from a perusal of the list of office holders in the various branches during the period under review, it would seem that the principle was, in fact, adhered to: in very few cases is the branch secretary or treasurer found to have served for more than two years, and in most cases the positions changed hands well before then. Nevertheless, these positions did become the sinecure of a small handful of senior members in each branch, who simply rotated the posts among themselves.

The day-to-day running of each branch was left to the local executive (*al-haia al-idariya*). In theory, according to the regulations of the Hebron branch, there were to be ten members on each branch executive, including the chairman, the vice-chairman, the secretary, and the treasurer. In practice, however, the number ranged from as few as five (in Anabta in 1954) to as many as nineteen (in Jerusalem in 1950). The length of time each member of the executive was to serve appears to have differed from branch to branch. According to the regulations of the Hebron branch, for example, executive members were to serve for only a year, while in Nablus the regulations provided for each executive member to serve for three years, with one-third of the members being replaced each year. In practice, however, it does not seem that these regulations were strictly followed in most West Bank branches. In Jerusalem, for example, nine of the eleven executive members in 1955 had remained in office since 1950.[34] While in Nablus, four of the nine executive members serving in 1962 had been in office for between eight and ten years.

The regulations of the Nablus branch specified that a general assembly of all its local members was to take place annually. In theory the general assembly was meant to approve guidelines for the executive and the various branch officials. These assemblies were never convened, however, and the running of each branch was left entirely to the local executive.

In some branches in the West Bank other local functionaries were mentioned from time to time. In Jericho there was reference to a branch accountant (according to the regulations of the Hebron branch, there was in fact meant to have been accountant in every branch). The Nablus branch had its own official preacher as well as a member permanently charged with organizing the distribution of leaflets. There was also mention of an advisory council, functioning alongside the local executive in Nablus. The function of this latter body was not entirely clear, and there is no mention of it in the regulations, either of the Nablus or of the Hebron branch; it would seem that the advisory council in Nablus was simply a local copy of a similar body that existed in several branches in Egypt.[35]

The various branches organized a number of special activities in their area. Many branches ran scout groups (*al-firaq al-kashfiya*), also known as "The Wanderers" (*jawwala*). At the head of each such group was a leader (*rais*) appointed by the branch, who was sometimes known also as the "commander" (*qaid*) or "instructor." The groups were all affiliated to a national scout movement organized by the Brothers, at the head of which stood the Commander of the Brothers' Scout Groups in the Kingdom. The branches also organized sports competitions and drama groups. All these activities were initiated entirely at the branch level, with the sole exception of a national scout camp that took place in 1952. Even the existence of a national commander of the scout groups did not indicate anything like the overall control of the scout movement that pertained in Egypt.[36]

The local branches did not, however, confine their activities to the town or village in which they happened to be situated. Several branches sought to extend their operations to the surrounding villages or refugee camps. These efforts did not usually lead to the establishment of new branches in the peripheral areas, where most activities continued to be initiated and controlled by the branch concerned. Thus, for example, an instructor was sent out from Hebron to drill the scout troop in a nearby village, and teachers were sent from Nablus to work with students in another school or in the neighboring refugee camp. The larger branches would also send members on lecture tours in the surrounding villages, which on occasion actually paid the lecturers for their services. These lecturers would attempt to rouse their audiences to take a stand on certain issues and tried to activate the local teachers and students.[37]

Unlike in Egypt, there was no intermediate, regional, level between that of the local branch and the movement's central leadership. The administrative office (*al-maktab al-idari*) is mentioned in the files as being responsible for the election of the general supervisor, and there can be little doubt that this office was responsible for the administration of the movement not only in the West Bank but in Jordan as a whole. But, as we have already seen, the administrative office does not appear to have had much influence or control over the functioning of the local branches, which were, to all intents and purposes, quite autonomous. The general controller is frequently referred to in the security services' archives, but almost invariably in connection with the movement's relations with the regime, or visits to the branches on special, festive, occasions. There is no indication in any of the movement's reports that the general controller attempted to direct the activities of the local branches, as did his counterpart in Egypt through such centralized coordinating bodies as the general advisory council or the general secretariat.[38] It would seem that these bodies either did not exist at all in Jordan or were wholly ineffectual in practice. Whatever the case, the impression gained is that there was very little central control over the movement's activities in Jordan. It should be stressed, however, that in the early years of the Brothers' activities in Jordan, the general controller was preoccupied with a series of major confrontations with the regime and had little time to spare for organizational matters. The general controller for many years was Muhammad Khalifa, a man who had nothing like the stature or charisma of Hasan al-Banna in Egypt, and, accordingly, wielded far less influence over the local branches in Jordan than did al-Banna in Egypt. There were, however, periods when the name of the general controller was not even mentioned in the movement's papers, and it is not clear who, in fact, held the position.

The Moslem Brothers in Egypt devoted considerable attention to the various occupational sectors of the community—workers, farmers, students, professionals—and organized a women's movement.[39] The Brothers in the West Bank, on the other hand, appeared to have far less interest in sectoral activities, although there are isolated references to some. In 1954, for example, a conference of about one hundred workers belonging to the movement was convened. The participants in this conference resolved to set up a federation within the movement, to be headed by Mahmud al-Natshe, and announced that it would prepare a charter. Nothing more, though, was ever heard of this workers' federation. One of the reports mentions the existence of a "Workers' Section—The Revolutionary Islamic Workers' Command," but there is no further reference. Nowhere is there any mention of separate students' or farmers' associations. The existence of an affiliated women's movement is mentioned only in one locality, Tulkarm, and there is no information about its character or its activities.[40] The almost total absence of any reference to these various sectors would seem to indicate that the Brothers in the West Bank attached very little importance even to those sectors that were mentioned in the reports of the security services.

One other highly characteristic feature of the Moslem Brothers in Egypt which is absent from the descriptions of the movement in the West Bank was the wide range of communal activities organized by each branch, in mosques, schools, hospitals, and recreation clubs.[41] According to the charter of the Hebron branch, these activities were in fact meant to have taken place. In practice, however, they were minimal, restricted to the running of various clubs in the town. In Jerusalem the Brothers appear to have organized two local groups in 1953—"The Islamic Society for Construction in Jerusalem," and "The Muslim Charitable Society for the Reconstruction of Jerusalem." But here again there is no record of how these two societies functioned. In 1960 there were reports of a school for adult education which was opened in Jerusalem with government support. Its purpose was to teach the Koran and instruct the students in the Muslim way of life.[42] Again there is no further reference in our sources to this institution.

One final, fundamental difference between the movement in the two countries, was the total absence of any type of secret organization in the West Bank, along the lines of the highly conspiratorial paramilitary bodies that existed in Egypt.[43] This was not only indicative of the relative weakness of the movement in Jordan and its loose organizational structure, but a clear sign of its unwillingness to embark upon any aggressive action against the existing regime. It certainly testified to a total lack of commitment to overthrowing that regime by force and to seizing power in Jordan for itself. In this respect the Moslem Brothers in Jordan were a pale shadow of their far more aggressive and politically active counterparts in Egypt and elsewhere in the Arab world.

Membership

According to the regulations of the Hebron branch, there were three types of members: (1) Participating Member (*mushtarik*), who had to be a Muslim, at least twenty years of age, and who observed Islamic moral values. The participating member had to put down in writing his desire to join the movement, and his willingness to obey its commands, to support it, and to pay his monthly membership dues. (2) Full or Active Member (*amil*), who had to have been a participating member for at least six months, and who had satisfactorily carried out his obligations to the movement during that period. He had to be fully versed in the charter of the movement and its ideals, and was required to make the following oath (*baia*) before the chairman of the branch: "I swear by Almighty God that I will obey...and will constantly promote the call (*dawa*) of the Moslem Brothers and pledge [to undertake] *jihad* in its name and to carry out the conditions of membership and to have full faith in the leadership, to heed and obey. I swear to this in the name of God, and God is my witness." The Nablus branch required, in addition, that the candidate for full membership be recommended by two veteran members. (3) Supporting Member (*muazir*), who was a kind of honorary member who was not required to make any formal commitment to the movement, but who had assisted in some way, financial or otherwise. This form of membership was usually conferred on sympathetic outsiders by the branch executive.

These categories were very similar, although not identical, to those in Egypt. The main differences were that in Egypt the participating member was called a "candidate"; there was no pledge to embark upon *jihad* for the realization of the movement's aims; and members were expected, wherever possible, to contribute more than just their monthly subscriptions.[44]

When it came to the expulsion of a member, the regulations laid down in the Hebron charter were almost identical to those governing the movement in Egypt. A member who had erred would be warned repeatedly to mend his ways and if he failed to do so he would be expelled. But while in Egypt only the general supervisor could authorize the expulsion of a member, in the West Bank this authorization was the prerogative of each local executive—a further indication of the highly decentralized nature of the movement in Jordan.

The regular reports of the different branches in the West Bank make very few references to the payment of membership dues,[45] and no reference at all to the oath-taking ceremonies prescribed for new members in the Hebron and Nablus regulations. It would seem that neither requirement was very closely observed, and revenue from membership dues would seem to have accounted for only a very small part of the movement's income in the West Bank—the bulk coming from either private donations or public fund-raising activities. In any case, the apparent failure of the Brothers in the West Bank to follow these two very basic practices further reveals the loose structure of the movement there and the rather tepid commitment of its members. As a legal movement, the Brothers in the West Bank had no need of the tightly knit clandestine structure that did so much to consolidate the movement in Egypt. On the other hand, the movement did not take full advantage of the benefits that derived from its legal status—the ability to raise funds openly, to set up various clubs and organizations that would broaden its popular base, and to maintain close ties with the regime. The situation was very different in Egypt, where the Brothers took the fullest possible advantage of their legal status while at the same time building up a comprehensive clandestine organization that would enable them to continue functioning if ever they were forced to go underground. It would seem that the Brothers in Jordan were in a sense damned by their relationship with the regime: it left them with very little popular appeal as a legal movement, yet at the same time made it unnecessary for them to evolve as an effective underground movement.

It appears that the movement in Jordan placed very little importance on special uniforms or other symbols. The Irbid branch, according to one report, did require its members to wear khaki uniforms and berets,[46] but this appears to have been an exception. The movement's emblem—two crossed scimitars embracing a Koran—did appear at the head of some of its publications. Party symbols played a far lesser part in the West Bank than they did in Egypt, where distinctive uniforms and emblems were an important part of the Brothers paramilitary image.[47]

Membership Structure

It is, for several reasons, impossible to estimate the precise numerical strength of the Brothers in the West Bank. Although the leadership of the movement was more or less stable, it did not have a fixed membership in the way the Qawmiyun or the Communists did, and its members were not at all as committed or active. The Brothers in the West Bank were a largely amorphous movement, and the size of its rapidly fluctuating membership depended on certain transitory political events or even on the changing relations between the various large clans. Moreover, even those who did consider themselves to be regular members did not always participate in the movement's activities. Thus reports on the Nablus branch—one of the largest in the West Bank, with a claimed membership of several hundred—as few as thirty members were reported to participate in some of its activities.[48] The distinction between member and supporter or sympathizer was not always clear, as the movement frequently functioned outside the confines of its own framework. The fact that the Brothers in the West Bank was a legal movement also makes it difficult to assess its numerical strength, as the authorities saw comparatively little need to keep a close check on its membership or on the numbers attending its various functions. A perusal of the reports on their membership submitted by branches in the northern part of the West Bank reveals the great fluctuations that took place in the number of members—and also casts serious doubt on the reliability of many of these reports. The chairman of the Nablus branch reported in 1950, for example, that membership had grown from two hundred to three hundred during the year, and that only three members had left the movement.[49] At the end of 1955, a report prepared by the security services placed the numerical strength of the Nablus branch at just two hundred. In July 1954, a new branch was opened in the village of Anabta with great pomp and ceremony. By the end of that same year, however, the security services reported that the branch had declined from a vibrant group of keen activists to a handful of youths who would meet from time to time in a local coffeehouse to play table tennis. In Jenin, the branch declined similarly after its establishment at the end of 1954—but here the reason given by former members was that the local chairman, who happened also to be the Mufti of Jenin, had turned the branch into a personal club to further the interests of his family in the town.[50] There is a total absence of information on membership numbers for several key branches, including Tulkarm, Tubas, and even Jerusalem. The Hebron branch, which was one of the largest and most stable in the West Bank, also poses a problem—should only the one hundred odd persons who regularly attended branch functions be considered members, or should the title apply to the three to four hundred persons who showed up periodically at special events, particularly those attended by the general supervisor?[51]

Nevertheless, it is possible to arrive at a fair estimate of the movement's strength in the West Bank during its first two decades. Taking the 750 members recorded in the files of the security services as a basis, and adjusting this figure to account for those places for which no figures have been recorded (estimating an average of 30 members for a small branch and 100 members for a larger one such as Jericho or Jerusalem), we arrive at an approximate membership of between 700 and 1,000. This must be viewed not only as a very approximate figure but also as a combined one, representing an accumulated high over the twenty-year period, while the total membership of the movement in the West Bank in any specific given movement was considerably smaller.

The geographical makeup of the movement's membership in the West Bank can be adduced from the lists compiled by the Jordanian Security Services. Of the 700 members on file whose place of abode is recorded, some 35 percent (about 250) lived in Nablus and its immediate vicinity; about 18 percent (135 members) lived in the towns and villages of the northern West Bank (Jenin, Tulkarm, Qalqiliya, Anabta), about 20 percent (150 members) lived in the Hebron area; 15 percent (110 members) lived in the Jerusalem area, and the remaining 12 percent lived in Bethlehem, Jericho, and the adjoining refugee camps. The concentration of members in Nablus and the north (which together accounted for over 50 percent of all members) and in Hebron was due to the conservative, traditional nature of the population in those areas compared with that of Jerusalem, for example, which had undergone a much deeper process of modernization, and was consequently less sympathetic to the fundamentalist thinking of the Brothers.

It is somewhat more difficult to arrive at an accurate picture of the social makeup of the movement's membership. Unlike in the case of the Communists the security authorities did not consider it worth their while to compile detailed files on the known members of the movement; and the Brothers themselves, for their part, appear to have attached little importance to such details. Only with reference to the leadership of the various branches does anything like a clear picture emerge. The most striking feature is the preponderance of religious functionaries of one sort or another on the branch executives. In the Jerusalem and Hebron branches during

the 1950s some two-thirds of the executive members held the title
"shaykh" (a venerated, old man) or *"hajj"* (someone who went as
a pilgrim to the Holy Cities of Mecca and Medina), and the situation
was somewhat similar in other branches as well. The branch executives included several leading figures in the economic, social, and
religious life of the West Bank. The executive of the Jerusalem
branch in the mid-1950s included Shaykh Muhammad Ali al-Jabari
and the historian Arif al-Arif.[52] In Nablus the executive included
members of such prominent families as the Nabulsis, Tuqans, and
al-Masris.[53] Reports on gatherings of the movement in various parts
of the West Bank included among the participants village *mukhtars*
and other local notables, as well as a wide range of intellectuals—
lawyers, physicians, pharmacists, teachers, students. Another group
that appears to have been fairly prominent in the movement was
the National Guard. Almost every branch had a few Guardsmen as
members, and it was reported that most of the Civil Guardsmen in
the village of Sur Bahir (near Jerusalem) were in fact members of
the movement.[54]

Teachers and students comprised a fairly prominent group, engaged in quite a wide range of activities—painting posters, participating in demonstrations, and preparing educational programs that
were presented before the public in an attempt to communicate
the movement's political and moral values. Their activities were not
confined to those villages where there were permanent branches
but extended to the outlying areas. Emissaries—sometimes themselves teachers—would be sent out from the larger centers to organize teachers and students in the surrounding villages. Students, of
course, made up the bulk of the Brothers' scout movement, the
"Rangers." Even so, the movement appears to have devoted comparatively little attention to the student population of the West
Bank, and it was considerably less successful in this sector than
were most of its political rivals. An indication of this can be seen
in the results of the national elections to the Students Committee
in 1957, when the Communists won five seats, the Baathists four,
and the Moslem Brothers none at all.[55]

Worthy of special mention was the Brothers' success in the refugee camps. Branches were opened in all the larger camps, and were
fairly active and attracted a considerable following. Even on the
East Bank, the Brothers had some success among the refugees, and
of the 150 members listed as belonging to the Irbid branch, the
bulk are described as refugees.[56] It was not easy for any movement

to operate successfully in the camps, which makes the Brothers' achievement even more noteworthy.

Among the upper echelons of the movement's leadership, those involved in religious instruction and guidance were the most important. These were not necessarily professional functionaries (*muftis* or *qadis*), but were quite often simply highly observant and devout lay Muslims and were revered as such by their followers. At the next level were the village *mukhtars* and large property owners. The two groups were frequently inextricably intertwined, and together they formed the basis of the movement's leadership. In other words, it appears that members were co-opted to the local branch executives on the strength of their economic and social standing in the community, and by virtue of the fact that they formed an important part of the social establishment in the West Bank. These local leaders were also men closely identified with the regime—a village *mukhtar*, or religious functionary, was, in fact, part of the administrative establishment in Jordan.

In examining the makeup of the movement's members—their social class and whether they were refugees or veteran residents— we have to rely on the lists of 750 names compiled by the security services between 1949 and 1967. The occupations of about half this number were recorded. The largest group, some 25 percent of all members, comprised merchants and urban property owners. These definitions were used rather loosely, and a "merchant" could be anything from a stall owner to a large-scale retailer or wholesaler, while "property owners" did not necessarily refer to owners of large tracts of real estate. In any case, the groups clearly included all urban self-employed other than professionals. Then came three other groups, each of which accounted for about 13 percent of the movement's membership. These were craftsmen (mainly cobblers but also tailors, carpenters, and mechanics), laborers (prominent were printing workers), and teachers. Farmers (including rural property owners) and students came next, each group comprising about 8 percent of the movement's members. The students were usually organized into groups and rarely joined the movement as individuals. This pertained particularly to the branches in Burqa and Hebron, where individual teachers appear to have had considerable success in recruiting their students to the movement. The balance of the movement's membership was made up of three groups, each accounting for about 6 percent of the total membership—the professionals (lawyers, physicians, and accountants), clerks, and religious functionaries.

The makeup of the movement's membership in the larger towns broke down in the following way. In Hebron, merchants and property owners made up 40 percent of the members, followed by teachers (20 percent) and students (also about 20 percent). In Nablus, the picture was somewhat different, with craftsmen particularly prominent. Craftsmen made up some 30 percent of the branch's members, about the same proportion as merchants and property owners; then came laborers (about 20 percent), followed by teachers, professionals, clerks, and religious functionaries (each about 5 percent). The "proletarian" nature of the branch reflected Nablus' position as the leading commercial and light-industrial center in the West Bank. There is insufficient information in the files on the membership of the Jerusalem branch to enable an analysis of its social composition. In the smaller towns and villages, farmers, teachers, and merchants were the most prominent groups, each comprising about 20 percent of the membership. A relatively large proportion of the movement's members were refugees, or former refugees. The files show that some 20 percent of members came originally from towns or villages now in Israel, or lived in refugee camps.

To sum up: the movement appears to have drawn its membership from all sectors of the population, with the urban self-employed (merchants and property owners) predominating. Clerks (the group from which the Brothers drew much of their support in the Egyptian cities) constituted a surprisingly small element in the West Bank, as did professionals. Although in absolute numbers religious functionaries did not figure prominently in the movement, it has to be remembered that they were a very small group and most of them in the West Bank were in one way or another involved with the Brothers. The bulk of the movement's members were from conservative religious backgrounds, which would account for the dearth of professionals in its ranks, as professionals tended to have a more westernized or even radical world-view.

The makeup of the movement in the West Bank was very different from that of its counterpart in Egypt. The population in Jordan, including the West Bank, was far more conservative than in Egypt, and had undergone a far lesser degree of westernization. This was reflected quite unmistakably in the social composition of the movement in each of the two countries, and also explains the relative lack of success enjoyed by the Brothers in Jordan compared with in Egypt. P. M. Mitchell, in his study of the Moslem Brothers in Egypt, notes that the movement there drew most of its support from "the Muslim middle-class." This was true of the West Bank as well. But Mitchell goes on to note that in Egypt the great majority of the movement's members were students, civil servants, teachers, clerks and office workers, and professionals.[57] In the West Bank, on the other hand, these groups were clearly in the minority. The reason for this was the rudimentary nature of both the government administrative apparatus and of private commercial enterprise in the West Bank compared with Egypt, where both sectors provided a livelihood for hundreds of thousands of white-collar workers. This was true even after the West Bank was annexed to Jordan in 1950, when, although the total number of white-collar workers in the area did increase, they still accounted for a very small part of the population. Also, the migration of educated workers from the West Bank to the East Bank in search of work was far less radical a social change than the migration from village to town in Egypt, where the resulting sense of uprootedness provided a considerable boost to the movement. In the West Bank, educated workers found themselves attracted to the radical left-wing parties. The dearth of professionals and the preponderance of merchants and property owners among the movement's members in the West Bank is a striking indication of the fundamental way in which the West Bank movement differed from its counterpart in Egypt.

Activities

Because they were a legally approved association, the Moslem Brothers in Jordan were able to engage in a wide variety of activities and to address themselves to several different sectors of the population. Routine activities took place, for the most part, in the movement's clubhouses. These clubhouses might be only a rented room in the local village coffeehouse or even the private home of one of the members. But the existence of a fixed meeting place in each branch was one of the characteristic features of the movement and in the larger centers the meeting place was a genuine clubhouse. Thus, in Nablus, the local branch rented the old municipal building for its activities; in Hebron, the movement met regularly in the al-Tamimi clubhouse in the center of the town; and in Jerusalem, after first meeting in rented rooms belonging to the Islamic Council and then in rooms near the Temple Mount, the local branch built its own permanent clubhouse behind Herod's Gate in the Old City.

Activities in the clubhouses were usually conducted in small groups or circles. Efforts were made to cultivate a recreation-center atmosphere in order to attract members of the general public. Various courses (such as typing) were held and a number of different sporting activities (weight lifting, table tennis, and so forth) took place.[58] Nevertheless the major emphasis was placed on the dissemination and inculcation of the movement's ideology. In the larger centers regular ideological meetings were held in the clubs at least once a week[59] (they were less frequent in the smaller centers). The gatherings were either addressed by a lecturer or devoted to lessons on religion. These lectures and lessons were sometimes held outside the clubhouses, occasionally in a park or some other public place, in order to reach a larger audience. Attendance at the meetings was by no means regular. About one hundred members usually attended in Hebron and Nablus, but that number more than doubled if the general supervisor was scheduled to speak.[60] Apart from religious instruction, a wide range of subjects was discussed at these gatherings. Speakers constantly harangued their audience about the gulf that existed between the Islamic ideal and the loose way of life in Jordan—a topic the Brothers had expounded in the mosques on more than one occasion. Purely political matters were also raised: Israel and the British and American imperialists were frequently the targets of bitter diatribe.

In addition to these regular meetings, the Brothers also held special festive gatherings, usually on the various Islamic holy days. Such gatherings were regularly held on Badr Day, Laylat al-Isra wal Miraj (the holy day commemorating the Prophet Muhammad's nighttime journey to Jerusalem and his ascent to Heaven), the Muslim New Year, and Mawlid al-Nabi. These festive gatherings were usually held only in the larger centers but occasionally in the villages as well. Occasionally, when an especially large attendance was anticipated, the gatherings took place in schools or even cinemas. Invitations were sent out in advance and the events were usually well attended; as many as five hundred members were reported at some of these gatherings in Hebron and Nablus, although the average attendance was about three hundred.

Another characteristic activity of the Moslem Brothers in Jordan was the use of the Friday sermon in the mosques to communicate their ideological message. This was greatly facilitated by the fact that the movement included in its ranks many practicing religious functionaries. The mosques were usually also the rallying point for many of the movement's demonstrations. Leaflets too were often distributed after Friday prayers.[61]

A popular way of reaching the general public was through the presentation of dramatic works designed around the movement's ideology. Between 1951 and 1953, for example, the dramatic circle run by the Moslem Brothers' sports club in Tulkarm staged a production, dealing with the question of poverty at the movement's branches throughout the West Bank, and drew large audiences. In 1953 high school students put on two plays about the Moroccan liberation strugge, "A Day of Combat in Marrakech," and "The Unknown Soldier." The Brothers sought to attract those who were disinclined to attend educational plays or intellectual lectures by organizing public sports events. These were also an important means of raising funds for special causes sponsored by the movement—such as the independence struggle in Algeria, or anti-illiteracy and -poverty campaigns in Jordan itself. The main competitions were wrestling, football, and swimming. There was considerable public interest in the sports events. Occasionally the organizers tried to persuade the spectators to remain after the competition was over, and take part in a political discussion. Apart from their value as fund-raising activities and forms for disseminating ideas, the Moslem Brothers saw sports as an important unifying force, a means of developing close bonds between members in preparation for the battle against the Zionist enemy. Muhammad himself, the movement's ideologues pointed out, was an accomplished horseman and archer.[62]

One type of activity that greatly worried the authorities, and consequently spawned several reports in the security services' archives, was scouting, which included field exercises and weapons training. There were organized troups of scouts in Nablus, Hebron, and Jerusalem, and also national scout camps. There are several reports on weapons training, dating mainly from the mid-1950s and 1958. This activity was of dubious legality, and was on occasion clearly illegal. Weapons training was often carried out in secret at night; groups of Brothers would sometimes take bus rides to some isolated locality where their arms and ammunition were carefully hidden, practice, and return home individually. Occasionally they would leave the towns quite openly, carrying their weapons with them and practicing in the surrounding countryside. These exercises usually took place on Fridays. Sometimes, trainees would go out into the field and live in training camps for a certain period. Their instructors would come out during the day, train them, and return home in the evening. In 1955–56, the Brothers began to train on weapons smuggled in from Sinai. After the 1956 Suez Crisis, when the Middle East became relatively quiet, the Hebron branch reached an agreement with the local army commander whereby members of the branch would receive regular training in firearms from instructors provided by the army. At least until 1956 the Moslem Brothers fervently supported the National Guard, which they saw as the spearhead of the future struggle against Israel (as we have noted, the movement was extremely suspicious of Glubb Pasha's Arab Legion).[63]

The differences in the structure and organization of the Moslem Brothers in Jordan compared with their counterparts in Egypt were, of course, reflected in the activities of the movement in each of the two countries. The sporadic weapons training undertaken by members of the movement in Jordan almost invariably with official sanction was a pale reflection of the highly organized clandestine military operations of the Brothers in Egypt. Even the various gatherings and functions organized by the Brothers in Jordan paled to insignificance when compared with the "Popular Congresses" and the festive gatherings held to mark Badr Day and other Muslim holy days in Egypt.[64] The far more modest range of activities of the movement in Jordan attested to the more circumscribed, conservative nature of the movement in the West Bank.

Finances

There is little information on the movement's finances during the first years of its existence in Jordan. There are hints, however, that during these years, the late 1940s and early 1950s, the Brothers in Jordan received considerable financial support from their parent movement in Egypt. It is also quite likely that the sources of income tapped in later years were also available to the movement then, though there is no direct evidence of this. In any case, the end of the 1948 war found the Brothers with considerable funds deposited in the al-Umma Bank in Jerusalem. These funds, along with money deposited in other banks, were frozen by the authorities until the legality of the movement had been established. According to their own testimony, the Brothers lent some £2,500 to the Ahmad Hilmi, prime minister in the All-Palestine government and an Egyptian protegé. When their financial situation later deteriorated in 1953, the Brothers appealed to the Arab League for the return of the loan. The situation grew progressively worse, and by the following year, 1954, there was not enough money to pay the rent on their clubhouse in Nablus.[65]

It appears that the position improved somewhat in 1955 (the movement in Egypt, then being hounded by the authorities, had apparently transferred some of their finances to Jordan), and there were even discussions with the movement in Syria concerning the possible transfer of money from Jordan to there.[66] In the mid-1950s there were four principal ways of raising funds. The first was through membership dues, but it seems that little money was ever raised from this source. Very few branches regularly reported the collection of membership dues, and the absence of such reports from other branches would seem to indicate either that dues were not collected or that little importance was attached to them as a source of revenue. A rather more effective source appears to have been the ad hoc collections made after the various gatherings and functions organized by the movement.[67] Special fund-raising campaigns were also initiated, usually for a special project. Donations often came from individuals who were not formally affiliated with the movement but chose to support it for one reason or another, and sometimes even from charitable organizations. The third means of raising at least limited sums of money was the sale of the movement's publications.[68] Most of the publications put out by the movement were, however, usually given away free of charge. Finally, an extremely lucrative source of income was the plays and sporting events organized by the movement. Tickets were sold for most of these events and were often tax-exempt. Although the income was earmarked for some specific cause (such as the war in Algeria or the Brothers' anti-poverty campaign in Jordan), it is highly probable that at least a portion of the money raised was used to finance the movement's regular activities.

Publications

The Moslem Brothers put out a wide range of publications in Jordan, the most important being their newspapers and magazines. *Al-Kifah al-Islami* ("the Muslim Struggle"), a weekly edited by Muhammad Khalifa, was the first. It began publication in late May 1954, but soon folded. It resumed publication on August 8, 1954, but was closed down after just two issues. The weekly was resurrected at the end of 1956, under the editorship of Muhammad Madi al-Qadi, who edited it throughout 1957. Following the publication of an article claiming that the Moslem Brothers had decided to take a motion of non-confidence in the government but had been prevented from doing so for unspecified reasons, *Al-Kifah al-Islami* was closed down for a third time, on October 7, 1957.[69] From its first appearance, the weekly was professionally produced and well printed. The front page was headed by the name of the paper, and between the two words was a hand grasping a flaming torch. Below this symbol, in small, decorative script, was a quotation from the Koran particularly favored by the Brothers: "Among the believers are men who were true to their covenant with God."[70] The publication regarded itself as "purveyor of the truth, in a spirit of dedication, to the entire community—to workers, clerks, students, the army, to men and to women." It pledged itself to deal with a wide range of issues, including those of interest to the military and students, as well as to give coverage to sports, culture, economics, family affairs, and general news. It also promised to feature stories and other fiction.

In June 1959 the Moslem Brothers brought out a new monthly called *Jaridat al-Saff* ("Paper of the Rank-and-File"). The six-page publication, printed in Amman, was highly critical of the regime and never distributed openly, but passed from hand to hand.

On June 15, 1960, the independent daily *Al-Manar* ("The Lighthouse") began to appear. Although it was not formally associated with the Moslem Brothers in Jordan, the paper—edited by Kamal al-Sharif, deputy secretary-general of the Islamic Congress's permanent office, aided by his brother, Mahmud—clearly presented the movement's point of view and became the most important channel for the dissemination of its ideas among the public at large.

In addition to its regular publications, the Brothers distributed large numbers of leaflets. This was in fact the movement's most common means of mass communication, and the various leaflets and pamphlets distributed by the Brothers in the West Bank spelled out their position on a wide range of issues. Some leaflets were professionally printed, with the movement's emblem prominently displayed, but most were simply duplicated from wax stencils. At the head of each leaflet were invariably a number of religious slogans, such as "God is great and unto Him all praise" (this frequently appeared at the end of the sheet as well); "God is great and *jihad* is our way"; "In the name of God, the Compassionate, the Merciful"; "Praise unto God and prayers and peace unto the Prophet of God, unto the members of his house, his companions, and unto those who follow him." At the end of each leaflet, in addition to the usual closing ("Peace be unto thee and God's mercy and blessings") there would often appear a quotation from the Koran in some way related to the movement's ideology, intended to stress the oneness of God, the faith of the believers in Him, and the importance of unity and companionship among all members of the community of believers.

The leaflets dealt for the most part with foreign or inter-Arab affairs, and tended to steer clear of domestic politics. In the 1954–55 period, they bitterly attacked Abd al-Nasser for the harsh steps he had taken against the Brothers in Egypt. In 1956, Israel and the imperialists were prominent targets of attack, as the leaflets came out in support of the nationalization of the Suez Canal and the struggle of the Egyptian people and their leader. Many of the leaflets throughout the period under review, dealt with the Palestine disaster and how it might be avenged. In the mid-1950s the liberation struggle against France in Algeria was a favorite topic, along with attacks on Nuri al-Said of Iraq. In later years, too, the pamphlets reflected the Brothers' stand on major events in the Arab world or on the ties between the various Arab countries and the imperialist West.[71] Some of the leaflets did deal with domestic issues both in Jordan and in Egypt, calling for greater adherence to Muslim religious values and practices or for attendance at rallies to mark Muslim holy days. These were, however, rather less common than those leaflets dealing with purely political matters.

Some of the leaflets were printed locally in the West Bank, others were brought in from Amman. They were distributed in a variety of ways—directly to members, outside the mosques after Friday prayers, in coffeehouses or on the streets, and sometimes even through the mail. From the limited information we have on this point, it would seem that the leaflets were distributed by members officially charged with this task or by groups of youngsters belonging to the movement.[72]

Finally, the movement published several books and pamphlets. A full-length book *Al-Islam wal-Hukm* ("Islam and Government") by an anonymous author, was distributed in 1952. In the early 1950s a pamphlet entitled "The Moslem Brothers and the Palestine Problem" appeared; in 1957 a pamphlet on the repression of the movement in Egypt was put out entitled "The Moslem Brothers

Are Being Persecuted." A very popular book among members of the movement on the West Bank was Shaykh al-Nabhani's *The Islamic Regime*, which described the ideal form of government in an Islamic state. The Nablus branch published in 1951 a special pamphlet to mark Laylat al-Miraj. The sixteen-page pamphlet, entitled "The Story of the Arab Prophet on the Night of His Nocturnal Journey," deals with the Prophet Muhammad's miraculous journey to heaven and also outlines the duties and obligations of the movement's members. Some of the pamphlets were really no more than expanded leaflets, and dealt with subjects in the gray area between topical events and ideology. Such a leaflet was that written by the general supervisor Khalifa in 1956, "We are the Victors," which called on members to support the National Guard, the best guarantor of the country's security and the eventual victory over Israel. Another volume that was widely read by the Brothers in the West Bank, even though it was not actually written by a member of the movement, was "The Mission of Holy War," written by Kamal al-Sharif, deputy head of the General Islamic Congress in Jerusalem, and published by the Congress. The book was dedicated to the National Guard, whose ideals it set out to portray.[73]

Ties with the Brothers Elsewhere in the Arab World

The Moslem Brothers in the West Bank maintained far closer ties with the movement in Egypt than with that anywhere else in the Arab world. In the first place, there were strong personal and family ties between members of the movement in the two countries. Said Ramadan, for example, secretary of the Islamic Congress in Jerusalem and one of the Moslem Brothers' most active members in Jordan, was the son-in-law of Hasan al-Banna—founder of the movement in Egypt—and in the early 1950s was still considered to be a member of the Egyptian movement. In another case, one of the leading members of the movement in Hebron moved to Egypt, to return to the West Bank some years later as an emissary of the Brothers in Egypt.[74] The Jerusalem branch, when it was first established in 1946, came under very strong Egyptian influence, both ideologically and organizationally.[75] Until 1954 the Brothers in the West Bank received considerable ideological material from Egypt in the form of books and pamphlets, but this ceased after the Egyptian Brothers were outlawed. Before the Brothers were outlawed in Egypt, the general supervisor of the movement there, al-Hudaybi, was invited to visit the West Bank. He was at first refused entry into Jordan, following a public outcry that was in all probability instigated by the Jordanian authorities themselves. Eventually, he was permitted to enter the West Bank, where he was warmly welcomed. Al-Hudaybi was followed by several other emissaries from the Egyptian movement.

The West Bank movement also received visitors from other Arab countries. In 1953 a group of scouts from the movement in Kuwait visited the Jerusalem and Hebron branches, starting a tradition that continued for several years. In the mid-1950s, groups of Brothers from Syria visited the headquarters of the Islamic Congress, and one group also visited the Hebron branch.[76] There was also a fairly regular written correspondence between the movements in Jordan and Syria. The Brothers' executive office in Damascus would from time to time send communiqués and commentaries on various political developments in the Middle East, and there can be little doubt that the Syrian movement, like the Egyptian, had a considerable influence on the West Bank Brothers. In 1956 the leader of the movement in Beirut, Muhammad Umar Dauq, was reported to have paid a visit to the Nablus branch. At the beginning of the 1960s a visiting preacher from Iraq, Muhammad Mahmud al-Sawwaf, visited several branches in the West Bank and harangued his listeners about the need to embark upon a holy war to liberate Palestine. Members of the movement in Jordan also visited branches in the other Arab countries. It should be noted, however, that all the information we have points to direct contact only with other Arab countries, and nowhere is any mention made of visitors from other parts of the Muslim world. The reason for this is that such visits were usually made to the Islamic Congress in Jerusalem (see next section).

There was some exchange of material among the branches in the various Arab countries, and in some branches in the West Bank it was possible for members to read newspapers and publications put out by the Brothers in other countries, even if they were usually well out of date. Thus one of the reports in the security services' archives tells of a West Bank Brother who admitted under interrogation that he had passed on copies of newspapers published by the movement in Baghdad ("Muslim Friendship"), Egypt "The Moslem Brothers"), and apparently Syria (*al-Shihab*—"The Meteor").[77]

The General Islamic Congress

Although it was not identical with the Moslem Brothers, the General Islamic Congress in Jerusalem was controlled by leading members of the movement and very much reflected the Brothers' outlook.

On October 4, 1953, the Moslem Brothers held a traditional gathering in Jerusalem to mark the night of *al-isra wa'l-miraj*. This was attended by visiting religious leaders from several Arab countries, none of them formal members of the movement. It was decided that the annual Holy Day should be marked each year by a similar gathering in Jerusalem of representatives from all the Muslim countries. The occasion, it was decided, would be dedicated to the problem of Palestine, especially as it affected Jerusalem. A permanent office was set up in Jerusalem, called *al-isra wa'l-miraj*, and a charitable body called "The Moslem Charitable Society for the Rehabilitation of Jerusalem, Ltd." was founded.[78] The new office, which maintained close ties with the Iraq-based "Organization for the Salvation of Palestine," decided to convene an all-Islamic Congress to be attended by representatives from the Arab countries, the Arab League, and the Islamic countries, as well as Muslim representatives from Europe, America, and the Soviet Union. The Congress met for the first time from December 4 to December 10, 1953. In addition to the usual resolutions—attacking the imperialists, calling for the restoration of Palestine to its rightful owners, and condemning the repression of Muslims behind the Iron Curtain—the Congress also passed several practical, operative resolutions. It was decided to set up a fund to finance the economic reconstruction of Palestine and especially of Jerusalem; to call on the Muslim countries to contribute toward the upkeep of the al-Aqsa Mosque and Dome of the Rock in Jerusalem; and to aid the Arab League in its efforts to safeguard Muslim sites in Jerusalem over which rival interests were seeking to gain control. A number of political resolutions were also adopted which, although having little operative significance, reflected the ideological outlook that united those attending—the reopening of the Hejaz railway, the establishment by every Muslim country of a consulate in Amman; the observance of Palestine Day on Rajab 27 each year; and the establishment of an Islamic political bloc, along the lines of the Eastern and Western blocs dominating the international scene. Taken together these resolutions all point to a strong pan-Islamic sentiment and attempts to bring the Palestine problem to the forefront of attention throughout the Islamic world, to involve all Muslims in the struggle to find a solution to that problem, and to strengthen the position of Jordan in the international and inter-Arab arenas and gain support for its hold on the West Bank. All this was entirely consonant with the political and ideological aspirations of the Moslem Brothers. At the end of the first Congress, a World Committee comprising seven members, four of them from Jerusalem, and a twenty-four-member Council were elected. Said Ramadan, who was shortly to become general supervisor of the Brothers in Jordan, was elected secretary-general. Kamal al-Sharif, who was closely associated with the movement, was elected director of the Congress's permanent office and Ramadan's deputy.[79]

Although it was decided in principle that the Congress would convene annually, it did not meet again in Jerusalem until 1959. The main reason for this was the intervention of the Jordanian authorities. At the beginning of 1954 members of the permanent office, including Ramadan, were prevented from entering the country, and the next year, 1955, the authorities explicitly forbade the holding of the Congress in Jerusalem. In the summer of that year the Congress's office in Jerusalem was closed down, and the intense efforts to have it reopened had little effect. The office was eventually reopened in 1956, after being closed for about twelve months. The Congress was convened in 1956 in Damascus, and another three years passed before it returned to Jerusalem.[80] Except for the twelve-month period in 1955–56, however, the Congress office in Jerusalem was active throughout the period under review.

The main activity of the office in the mid-1950s was the collection of donations from throughout the Islamic world and the allocation of these funds either to the projects specified by the donors or to projects decided on by the Congress. The office also worked very closely with the National Guard in a number of different ways. For example, the office took responsibility for the fortification works in four villages near Jerusalem and Hebron, and when they were completed, handed them over to the army. It also provided several other villages with building materials and other aid so that they could construct their own fortifications, and made sure they received proper instruction from members of the office or the Moslem Brothers. In Jerusalem, according to Congress sources, more than 5,000 Jerusalem dinars were spent by the office on the construction of barricades in several quarters. The office, again according to Congress sources, spent some 14,000 dinars on food and uniforms for National Guardsmen in the West Bank. That same year, 1954, a Kuwaiti delegation donated 10,000 dinars to the National Guard, of which it was specified that part had to go to

Guardsmen serving in Jerusalem. The money was, it would appear, channeled through the Congress.[81]

The Congress office also engaged in a wide range of propaganda activities, usually focusing on furthering the interests of Jerusalem. Leaflets were distributed protesting the proposed internationalization of Jerusalem. Members of the office also visited forward positions of the Arab Legion, and delivered religious sermons to the soldiers serving there. On a local level representatives of the office, who were often also among the leading Brothers in the West Bank, delivered lectures to the Jerusalem population which generally reflected the ideas and thinking of the movement.[82]

At the beginning of July 1956 the Jordanian authorities lifted its ban on the Congress, and its leaders were permitted to return to Jerusalem. These included representatives from Syria, Lebanon, Saudi Arabia, Egypt, Pakistan, and even the Soviet Union. They explained that their return had been made possible by the removal of "the dictatorial imperialist regime"—the inference was to the dismissal of Glubb Pasha and the elimination of direct British influence in Jordan. A new era of close cooperation between the Council and the Hashemite regime ensued. In 1957 a mass parade of scouts and National Guardsmen was held in the plaza of the Dome of the Rock, and the gathering was addressed by the deputy director-general of the Congress, Kamal al-Sharif. After the speech, copies of Sharif's "The Mission of the Holy War," with a preface written by King Husayn, were distributed. This sudden rapprochement was probably due to the king's growing need for support as his showdown with the government of Sulayman al-Nabulsi approached. The ploy worked, and the elements associated with the Congress—most prominently the Moslem Brothers—did rally to his support when the showdown finally came. Furthermore the king probably hoped to gain the support in other Arab countries of the Brothers and other organizations associated with the Congress. On February 5, 1959, the Congress was convened for the third time, in Jerusalem. The participants launched a spate of vitriolic attacks on the Nasserite regime in Egypt,[83] and in this way did much to serve the political interests of Hashemite Jordan. The fourth Congress was convened the following year, at the end of January 1960, followed a year later by the fifth Congress, in mid-January 1961. King Husayn addressed the latter gathering, followed on the podium by Kamal al-Sharif. Eleven delegates from Muslim countries in

Asia and Africa attended, and greetings were cabled by the heads of many states throughout the world. The Congress discussed and passed resolutions on the events effecting Muslims in countries as far afield as Algeria, Palestine, the Soviet Bloc, Eritrea, and Indonesia.

It is difficult to define precisely the relationship between the Islamic Congress and the Moslem Brothers. It is clear beyond all doubt, however, that the leading members of the Congress were also members of the Brothers and frequently represented the views of the movement. The Congress office, situated in the Old City of Jerusalem, was frequently used by the Moslem Brothers in the city to hold meetings and to house visiting guests. The duplicating machine in the office was also used by the Brothers to roll off leaflets. Moreover, the general supervisor of the Brothers in Jordan, Abd al-Rahman Khalifa, was responsible for auditing the Congress' books.[84]

In the final analysis, the Congress did tend to support the Brothers on almost every issue and it would seem that it was in fact little more than a "front," designed to extend the influence of the movement beyond the ambit of its official members. The movement probably also hoped the links that the Congress managed to forge with influential Muslims throughout the Arab and Islamic worlds would help it to strengthen its position in Jordan and increase its following there.

IDEOLOGY

The Charters

The charters of the three largest branches in the West Bank are available to the researcher—those of the Jerusalem and Nablus branches, both dating from 1946, and that of the Hebron branch, dating from 1949. The Jerusalem document is called "The Basic Charter of the Moslem Brothers Association in Palestine," and although it was in fact adopted by other branches in the West Bank (Bethlehem, for example, in 1949), it never became the exclusive charter of the movement in the area. The charters of the three large branches are nevertheless very similar.

All three display the unmistakable influence of the movement in Egypt. As we have already seen, there were a number of differences in the way the movement was organized in each of the two countries. Ideologically, however, the two movements were virtually identical, with the Jordanian Brothers adopting whole-cloth most of the fundamental ideals and principles evolved by its older, better-established counterpart in Egypt. This is abundantly clear from the six basic "goals" the movement set itself, in both Jordan and Egypt: (1) the "educational goal" of purifying Islam through a return to its original, pristine principles, and adapting these principles to the requirements of the modern world; (2) the "practical goal" of unifying the Muslim countries by coordinating their world outlooks and by bringing their peoples into close contact with each other; (3) the "economic goal" of developing the Islamic world and assuring the equitable distribution of wealth among the different Muslim nations; (4) the "social goal" of encouraging a tradition of charity and almsgiving, and eliminating poverty, ignorance, and disease; (5) the "national goal" of instilling a spirit of (Muslim) patriotism in the population of the (Muslim) nation; and (6) the "global goal" of making Islam the basis of an unrivaled world culture. The only difference among the branches in the definition of these six goals is to be found in the Jerusalem charter, which defines the "national goal" as the "patriotic-national goal" (*watani-qawmi*) and stresses the need to work for "the salvation of Palestine and the safeguarding of the integrity of the Arab Muslim homeland...and to strive for the realization of Arab unity and the Islamic commonwealth." This tendency to stress local Palestinian patriotism and nationalism grew increasingly strong in the course of the 1950s and 1960s.

Positions on Religion, Society, and Politics

The Moslem Brothers in the West Bank expressed their religious, social, and political ideas in a variety of ways during the period under review—in publications, in sermons, in lectures, in study groups, and at festive gatherings. Their fundamental position on these issues was basically that of the movement in Egypt.

The overriding concern was, of course, the relationship between state and religion. The Brothers held, dogmatically, that religion and state were inseparable, and any such separation was the result of an alien Christian-European creed. Islam was not only the personal religion of the individual, a matter between man and his God, they argued, but it was also the basis of "law...and political order."[85] This was not just a statement of a general truth; the movement in the West Bank constantly attacked what they saw as specific deviations from this principle in the everyday life there. Jordan, like Egypt and several other Arab countries, had a constitution modeled on that of France. The Moslem Brothers, both in Egypt and Jordan, bitterly attacked the adoption of a Western-type constitution in their countries, seeing it as a heresy and one of the causes of division in the Islamic community.[86] The general supervisor of the movement in Jordan, Abd Al-Rahman Khalifa, claimed that the foreign constitution had robbed the country's qadis of their recourse to Islamic tradition, and instead of being able to pass their judgments on the basis of the righteous precepts laid down by the caliphs and sages of Islam, they had now to turn to those borrowed from the infidel. In this way, he concluded, the laws of Islam were being forgotten and the Koran neglected.[87]

Given the not insignificant percentage of Christian Arabs living in the West Bank, and the fact that the Moslem Brothers had on more than one occasion been suspected of sowing dissension between Muslims and Christians there, the movement felt obliged to spell out the place they envisaged for Christians in the future Islamic state. In an effort to assuage the fears of the Christians, the movement pointed out that in the original Islamic state the rights of religious minorities (*ahl al-dhimma*)[88] were rigorously protected, and that in the future Islamic state, not only would their rights be protected but *dhimmi* would have equal rights with Muslims. This approach was not, of course, that sanctioned by Islamic tradition, which denied to *ahl al-dhimma* many of the rights to which Muslims were entitled. It was, however, perfectly in keeping with the position of the Moslem Brothers in Egypt, who drew a clear distinction between foreign Christians and the indigenous "Eastern" Christians who were equal to Muslims in every respect other than their religious beliefs.[89] In practice, however, the situation was very different, and the Brothers displayed much of the traditional Islamic contempt in their dealings with the local Christian Arabs. In 1962, for example, the Christian director of the General Security Services in Jordan was dismissed from his post. The move was welcomed by the Brothers, who noted that in a state with an Islamic constitution, it was unthinkable that the director of the security services should be anything but a Muslim.[90]

The Islamic State of the future, which would be modeled on that of the Prophet Muhammad and the first four caliphs, would also be the ideal state in modern terms—for Islam was not a reactionary religion, as its Communist and nationalist detractors claimed, but the most progressive of all faiths. Islam was founded on fundamentally democratic principles and insisted on strict social justice or, in traditional terms, Islam was based on "justice, obedience, and consultation."[91]

In the area of social justice, which was somewhat less esoteric than the dogmatic questions of religion and state, the Brothers in the West Bank displayed rather greater interest. But even here their treatment tended to be cursory and very superficial, stressing broad generalizations such as the need to return to the pure, all-embracing tenets of early Islam and the full social integration of the Islamic community. This required greater attention to the weaker members of that community—the poor and the underprivileged. The movement also made specific demands for greater social equality, and greater readiness on the part of the privileged to help their less fortunate fellows by contributing to the common good and performing good works as laid down by the Islamic religion. The Brothers initiated a number of anti-poverty projects, similar to those undertaken by their Egyptian counterparts, but it is not clear just how effective these were. The movement's representatives in parliament were even prompted to table a no-confidence motion in the government at the beginning of 1963 because it had failed to nationalize various sectors of the economy (as required, they claimed, by Islam) and because workers weren't sharing in the profits or decision-making processes of the various economic enterprises. All this clearly reflects the thinking of the Egyptian movement's founding father, Hasan al-Banna, who saw the creation of a society based on equality and economic justice as one of the central injunctions of Islam.[92]

The Return to a Pure Islamic Moral Code

The Moslem Brothers in the West Bank did not reject outright (as did their counterparts in Egypt) the introduction of certain innovations from the West. They in fact very much favored any technological innovation that would help develop and strengthen the Islamic countries. The West Bank Brothers were, however, implacably opposed to the introduction of any social or ethical innovation. Such innovations, they maintained, ran counter to the spirit of Islam, were liable to damage its social fabric, and would lead ultimately to the destruction of Muslim society. Those Western ideas that did not threaten Islam were likely to prove advantageous to the Muslims, the Brothers appeared to adopt and "Islamize."

But the encroachment of Western values and a Western lifestyle on Muslim society was seen as part of a Christian-imperialist plot to undermine that society from within and rob it of the will and inner strength to combat its external enemies. In the view of the Moslem Brothers, the world of Islam was locked in a relentless struggle with Western civilization.[93] This attitude governed much of the political activity undertaken by the Brothers in Jordan and throughout the Arab world. Any phenomenon that they considered to be morally corrupt or associated with the destructive cultural infiltration by the West was condemned and made the subject of a vigorous public campaign.

At the beginning of 1955 the Brothers in the West Bank strongly criticized the Islamic Convention taking place in Cairo. In a special leaflet put out by the movement, the appearance of the popular Egyptian singer Umm Kulthum at the Convention was decried as an abomination.[94] The Brothers had good political reason to oppose the Convention, which was taking place under the auspices of a regime that was then bent on suppressing their brethren in Egypt, and which might also be seen as a rival to the Islamic Congress in Jerusalem. But that does not necessarily detract from the sincerity of their ideological opposition to Umm Kulthum's appearance, for they had clashed with the Hashemite regime in Jordan on several occasions over similar issues.

The Moslem Brothers had fixed repressive ideas about women and how they were expected to conduct themselves. Women were not permitted to use makeup or to over-adorn themselves, they were to veil their faces, and were not to appear in public "half naked." This, the Brothers maintained, was clearly laid down by Islam. The secretary of the Brothers' Hebron branch went even further and urged the government to bar women from holding any position in its service.[95]

The movement took a strong stand also on moral issues. Its representatives in parliament opposed the proposed 1960–61 budget for the Jordanian broadcasting services on the grounds that the latter aired "immoral" songs and music. The Brothers came out time and again against any form of entertainment which they regarded as unduly permissive—appearances by foreign dance companies, dance clubs in the various towns of the West Bank, and so on. They also criticized the government for issuing so many licenses to stores selling alcoholic drinks, and demanded that government officials be forbidden to drink wine in public. A similar demand, which seems strongly xenophobic, was made of the British officers serving with the Arab Legion: pending their ultimate dismissal, which the Brothers consistently demanded, their behavior should be kept on close rein, for their excesses were having a bad influence on the local Muslim youth. It would seem that the Brothers had little faith in the young generation and sought to put a stop to Jordanian students going abroad to study in the Western countries. While admitting the value of the scientific and technological knowledge that students obtained in the West, the Brothers were concerned that students were brought into close contact with a "pernicious" culture and acquired Western ways of behavior and thought which they brought back with them on their return to Jordan. On more than one occasion the Brothers expressed their exasperation at the younger generation's lack of respect for their movement's ideas, and complained that young people growing up in Jordan viewed anyone who sought to safeguard the sacred interests of Islam as a "reactionary," an "ignoramus," or even as "mentally deficient."[96]

Education

The Moslem Brothers placed very great stress on the importance of education. This is evident not only from their statements and writings but also from the very nature of many of their activities—their various anti-illiteracy projects, the study groups which they ran on a regular basis in their clubhouses, the public gatherings and festivities organized to mark occasions of historic or religious importance, and the physical and paramilitary training they offered to the youth of the West Bank. The Brothers declared quite specifically that their goal was "to provide the youth with a proper Islamic education in order to create a healthy society."[97] They argued that Islamic education had seriously declined in the West Bank under the British Mandate. As an example they cited the situation in Nablus. Nablus had always been renowned for its strong attachment to the values and ethics of Islam. Under the Mandate, however, the residents began to move away from these spiritual values, enticed by the allure of the materialistic world. Parents in the town stopped sending their children to al-Azhar in Egypt, the Brothers claimed, preferring to send them to foreign non-Muslim schools and colleges. The result was inevitable and before long, Nablus, once famous for its religious sages, was almost without such sages and deeply sunken in moral crisis. The Brothers argued that this process had been helped along since the end of the Mandate by the Hashemite regime—despite the fact that the foreign rulers had been replaced by Muslims. The Hashemites had done nothing to rectify the damage done by the British, the Brothers claimed, with the result that the situation had continued to deteriorate. The new regime went so far as to control religious instruction, by promulgating the Sermonizing and Instruction Law in 1955, under the terms of which all religious instruction in the mosques had to receive the prior approval of the chief qadi. This law contradicted the tenets of Islam, the Brothers claimed, noting that the discussion of spiritual matters within the walls of the mosque was a religious duty of the true believer. What was worse was the fact that while religious instruction was restricted in the mosques, the study of Islam was freely permitted in the various foreign missionary institutions, most of which were affiliated with one or another of the major churches and monasteries.

The Brothers criticized the regime's attitude toward education throughout the period under review. In 1961, for example, they condemned the changing of the name of the Education Ministry, from "al-Maarif" (literally, "knowledge" or "science," but with clear religious overtones) to "al-Tarbiya wa'l-Talim" (which means education and teaching in the purely technical sense). The Brothers saw this change as tangible proof of the growing alienation from religion in the country's education system. Also in 1961 the Brothers complained that teachers of religious instruction who retired were not being replaced. Two years later what was seen as a further deterioration in the field of education prompted a vote of no confidence by the movement's representatives in parliament. In tabling the motion the Brothers claimed that there was insufficient religious instruction in the kingdom with little being done to encourage the spread of Islamic values beyond the weekly sermon in the mosque.[98]

Missionary Activity

The Moslem Brothers exhibited considerable anxiety about missionary activities in Jordan, seen as the very essence of the type of political, religious, and cultural dangers facing the Muslims. According to the movement, the activities of the foreign philanthropic organizations (the various medical and social welfare groups) were not really intended to provide aid to the needy, as they professed, but rather to entice this vulnerable sector of the community away from its Islamic affiliation. Still more insidious were the educational activities of the missions: all these educational institutions the Brothers claimed, were engaged in "missionary propaganda" and constituted a threat to Islam. The missions placed great emphasis on the study of Islamic history and religion. But these subjects were taught by Christian teachers using foreign texts, so there was always a grave danger of heresy.

The various orders, monasteries, and missionary institutions were working systematically and secretly toward a common long-term goal, the Brothers claimed. One of their ways of advancing toward this goal was the acquisition of Arab property, and the missionaries showed special interest in sites that had some religious significance. Their major interest was of course in Jerusalem, where, the Brothers claimed, the churches had acquired control of some 78 percent of all land in the city. In the wider Jerusalem-Bethlehem area, they controlled about 20 percent of all land. The Latin Monastery alone, according to the Brothers, had allocated one million dollars for the acquisition of land. The ultimate goal of the missionaries, who were aided and abetted by the Jews, was to seize control of the Temple Mount and rebuild the Temple on the ruins of the Dome of the Rock—after they had succeeded in placing the entire city of Jerusalem under Zionist control. Proof of the close cooperation between the Christians and the Jews in realizing this aim was seen in the Ecumenical Council's decision to absolve the Jews of the blame for Christ's crucifixion.[99]

The attitude of the Moslem Brothers in the West Bank to the missions was largely inspired by Hasan al-Banna, who saw the missionaries as the main agents of "cultural imperialism," which sought in the name of Christianity and on its behalf to annihilate Islam. The movement in the West Bank tended, however, to be much more vitriolic and outspoken in its verbal attacks on the missions than was its counterpart in Egypt. The obvious explanation for this was the intensive nature of missionary activity in the Holy Land. Apart from al-Banna's ideological opposition to the missionaries, then, there was the constant fear, especially in the 1950s, of their continuing drive to acquire more property. The Brothers feared that Muslims in the West Bank were threatened by two powerful enemies—the Christians and the Jews—and it was almost inevitable that they should suspect some form of close cooperation between them, this time with a new twist: it was not the Jews that were working for Western imperialism, but the Christian churches that were working for the interests of world Jewry.

Attitude Toward Political Parties in the West Bank

The Moslem Brothers were wholly opposed in principle to the very existence of political parties, which they saw as dividing the Islamic community and ultimately weakening it, making it easy prey for its enemies. Schism of any form was forbidden by God, and constituted a serious transgression.[100] It was in accordance with this belief (and perhaps for practical political reasons) that the Moslem Brothers refrained from calling themselves a "party," preferring the term "association" (*jamiya*). This view also governed the Brothers' attitude toward the other political parties in the West Bank. As it was the only legal party in the area, it had a great advantage over its political rivals in that it could disseminate its ideas, both verbally and in writing, quite openly. This advantage was most evident during the 1957 political crisis in Jordan, when the Brothers came out in support of the beleaguered king and attacked the "subversive" radical parties. It was at this time that the party recorded its most significant growth. Being the only legal party in the area, its political meetings became the only platform where supporters of the various parties could enter into public debate. Thus the meetings called by the Moslem Brothers, instead of remaining a platform for internal discussion, became the regular forum of interparty debate, with the various parties sending special representatives for precisely this purpose. Sometimes these meetings became so heated that the security authorities feared they might threaten public order. When the authorities did intervene, it is interesting to note, it was never to prevent the debates from taking place but simply to preserve public order.[101] This tolerant attitude may have derived from the perception that the Moslem Brothers, in their ideological clashes with the illegal opposition parties, represented positions akin to those of the regime and were in effect defending the regime against its detractors. It is testimony to the faith the authorities had in the Moslem Brothers and their ideology that they seem never to have thought for a moment that the more radical or nationalistic arguments would triumph in these debates.

The Liberation Party (Hizb al-Tahrir) was the opposition party most similar to the Brothers both ideologically and structurally, and was thus seen by the Brothers as their more serious rival. It was founded in 1952 by members who had left the Moslem Brothers, claiming that it was not sufficiently faithful to the tenets of Islam, and from the start there was bitter rivalry between the two parties. There were isolated attempts later at some form of cooperation or even unification, but these came to nothing, and the fundamental animosity persisted throughout the period. There was one instance of close cooperation between the two parties in October 1954, when the Brothers supported the Liberation Party's parliamentary candidate in Qalqilya and contributed greatly to his election. Between 1952 and 1956 several attempts at union were reported. In June 1953 representatives of the Liberation Party initiated a discussion with the Brothers in Nablus on the merger of the two movements into a single organization to be called "Islamic Brotherhood" (al-Ukhuwwa al-Islamiya). This was seen by the Liberation Party as a possible way to achieve legal status (which it had failed to obtain in its own right, despite persistent efforts). At the end of that same year another attempt at union was made, this time in Jerusalem. About a year later, at the end of 1954, the leader of the Liberation Party in Jordan, al-Nabhani, and the supervisor general of the Moslem Brothers, Hasan al-Hudaybi, attempted to arrive at some form of union between their movements. Contacts between the leaders continued into 1955.[102] All these attempts failed, however, more for reasons of personal rivalry than irreconcilable ideological differences. What ideological differences existed arose largely from the very fact of their separate existence. There were no further attempts at union after 1956, when the two parties entered into a period of unrestrained antagonism.

Each party did its utmost to vilify the other, through libel, public diatribe, and even by passing on damaging information to the authorities. The intensity of their rivalry was fuelled by the fact that the two parties had common roots and very similar platforms, and appealed to the same sectors of the population for support. This made it necessary for each party to play up the differences between them and also to point out what it saw as irregularities in the thought and political behavior of its rival. The debate was conducted on two levels—the purely political and the religious-ideological (which also had political and social implications). On the political level, each of the two parties accused the other of working for one or another foreign power. The Brothers accused the Liberation Party of working for the United States, which provided it with funds. No proof of this was provided, of course, but the ideology and political conduct of the Liberation Party did lend some credence to the accusation.[103] The Liberation Party for its part accused the Moslem Brothers of working for the British, which explained why the Brothers supported the British-dominated Hashemite regime in Jordan.[104] It would seem that the Brothers' constant call for the dismissal of Glubb Pasha and his fellow British officers from the Arab Legion, as well as their persistent demand that all trace of foreign influence be removed from Jordan, did not deflect this kind of accusation. In the religious-ideological sphere, each of the two parties were continually laying claim to be the only genuine, committed, and uncompromising bearer of the flag of Islam, the true interpreters of Islam in the complex political conditions of twentieth-century Jordan. The Liberation Party accused the Brothers of accepting the alien, non-Islamic concept of a separation between state and religion. They argued that the Brothers did not have a coherent position on economic and social issues, which Islam did have, and were lukewarm and quite unsuccessful in their struggle for the application of the laws of Islam in Jordan. The Brothers tended to respond to these charges of political opportunism in kind, making counter-charges rather than systematically refuting the accusations leveled by the Liberation Party. The basic charge the Brothers leveled against the Liberation Party was that its members made false claims to religiosity and piety, being in fact far from genuinely religious persons. Their creed was a "false creed" designed to mislead the Muslim community. The Brothers cited the Liberation Party as the most typical and pernicious example of *hizbiya* ("party-ism"), and the very creation of the party served to split the Muslim world rather than unite it.[105] The implication of the charge was, of course, that the Liberation Party's existence as a separate party had no legal sanction, and that the only legitimate bearers of Muslim hopes and aspirations were the Brothers.

There was a heated theological debate between the two parties on the question of the unified Islamic State of the future, and on the timing and nature of Islam's holy war, the *jihad*. The Liberation Party insisted on the creation of the Islamic State (without apparently going through a transitional phase of Arab unity) prior to the launching of *jihad*. The Moslem Brothers, on the other hand, argued that *jihad* should commence immediately, without waiting for the creation of the unified Islamic State. They accused the Liberation Party of prejudicing the interests of the Islamic nation by postponing the *jihad*. The Brothers sometimes defined *jihad* as an Arab war of liberation against the Western imperialists and against Zionism, and accordingly Arab unity was an essential prerequisite for such a war. Thus they placed far greater stress on the importance of Arab nationalism than did the Liberation Party, which was more committed to the notion of Islamic universalism. In view of the extremely sensitive nature of the subject (the Liberation Party was reluctant to give the impression that it was cool to the idea of Arab nationalism, while the Moslem Brothers were equally reluctant to create the impression that they rejected the notion of Islamic universalism), it was never broached openly. But from the plethora of oblique hints and innuendos that survive from the debates on the subject, a fairly clear picture emerges of just where each of the two parties stood.[106]

After the Liberation Party, the one most frequently mentioned in the Moslem Brothers' literature was that most diametrically opposed to them ideologically—the Communist Party. Their hostility to the Communists was total, and during the 1957 political crisis in Jordan they exhorted their members to hound Communists without mercy. Even after the crisis passed there was no rapprochement between the two parties and they remained bitterly hostile to each other.[107] Ideologically the Brothers viewed the Communists as the implacable foes of Islam, whose dogma contradicted the very essence of the Islamic religion.[108] The Communists were equally negative about the Moslem Brothers whom they saw as incorrigible reactionaries. The Brothers dismissed Communism in general, and Arab Communism in particular, as a false social creed. The Communists were also accused of murder and robbery "in the name of liberty and progress" in Iraq, and of crimes they had committed in Jordan in their quest to annihilate the Muslims.[109] In short, Communism was seen not only as the enemy of Islam as a religion but as the brutal foe of the Muslims as a people. While the Communists were cruel, cynical and paid only lip service to the concept of equality, the Moslem Brothers followed a creed that was progressive, democratic, and humanitarian.

The Baathists did not figure prominently in the writings of the Moslem Brothers. The ideas of their ideological leader, Michel Aflaq, were, however, anathema to the Brothers, as was the fact that Aflaq was a Christian. In the summer of 1963 the Brothers violently attacked the Baathist regime in Syria, claiming that Aflaq was running Syria, a Muslim country, according to alien notions derived from the Christian West. Aflaq was a racist, they claimed, just like his Christian mentors in the West, and his only aim was to divide the inhabitants of his country.[110] Another fairly common accusation leveled against the Baathists was that their governments in Syria and Iraq were guilty of the most heinous atrocities. Surprisingly, on the issue of Arab nationalism, where the ideologies of the two parties were clearly at odds, the Brothers tended to be lukewarm and even confused in their criticism. The Brothers were extremely reluctant to get too deeply involved in a debate that would reveal them as opposed to Arab nationalism as a result of their greater ideological commitment to the idea of pan-Islam. Pan-Arab sentiment was very deeply rooted in the West Bank, and the Brothers were obviously not willing to alienate the population by appearing to be going against this powerful current; instead they sought to divert it into channels that could in some way be reconciled with their own pan-Islamic aspirations. They preferred to keep their public debate with the Baathists on what was, for them, the safe ground of Muslim piety, and steer clear of the issue on which the Baath would have an obvious advantage.[111]

Religious provocation, then, was the outstanding element in the Moslem Brothers' struggle against its political rivals in the West Bank. The charge of heresy, atheism, or even of hostility to Islam was the movement's most powerful political weapon. Compared with the movement in Egypt, the Brothers in Jordan were far cruder and less restrained in their attacks on their rivals. Whereas the Egyptian Brothers were prepared to admit that Communism, though anti-Islamic, did espouse certain positive social principles, their counterparts in the West Bank credited the Communists with no positive attribute whatever, and even went so far as to accuse them of seeking the actual physical annihilation of all believers. The difference between the movement in each of the two countries is even more striking when it comes to relations with the other parties. Whereas the Brothers in the West Bank accused their rival parties of atheism, heresy, or even of taking orders from the Vatican, the movement in Egypt seldom went much beyond expressing its dissatisfaction with the deficient Islamic background and the moral corruption that characterized the leaders of its political rivals.[112]

The emergent picture is one of a party fighting for its political survival, bidding to outdo its rivals in the eyes of the public. The only party not vulnerable to such all-out attacks on religious grounds was, of course, the Liberation Party. The latter not only made its appeal to precisely the same sectors of the population as the Moslem Brothers, but even laid claim to a more coherent and rigorous concept of Islam. The very existence of the Liberation Party constituted a threat to the legitimacy of the Moslem Brothers, who wanted to be seen as the sole custodians of the Islamic heritage.[113] The great viciousness with which the Brothers attacked the Liberation Party is a clear indication of the threat they perceived in it, a threat far more severe than any posed by the nationalist of left-wing parties. Vis-à-vis the Liberation Party, the Brothers were forced to enter into serious debate on points of principle, and could not resort to their usual expedient of crude religious diatribe. Their basic charge against the Liberation Party was that it represented a false concept of Islam and assumed a self-image of sham piety. But in addition to this, and to some extent contradicting it, the Brothers accused the Liberation Party of driving a wedge into the community of believers by setting itself up as a separate party —which would seem to imply that their basic criticism was not of the ideology of the Liberation Party as such, but rather of what they saw as the personal political motivation of its leaders.

Attitude Toward Arab Regimes

The Regime of Abd al-Nasser in Egypt

Immediately after the Free Officers' revolution in Egypt, the Brothers announced their full support of the new regime, which they described as "The Moslem Brothers Regime." Its aims, they believed, were to oust the British from Egypt, to eliminate corruption, and to assure a genuine Islamic form of government. Of course, the Moslem Brothers identified fully with all of these objectives.

The murder of Hasan al-Banna was associated with the era of imperialism under Faruq, and the revolution was seen as a bright new page in Egyptian history.[114] Much of this early enthusiasm was, of course, misguided, and the adulation of the coup by the movement in the West Bank was grossly premature. Thus the suppression of the Moslem Brothers in Egypt in 1954 came as a profound shock. Cables in protest were sent to the Egyptian president and to the Egyptian revolutionary leadership, calling for the release of all Brothers under detention and accusing the authorities of disloyalty and anti-revolutionary behavior. These protests were, however, expressed with restraint.[115] It appears that early in 1954, before the Egyptian authorities took repressive measures against the Moslem Brothers, a heated debate had taken place among members of the movement in the West Bank over the extent to which they should demonstrate their solidarity with the Egyptian movement. The veteran members, including the general supervisor and most of the religious functionaries, argued for playing down the link between the two movements and projecting a more independent image. Other members supported full identification with the parent movement in Egypt, and lost no time in attacking Neguib and his government over repression of the Egyptian Brothers. The arrest of the general supervisor in Cairo and the accusation that the Moslem Brothers in Egypt were involved in a plot against the life of Abd al-Nasser provoked must hostility against the movement in the West Bank. Anonymous leaflets were circulated in which the movement was characterized as the "Association of Infidel Brothers." The Jordanian Security Services even feared at one point the outbreak of terrorist violence.[116] It was at just about this time that the Brothers in the West Bank came out openly against the Egyptian regime and in support of their beleaguered comrades in Egypt. They distributed a leaflet accusing Abd al-Nasser himself of having planned the abortive attempt on his life and then blaming the Moslem Brothers. To protest the execution of several Brothers in Cairo, many Jerusalem merchants closed their shops for two hours. At their weekly meetings throughout the West Bank the Brothers bitterly attacked the Nasserist regime in Egypt and accused them of brutality, torture, and even murder, likening the regime to that of Atatürk in Turkey. During 1954 and 1955 the Brothers relentlessly attacked the domestic and foreign policies of the Egyptian regime. Abd al-Nasser's policies aimed at the destruction of Egyptian society and its moral foundations, they charged. He was a bloodthirsty dictator and his guarantees of the British evacuation of Suez were all lies. Abd al-Nasser was, in fact, an imperialist agent posturing as a nationalist leader. He was hounding the Moslem Brothers in Egypt because they alone had criticized his shameful capitulation to the British. Ultimately, the Brothers in the West Bank went so far as to call for a *jihad* against the Nasserist regime, aimed at its overthrow. The gravest charge the Brothers leveled against the Egyptian government was the one they most frequently directed against their domestic rivals in the West Bank—that of "heresy" and of waging "a war against Islam." Abd al-Rahman Khalifa sent a letter to Abd al-Nasser, couched in the most extreme language: "It has become clear to all the world just how much you hate Islam and the Muslims."[117]

July and August of 1956 marked the start of a dilemma that was to trouble the Moslem Brothers in the West Bank for years to come. Abd al-Nasser's nationalization of the Suez Canal was enthusiastically received throughout the Arab world, and joyful crowds thronged the streets of the West Bank immediately as the news was announced. The Brothers could not afford to remain aloof from the celebrations,[118] particularly as the expulsion of the British infidel from Egypt had long been one of the movement's dearest aspirations. On the other hand, the Moslem Brothers' hatred for Abd al-Nasser remained strong as ever, and they were quite simply unable to forgive him for his brutal suppression of their brethren in Egypt. They tried to extricate themselves from this dilemma by separating the two issues entirely, praising Egypt's nationalization of the Suez Canal while continuing to condemn Abd al-Nasser. This ruse worked well when it came to printing leaflets.[119] The obvious contradiction could not, however, be easily resolved in the give-and-take of everyday political discourse, in the process of which the Brothers' hatred of Abd al-Nasser tended to overshadow their enthusiasm for the nationalization. There was nevertheless a perceptible moderation in the movement's criticism of the treatment of the Moslem Brothers in Egypt, apparently in deference to the popular mood in the West Bank. Later, members of the movement actually took part in public demonstrations supporting the nationalization of the canal, giving no indication whatever that their view of the Egyptian regime responsible for that nationalization was in any way different from that of their fellow demonstrators.[120]

This sense of ambivalence in the Moslem Brothers' attitude to the Nasserist regime in Egypt disappeared temporarily during the tripartite invasion of Egypt in 1956 by Britain, France, and Israel. Within the content of this new situation—a Muslim country under attack by its Christian and Jewish foes and the Hashemite king himself entering into an alliance with his erstwhile enemy—the Brothers came out openly and unreservedly in support of Abd al-Nasser and his regime. In a cable sent to him by the movement's executive office in Damascus at the end of October 1956 and signed by Mustafa al-Sibai, leader of the movement in Syria, Muhammad al-Sawwaf, leader of the movement in Iraq, and Abd al-Rahman Khalifa, leader of the movement in Jordan, the Egyptian leader was given the Moslem Brothers' official blessing, at least while his country was under attack. The movement's leaders made it clear that they were paying no attention to Israel's attempts to sow dissension in the Arab world by spreading false rumors that Abd al-Nasser was still persecuting the Moslem Brothers in Egypt. They affirmed that the Egyptian people were in fact firmly behind their leader. The movement sent its best wishes to the Brothers in Egypt, who were in the vanguard of the fight against the invaders, proclaiming that Moslem Brothers throughout the Arab World would make every sacrifice to defend "dearest Egypt, which is part of the noble Islamic homeland," by launching a Muslim-Arab *jihad* against the imperialists and their Zionist allies. Other leaflets in support not only of the Egyptian people but also of their leader appeared in the West Bank during November 1956, and the movement even called on its members to volunteer for military training in response to the attack on Egypt.[121]

Just as the first honeymoon between the Moslem Brothers and the Free Officers regime in Egypt soon passed, so too did the period of solidarity engendered by the tripartite invasion of Egypt in 1956. At the beginning of March 1957 Israel completed its withdrawal from Sinai and the Gaza Strip. Abd al-Nasser lost little time in returning to his old ways of hounding the Moslem Brothers. At the end of May 1957 Egyptian officers and policemen allegedly massacred a large number of jailed Brothers, an event that effectively ended what remained of the truce between the movement in the West Bank and the Cairo regime. The Moslem Brothers' executive office put out a communiqué condemning the massacre as unprecedented in the history of the Arab people. The communiqué compared it with the atrocities perpetrated by the Zionists or by the French in Algeria. The "New Pharoah," who had been too cowardly to put up a decent fight against the Zionist invaders in Gaza and Sinai, thought nothing of using the arms he had hoarded to strike at the defenseless Moslem Brotherhood.[122] This communiqué effectively erased every trace of rapprochement. No longer was any distinction made between Abd al-Nasser's domestic and foreign policies—he failed to use his vast military might to fight the enemies of the Islamic community but rather turned it against believing Muslims at home.

In early 1962 Abd al-Nasser became deeply embroiled in the Yemen. The Moslem Brothers in the West Bank, who closely identified with Saudi Arabia, were quick to pounce on this example of

Egyptian perfidy and unleashed the anti-Nasserist venom that they had kept tightly bottled up for the past three years. They put out leaflets reproducing excerpts from the Saudi press in which Abd al-Nasser was denigrated as a Communist, a heathen, and an atheist. For good measure the Brothers added a few uncomplimentary epithets of their own, reiterating their old charge that the Egyptian leader was bent on annihilating Islam and calling on all true Muslims to oppose him and come out in support of King Saud and King Husayn.[123] During this period, all of the Brothers' attacks centered on Egypt's foreign policy, and little was said of its policies at home. This changed in the summer of 1965, however, and from then until the end of the period under review, the Moslem Brothers in the West Bank took up an uncompromisingly hostile position on Abd al-Nasser's foreign and domestic policies alike, going so far as to fabricate charges in an effort to undermine his credibility even as a sincere Arab nationalist. In mid-1965 the Egyptian authorities once again started persecuting the Moslem Brothers there, following reports of an abortive anti-government plot in which the prominent Jordanian Brother Said Ramadan was allegedly implicated. The reaction of the movement in the West Bank was predictable, and no opportunity was lost to paint the blackest possible picture of the reign of terror in Egypt. In order to destroy Egypt's claim to leadership of the nationalist movement in the Arab world, the Brothers published copies of what was purported to be a secret circular put out by the Egyptian Ministry of Foreign Affairs. This circular contained a set of instructions to Egyptian embassies abroad, among which was a clear injunction that the problem of the Palestinian refugees was not to be raised, particularly in the U.S. and its Western allies. The embassies were instructed to say no more than that the UAR was doing its best to find a solution to the problem. As secret discussions were then going on between the UAR and the U.S. concerning the refugees as well as bilateral trade ties, any reference to the problem might prejudice the delicate negotiations. The Brothers called this circular the "Document of Treachery" which revealed the Egyptian leader as a man "prepared to sell Palestine for a mess of American pottage." It would not be long, the Brothers claimed, before even those fools who still idolized him would see Abd al-Nasser for what he really was, and the legend would be shattered.[124]

In summary, the attitude of the Moslem Brothers in the West Bank to the Egyptian regime appears to have been dictated by the attitude of the regime to the movement in Egypt. As the regime's attitude fluctuated between tolerance and brutal suppression, so that of the West Bank Brothers ranged from uneasy truce to uncompromising hostility. Egypt's foreign policy, for all the stress it placed on Arab unity and its anti-imperialist stance, only influenced the Brothers' attitude to the Cairo regime on two occasions—at the time of the Suez crisis and at the establishment of the UAR which was closely followed by Abd al-Nasser's bitter conflict with Iraq. It was no coincidence that precisely during these two periods of crisis the Egyptian authorities refrained from harassing the Moslem Brothers in Egypt: the regime needed all the support it could get, and preferred to postpone its confrontation with the Brothers to a more convenient time. These two periods of truce in Egypt made it easier for the Brothers in the West Bank to come out openly in support of Abd al-Nasser at a time when the area was seething with pro-Nasserist sentiment.

Saudi Arabia

The Moslem Brothers in the West Bank criticized the domestic and foreign policies of each of the major Arab countries. They strongly condemned Nuri al-Said's regime in Iraq for signing the Baghdad Pact and for its position on the Palestine question; Syria and Iraq under the Baathists were charged with racism, brutality, promoting dissension and schism, and religious persecution.[125] Only Saudi Arabia escaped censure, because of the alleged personal piety of the Saudi dynasty and the extreme conservatism it exhibited in upholding Islamic tradition and Islamic legal and moral practices. It would seem that this far outweighed Saudi Arabia's openly pro-Western orientation.

In 1954, however, a single member of the movement protested against King Saud's visit to Jordan: in a leaflet put out in the name of the Moslem Brothers on June 19, King Saud and his Hashemite host were implored to "safeguard religion." Deeply insulted, the Saudi monarch canceled his planned visit to the West Bank. The leadership of the movement in Amman was incensed at the incident and immediately published in the press a public apology. They noted that on the same day the leaflet was distributed, the leaders of the movement met with the two kings and presented them with the movement's blessings. To clear the matter beyond all doubt, they stressed that they had no quarrel with the king either on matters of religion or on affairs of state, the prime objective of the movement being to oust all "foreign elements" from the Arab and Islamic lands,[126] an objective that had already almost been achieved in the Kingdom of Saudi Arabia.

In the mid-1950s Jordan and Saudi Arabia began to draw closer together in the face of the growing Nasserist threat. This was a development clearly welcomed by the Brothers, and at the height of Jordan's conflict with Nasserist Egypt in August 1956, the local press reported that the movement's Jerusalem branch had invited the Saudi consul to be the guest of honor at its celebrations marking the anniversary of the *hijra*. In 1962, in the course of one of their many diatribes against Abd al-Nasser, the Brothers cited excerpts from Saudi newspapers in which the Egyptian leader was described as a Communist and an atheist, epithets which the movement heartily endorsed. The popular masses were called upon to rally round King Husayn and King Saud, "Protectors of the Holy Places," in their confrontation with Nasserist Egypt. The support for the Saudis reached an unprecedented level in 1965, to judge by a report in the Lebanese newspaper *al-Muharrir*, according to which Said Ramadan, one of the Brothers' most prominent leaders, had several meetings with Saudi officials in Amman in an effort to help further Saudi Arabia's goal of convening an Islamic summit and establishing an Islamic Alliance.[127] Whether or not the above report is true, the openly declared sympathy of the Brothers for the Saudis would have tended to encourage speculation along these lines and lend credence to such reports.

This sympathy clearly derived from the conservative nature of Saudi Arabia's domestic policies, and, in the 1960s especially, the desert kingdom stood as a bastion of Islam in an Arab world increasingly consumed by various secular left-wing ideologies. Above and beyond the ideological and political ties that clearly bound Saudi Arabia and the Moslem Brothers, there is also the possibility that the Brothers received some financial support from Riyadh. Rumors of such support were never confirmed and no proof is available. Nevertheless it is understandable that rumors of this nature should inevitably gain currency given the close ties between members of the movement and Saudi officials in Jerusalem.

The Arab Nations and Their Responsibility for the Palestine Tragedy

According to the Moslem Brothers in the West Bank, the various Arab countries bore the major responsibility for the humiliating defeat in Palestine in 1948. A wide range of accusations—from

charges of incompetence to the more serious of treason and be-
trayal—were leveled against the Arab regimes involved. The disaster
in Palestine came about, the Brothers declared, because the Arab
countries were unable to unite themselves for a concerted action.
This was due to the fact that the Arab leaders had adopted "an
empty and counterfeit Arab nationalism instead of [striving for]
Islamic unity." Loyalty to the tenets of their religion would lead
not only to unity and mutual solidarity, but also to a purity of
heart and a raising of moral values which would assure an ultimate
Arab victory over Israel far more certainly than would the mere
acquisition of arms. The Arab countries, the Brothers charged, also
relied far too heavily on "friendship with the West," thus greatly
restricting their freedom of action vis-à-vis Israel.[128]

The Brothers were not always so restrained in their criticism of
Arab states, and at times their attacks were much harsher. The disaster in Palestine came about "because of the treachery of the Arab
leaders and officers, who betrayed their men." It was the result of
a tripartite plot between the Jews, the Arab leaders, and the latter's
masters, the imperialists. Some of these leaders gave the impression
of being true believers (in Islam) and devoted to the well-being of
their countries when they were in fact nothing more than "the
Knights of Imperialism" totally subservient to the "Zionist Mon-
strosity."[129]

Usually, however, the Moslem Brothers were much more restrained than this in their attacks on the Arab regimes. Given their close
political ties with the Hashemite regime in Jordan, their political
identification with Saudi Arabia, and their concern to maintain
good relations with the regime in Syria, this was hardly surprising.
Nevertheless, one cannot deny the authenticity of the Brothers'
accusations against the Arab leaders concerning their responsibility
for the defeat in Palestine, and there is little doubt that the Brothers firmly believed these leaders were directly to blame for the
worst tragedy ever to befall the Palestinian people.[130]

Imperialists and Imperialism

When they referred to imperialism or to the imperialist powers,
the Moslem Brothers generally meant the Western countries and
Western imperialism, as it was these countries whose political presence and power was most directly experienced in the Middle East
and North Africa. They were careful to point out, however, that
the Communist powers were also imperialistic and just as much of

a threat to the Arab world as were the Western imperialists: "the Western frogs and the Eastern monkeys" alike threatened the existence of Islam. It was incumbent upon all Muslims to fight both, present a solid Islamic front against them, and on no account ally themselves with either one.[131]

The threat of Communism, according to the Brothers, lay mainly in its ideology and was thus rather remote—unlike that of Western imperialism which was concrete and immediate. The West, the Brothers believed, posed a triple threat to the Arab world: cultural, economic, and military. The culture and moral threat was viewed as every bit as grave as that of direct military intervention. By exporting its culture to the Islamic world Western imperialism was deliberately attempting to undermine Arab-Muslim society, which more than any other Muslim society had succumbed to the drug of Western culture. By managing to infiltrate its way of life and moral values into large parts of Muslim society, Western imperialism had managed to sow the seeds of dissension and thereby weaken the Arabs to such a degree that they were now feeble and backward and wholly subservient to the will of the imperialist powers. Only the uprooting of all traces of Western influence and the return to the values of pure Islam would revive and reunite the Arab nation and enable it to fulfill its role as the standard-bearer of Islam.

The threat of economic domination by the West troubled the Moslem Brothers rather less, but even so they displayed a coherent and consistent awareness of the grave political implications of such domination. They opposed any form of Western economic assistance to Jordan, believing that it would make the country even more subservient to the West than it already was, paving the way for its eventual physical conquest. They openly opposed American aid for a government agricultural project in 1954, for example, and consistently opposed all Western financial aid to the Jordanian army. In January 1957 the Brothers joined their nationalist and Communist rivals in supporting Jordan's agreement with Egypt, Syria, and Saudi Arabia whereby Arab aid would replace Western aid, as a first step toward the official abrogation of the country's 1948 treaty with Britain. The Moslem Brothers continued to support the anti-Western measures taken by the Nabulsi government, and rejected outright an American offer to provide King Husayn with military aid, in place of that he was to receive from the wealthier Arab countries. But as the showdown approached, and the authorities began to crack down on the nationalist and Communist movements in Jordan, the Moslem Brothers abruptly dropped the subject of Western imperialism's political and economic penetration of the area. Once the storm blew over, the Brothers reverted to their previous position and, from June 1958 on, attacks by the movement on the Western imperialists were reported from time to time.[132] The most obvious imperialist threat, the one demanding the most intensive and urgent attention, was, of course, the Western powers' direct military penetration of the area. The Brothers in the West Bank were primarily concerned with the West's military aspirations in the Arab East, where the British and the Americans had connived at the creation of the State of Israel, "supported the Zionists, training them in hostility toward us, and was supplying them with arms and ammunition."[133] They were also concerned, however, with the direct military occupation of the Maghreb by the Western powers, and paid particular attention to Algeria's struggle against the French. The liberation struggles against the French in the Maghreb received more attention from the Moslem Brothers in the West Bank than any other political issue in the Arab world, barring Palestine. Their support for the "holy war against the French oppressor" was expressed in public meetings, in leaflets and in the press, and through various fund-raising projects.[134] The Arab governments were asked to expel all French diplomats and citizens from their countries, impound all French property, and even to seize young Frenchmen as hostages. Simultaneously, the Arab governments were asked to provide the Algerians with financial and military support, as well as with volunteer fighters from their own countries. The liberation struggle in North Africa was, in the view of the Brothers, a genuine *jihad*, and as such should be fought under the banner of Islam, not according to "the principles of Marx and Lenin" (a swipe at the part played by the Communist Party in the Algerian war).[135]

Israel

To the Moslem Brothers Israel was the epitome of evil. In their attitude toward the creation of the Jewish state, the Brothers found themselves caught up in a contradiction not uncommon in Arab nationalist thought. On the one hand, Israel was merely the creation of the imperialist powers: Israel did not exist in its own right and was no more than a tool in the hands of its imperialist masters. On the other hand, however, Israel was portrayed as the outpost of a world Jewry that wielded immense power.[136]

The Brothers were caught in a similar contradiction when it came to the question of Israel's might and durability. It goes without saying that they did not recognize Israel's *right* to exist, but it would also appear that they doubted the Jewish state's *ability* to survive. Israel was not, in their eyes, a natural entity, and would thus probably collapse and disintegrate on its own. It was in a state of chronic economic crisis, and its army was cowardly, feeble, and ineffective —as its performance proved, restricting itself to small-scale reprisal raids designed to terrorize the Arab border areas. Yet at the same time Israel was also viewed as an extremely dangerous enemy. The Jewish state emerged as the result of the unflagging belief of the Jews in their God-given right to Jerusalem and in their right to return to the land of their forebears.[137] The religious faith of the Jews and their tenacious belief in their right to return to Palestine were often referred to not, of course, in order to lend credence to that right, but rather to serve as an example to the Muslims how a religious faith could lead to ultimate redemption. Nevertheless, the reference clearly indicates a recognition, whether conscious or not, of the Jewish people's religious attachment to Palestine and as such represents a more balanced and objective view of the Jewish state than that normally expressed in the Brother's diatribes against Israel. It also recognizes, tacitly at least, the vitality of the Jewish state. At least one of the movement's speakers suggested that the Arabs may in fact have been quite mistaken in their assessment of Israel's strength and capacity for survival: "eighteen years have now passed for this 'imaginary' Israel, and it is still growing stronger, richer, and more populous." Another speaker noted that "the Jews have demonstrated their dauntless will in establishing their state, while we do a lot of talking and little doing."[138]

When it came to analyzing the aspirations and objectives of the Jewish state, any doubts about Israel's strength seem to have been quite forgotten. The Zionist state aspired, the Brothers believed, from the day it was created, to expand into vast tracts of Arab territory. Its initial objective was to establish a Jewish kingdom extending from the Nile to the Euphrates. But that was not all. The Jewish state had designs also on the Hejaz, which they hoped to reconquer and return to what they claimed was the ancient settlement of their ancestors in the holy city of Medina. The first stage in Israel's thrust toward the Euphrates was the series of reprisal raids which the Jewish state conducted along its borders. These raids, which were on other occasions cited as proof of the cowardliness and ineffectiveness of the Israeli army, were now seen as part of a careful plan designed to sow terror and destruction in a continually expanding arc surrounding the Jewish state, causing a mass exodus of the Arab population and its replacement by Jewish settlers—until eventually all the Arab countries bordering on Israel were emptied of their original inhabitants and incorporated into the grand Zionist empire of the future.[139]

Nationalism, Arabism, and Islam

In defining the bases of their political identity, the Moslem Brothers had to use the terms current in the Arab world and hence familiar to the local population in the West Bank—terms such as Arabism, Nationalism, Unity, Islam, as well as various combinations, like Islamic Unity. This terminology was used very loosely, however, and the vagueness concealed a good deal of contradiction. There was moreover a clear distinction between the way these terms were used in the Brothers' public proclamations, the way they were used implicitly and only half-consciously, and the manner in which they related to the movement's actual political performance.

In spelling out their fundamental position for the politically aware masses in the West Bank, the Brothers chose to use, not without some reservation, the term "Islamic unity." The concept of political unity was, of course, a secular one most closely associated with the thought of Arab nationalists and as such was not entirely to the taste of the Brothers. Nevertheless, given their awareness of the great emotive power of the term "unity" among the Arab masses, the Brothers decided for what were tactical rather than ideological reasons to take over the concept and use it to divert the popular hunger for unity into what they considered the "correct" —Islamic—channel.[140] Unity was the political goal, but it was to be *Islamic*, rather than merely Arab, unity. Once Islamic unity had been realized and a great Islamic Bloc extending from Morocco to Indonesia had come into being—equaling the two great power blocs presently dominating the world scene—only then would Islamic civilization be raised from the position of subjugation to which it had been condemned by Christian imperialism.[141]

Diametrically opposed to Islamic unity was the secular concept of Arab nationalism, to which the Moslem Brothers were wholly opposed. Both the style and the content of their diatribes on this subject give the impression, however, that their rejection of the notion of Arab nationalism was as much tactically as ideologically motivated, and formed an integral part of their rivalry with the nationalist parties in the West Bank. Nationalism, the Brothers maintained, was "anti-Islamic" in that it separated from the fold of Islam millions of Muslims who did not happen to be Arab. What is more, nationalism was an abomination, for it was a concept invented by such mortals as the infidel Aflaq, while Islamic unity was based on an article of God-given faith. The nationalism of Aflaq and his ilk represented a return to the notions of pre-Islamic tribalism. It was an ideology disseminated by power-hungry Arab dictators, and represented the first step toward complete heathendom.[142] While the Moslem Brothers in Egypt drew fine distinctions among the various types of nationalism with respect to the degree of their legitimacy,[143] the movement in the West Bank rejected the concept of *qawmiya* in toto. This would seem to indicate not only the general lack of intellectual sophistication on the part of the Brothers in the West Bank, but also their strong fear that by recognizing in any form the concept of *qawmiya* they would be according a degree of legitimacy to their nationalist rivals there.

One of the most telling arguments used by the nationalists against the Moslem Brothers was that by denying Arabism as the supreme basis of political identity and positing Islam in its stead, the Brothers were guilty of creating a schism between Moslems and Christians, thereby gravely weakening the Arab countries. This charge carried a great deal of weight in the West Bank, where there were large concentrations of Christians in Jerusalem and the surrounding towns. The Brothers responded to the charge in two ways—by making the countercharge that nationalism was a divisive force even in the Arab world, citing the Kurds in Iraq as an example, and by attempting to refute the accusation by proving that they had no intention to discriminate against the *dhimmi* and that the latter had always had an important and positive role in Islamic history. Moreover, they pointed out, Christian Arabs had always sided with their Arab brothers during confrontations with the Christian West, as the Egyptian Copts had fought against the Christian Romans, and the Christians in Persia had fought alongside their non-Christian brethren.[144]

The Brothers tended not to differentiate between pan-Arab nationalism and the regional nationalism of the individual Arab states. From their point of view, both forms were unacceptable. The very division of the Middle East into separate countries was, the Brothers argued, the result of imperialist machinations in the area. Following the principle of divide-and-rule, the imperialists had succeeded in carving up the area into a series of small, self-concerned states. These countries subsequently became embroiled in conflicts among themselves, and their attention was diverted from their real, common, enemies—the imperialists, the Christians, the Jews, and the Zionists. Up to this point, the Moslem Brothers were subscribing to a view widely held in the Arab world, even by the nationalists. But from here on, the Brothers evolved a theory entirely of their own. The selfish local-patriotism of the individual Arab states led these states to take steps that were harmful to Islam and which ran counter to its basic principles. Thus, for example, there were certain Arab countries that supported (non-Muslim) India against (Muslim) Pakistan over the Kashmir question, simply because India had agreed to back them on some other issue. Similarly, certain Arab countries chose to ignore the persecution of Muslims in the Soviet Union and China, again because the two Communist powers were providing them with political or economic support.[145]

The Brothers' strong objection to Arab nationalism as being "anti-Islamic" did not prevent them from supporting the concepts of Arabism or Arab Unity. They believed that the 80 million Arabs, once politically united, should in fact serve as the kernel from which would spring the ultimate unification of the world's 500 million Muslims. This concept of Islamic Arabism—"the Arabism of Muhammad from which sprang forth Islam"—should be encouraged, the Brothers maintained. Arab unity under the banner of Islam was not only a legitimate objective but an essential one.[146]

In doctrine, then, Arabism was clearly subservient to the ideal of Islamic universalism. In practice, however, the Brothers tended to stress their Arab identity rather than their identity as Muslims. Their speakers would frequently refer to the idea of Arab unity or "the united Arab state," not as a first step on the way to Islamic unity, but as an essential prerequisite for the "liberation of the Arab world from imperialism."[147] The Brothers displayed a similar Arab insularity with regard to their view of *jihad*. This they saw primarily as a means toward the redemption of Palestine and the ousting of imperialism from the Arab lands. Not once was it referred to in its classical sense, as a global war waged by Islam against the infidel. A similar attitude appears to have motivated their constant appeals to the Islamic world to come to the aid of the Arabs.[148] Appeals to the Arabs to rally for non-Arab Muslims were much rarer, and were usually made more to embarrass or chastise the radical Arab leaders for abandoning their allegiance to the rest of the Islamic world than to garner any effective support for the downtrodden Turcomen or Tibetans.

In terms of practical political performance (as reliable an indicator of basic attitudes as are professed ideological principles), there is no mistaking the primacy for the Moslem Brothers of the question of Palestine and other exclusively Arab issues. Political affairs of the non-Arab Islamic world were very much a secondary concern. And whenever the Moslem Brothers called on the Jordanian regime to engage in a show of solidarity, it was invariably in support of some Arab cause.[149] Thus while the Moslem Brothers in the West Bank were probably quite sincere in their commitment to the basic principles of their movement, they displayed an unmistakable drift toward the notion of Arab nationalism and away from that of Islamic universalism. This was very likely due to the political realities of the West Bank, where Arab nationalism—as a concept embracing a sense of particularist Palestinian identity (in the case of the Brothers)[150] or as the sole basis of political identity (in the case of the Qawmiyun)—held a tremendous attraction for a population thoroughly convinced that in order to regain its rights in Palestine it required massive support from its fellow Arabs. The notion of pan-Islamic solidarity, for all its ideological importance, was not seen as having any immediate political relevance. When it came to deciding who they were to support—the Arabs in Algeria and Morocco or the Muslims in India—the West Bank Brothers unhesitatingly opted for the former.

The Moslem Brothers in Egypt had a somewhat similar attitude to the question of Arabism and Arab unity—their wretchedness was also the wretchedness of Islam, while in their redemption lay that of Islam as well.[151] But in Egypt too this was only theoretical, and in their public proclamations and political conduct, the Brothers there displayed very little interest in the Arab world—with the single exception of Palestine. The movement in the West Bank displayed a far greater degree of awareness of and involvement in the developments in other parts of the Arab world—in the Fertile Crescent, because of the traditional affinity felt for the population, and in Egypt, because of the strong organic bonds that linked the movements in the two countries. Added to this was the fact that the West Bank was far more dependent on help from the rest of the Arab world than was Egypt. The result was that, while both movements recognized the theoretical legitimacy of pan-Arab aspirations, the movement in the West Bank was far more actively involved in the affairs of the Arab world than was the movement in Egypt.

Palestine

The powerful attraction that Palestine, particularly Jerusalem, held for the Moslem Brothers lay first and foremost in its religious significance. The place of Jerusalem in Islam was the basic reason given by the Brothers whenever they called for the liberation of Palestine from the Jews: "This country[152] belongs to the Muslims." This concept of Palestine's sacredness as the main reason for the struggle against those who had usurped it was common to the movement in the West Bank and Egypt alike,[153] although the Brothers in the West Bank were somewhat more extreme in making the claim that God "favored Palestine over any other Arab country,"[154] an indication of the degree to which the element of Palestinian identity had become intertwined with their religious ideology.

The Brothers believed that in order to triumph it was necessary first to "return to Islam and observe the Islamic Law, and to act in concert according to the Koran." But while representatives of the movement in Egypt assured their brethren in the West Bank that a return to Islam would result in the ultimate demise of Zionisn and of the Jews, the Brothers in the West Bank itself preached that a return to religion would assure the "restoration of Palestine."[155] In the West Bank it was identification with Palestine, as opposed to the political-ideological identification felt by members of the movement in the other Arab countries.

The Moslem Brothers' concept of *jihad* sheds further light on this view of the liberation of Palestine as a sacred religious duty. As we have seen, the liberation of Palestine was seen as the primary objective of *jihad*. In other words, whenever the Brothers in the West Bank spoke of *jihad* they meant primarily the liberation of Palestine from its Zionist usurpers.[156]

The position of the Brothers on the Palestinian refugees was very similar to that of the Qawmiyun and other nationalists in the West Bank. They were wholly opposed to solving the problem by settling the refugees in Jordan or any other Arab country, rejected any attempt to rehabilitate them, and demanded that they be allowed to return to their original homes in Israel. The Brothers were, however, prepared to accept some improvement in the material conditions of the refugees in the camps pending their eventual return to their homes.[157]

The Moslem Brothers differed considerably from other parties in the West Bank in the solution they posited for the Palestine problem. As we have seen, the Brothers frequently called for Arab unity as an essential prerequisite for the liberation of Palestine. In this they did not differ from the Qawmiyun. They were not, however, entirely consistent on this point. There were periods when the Brothers bitterly attacked their fellow Arabs, doubting that they were really prepared to come to the aid of the Palestinians. These periods of disillusion were particularly common in the late 1950s and early 1960s. On one such occasion the head of the Nablus branch proclaimed: "We must stop waiting for a solution to the Palestine problem. We must build up an army to restore Haifa and Jaffa." The Islamic Congress which met in Jerusalem in 1953 also called on the refugees to organize themselves into a fighting force. In subsequent years as well, there were frequent similar proclamations, accompanied by expressions of disappointment in the failure of the Arab and Muslim countries to come to the aid of the Palestinians. This issue was of such great importance to the Brothers in the West Bank that they were even prepared to enter into open conflict with the Hashemite regime whenever it seemed to be postponing the war of liberation.

Given the deep apprehension that the Arabs would leave the Palestinians to their fate, and the awareness that the latter might have to depend on their own resources, it is not difficult to see why the Brothers were so enthusiastic in their support of the National Guard. This paramilitary body was made up almost entirely of Palestinian villagers, unlike the Arab Legion which recruited the bulk of its members in Transjordan. The Brothers' close identification with the National Guard was thus, first and foremost, another expression of their marked Palestinian orientation. On more than one occasion they bitterly attacked the Legion for failing to react to Israeli raids on the border villages. They had no doubts about the National Guard and never once criticized it on any count. On the contrary, they were among its most ardent supporters and consistently lobbied for the diversion of more state funds to the force, which they felt was being discriminated against in favor of the Legion.[158]

Not satisfied with mere slogans, the Brothers also made concrete suggestions concerning the liberation of Palestine. Thus in a speech in Nablus they proclaimed that "the only way" to liberate Palestine was to set up training camps for Palestinian youth, next to the refugee camps, where they could receive military training rather than waste time playing cards in coffeehouses or waiting idly for their next handout from UNRWA. The Brothers called on the inhabitants of the West Bank and the refugees not to waste their money on radios and other luxuries but instead to buy weapons and prepare themselves for the "day of reckoning."[159]

On the notion of a "Palestinian entity," long before the Arab states had given their blessing to this concept, the Brothers had stated that the creation of a Palestinian entity was a positive and essential step. What is more, they had proposed as a subsequent step the creation of a "provisional Palestinian governnment," pending the final liberation of Palestine.

The Brothers went beyond just making proposals, and were actively engaged in the struggle for the liberation of Palestine. On the one hand, they did a great deal to persuade the refugees to turn down all offers of compensation and to stand firmly by their right to return to their homes.[160] On the other hand, they raised funds in a number of different ways for various purposes associated with the struggle—the improvement of the lot of the refugees in the camps, the fortification of villages bordering on Israel, direct financial aid to the National Guard, the dispatch of military instructors to the border villages, and the attempted creation of their own militia.

The firm insistence that the Palestinians should rely on themselves rather than on their Arab brothers (even though the responsibility of the Arab states to take up arms against Israel was repeatedly stressed) distinguished the Moslem Brothers from other parties in the West Bank, particularly in the 1950s. This local Palestinian patriotism dated back to the founding of the movement in Jerusalem in 1946. Local patriotism was a hallmark of the movement in Egypt as well, and it is quite likely that the vein of Palestinian patriotism so apparent in the al-Fath movement has its origin in Yasir Arafat's early association with the Moslem Brothers.[161]

5. The Liberation Party

ACTIVITIES

Development of the Party

The Liberation Party was founded in Jerusalem by a group of religious functionaries who had broken away from the Moslem Brothers. The initiative for the break came at the beginning of 1952, from a former disciple of Hajj Amin al-Husayni, Shaykh Taqi al-Din al-Nabhani. Al-Nabhani, a high school teacher in Jerusalem, was soon joined by three of his religious colleagues in Hebron: Asad and Rajab Bayyud al-Tamimi, and Abd al-Qadim Zallum.[1] At first the group met sporadically, mostly in Jerusalem and Hebron, to exchange ideas and to recruit new members. For the first few months the emphasis was on informal religious discussion and only at the end of 1952 did the group begin to take on the character of a political party.

On November 17, 1952, five members of the group (Taqi al-Din al-Nabhani, Daud Hamdan, Munir Shuqayr, Adil al-Nabulsi, and Ghanem Abdu) submitted a formal application to the Jordanian Interior Ministry for permission to establish a political party. The application, personally studied by Said al-Mufti, the interior minister and deputy prime minister at the time, was denied. The group was informed of the minister's decision through the office of the governor of Jerusalem in March 1953. The reasons given for the refusal, published by the Interior Ministry, stemmed from the nature of the proposed party's platform rather than from the composition of its membership. The applicants were told that the basic tenets of the proposed platform were contrary not only to the spirit but to the very terms of the Jordanian constitution. For example, it was pointed out, the proposed platform did not accept the principle of succession as laid down in the Jordanian constitution; instead, the platform called for an elected ruler. Furthermore, the

This chapter draws on the Hebrew version of 1972 prepared by Ella Landau and Rachel Simon.

platform did not recognize nationalism as the overwhelming political norm underlying the basis of the state, but rather the Islamic religion. In other words, the proposed party challenged the very legitimacy of the Jordanian regime and sought to drive a wedge between its citizens. The public interest, the group was told, would best be served by withholding the requested permission.

At first the group considered appealing the interior minister's decision to the Supreme Court, but soon decided to follow the path taken by the Moslem Brothers in Egypt. According to the Ottoman Associations Law, which was still in force in the West Bank, an association could be formed merely by announcing the intention to form it to the highest authority in the area, or even by publishing such intention in the local press. Accordingly, the group informed the governor of Jerusalem, the interior minister's representative in the West Bank, that it intended to form an association (*jamiya*) and not a political party (*hizb*). At the same time, the group announced its intention in a local newspaper, *al-Sarih*, and informed the interior minister that it had not really intended to form a political party and was therefore withdrawing its original application to form one—along with the minister's negative response to that application.[2] The authorities did not accept this formalistic ruse, however, and on March 25, 1953, the members of the group were arrested. They were released two weeks later but were placed under house arrest. The Interior Ministry took pains to inform the public that it had acted against the group not because of its Islamic beliefs, but because its activities were subversive and because it sought to overthrow the legitimate regime.[3] Throughout that year, however, the members of the group hoped that their party would be accorded recognition by the authorities, either in response to its request to the new prime minister, or as a result of a possible renewed alliance with the Moslem Brothers, who enjoyed official recognition. While the Liberation group never actually gained recognition, the authorities did in fact stop hounding it.

Occasionally calling itself the Liberation Party, but more often, the "Nabhanis" (after its founder), the group was active during its first year mainly in Jerusalem, Hebron, Nablus, and in the refugee camps around Jericho. In Hebron, the party attempted to preach its doctrine after the Friday prayers at the Cave of the Patriarchs; in Jerusalem, it set up a number of study groups, which met mostly in the evenings. The party made some attempts to organize secretly, in order to evade the surveillance of the security services. In Hebron, for example, it was decided that the party's views would not be disseminated by local members, who had been warned by the authorities, but by members from other towns in the West Bank; the latter, it was hoped, would be less well known to the local police. After receiving considerable financial aid from Lebanon, Taqi al-Din tried to set up several groups of ten members each, but the experiment failed, with the exception of a single group in Jerusalem.

Daud Hamdan's assertion that it would require only three months' preparation before the party would be ready to overthrow the Jordanian regime was soon found to be wholly unrealistic; Hamdan himself admitted as much at one of the party's closed meetings, granting that the preparations would take longer than he had originally expected, and that many more members would be necessary before an uprising could be attempted. Accordingly, efforts were made to increase the party's following by infiltrating the rural areas, with particular attention being paid to the village schoolteachers.[4] Some organizing was attempted in the villages of western Samaria, where several new branches were established, the most successful being at Azzun.

The party's major efforts continued to be aimed at the urban centers, however. In western Samaria, the principal targets were the towns of Tulkarm and Qalqilya. Other, less important branches in the area were established during 1954 in Jenin, Ramallah and al-Bira.

The general elections of that same year provided the party with the opportunity to disseminate its ideas to the public at large. Shaykh Ahmad al-Daur stood for parliament, and conducted a campaign throughout Samaria, including a number of appearances in Nablus. Al-Daur's candidacy indicated the growing self-confidence of the party, which was by now prepared to express its views openly, especially in the mosques. This was particularly true during the month of Ramadan, when popular religious fervor was traditionally at its peak.

In Jenin and Nablus, the party's candidates vigorously contested the elections; but its propaganda activities all but ceased following its defeat at the polls. Although Ahmad al-Daur was elected, his parliamentary duties in Amman removed him from his field of local activity in the Tulkarm-Qalqilya area. The party kept alive its activities in Nablus by bringing prominent members from Jerusalem and Hebron to deliver addresses in the mosques and to organize small study groups. In the spring of 1955, the Jordanian chief of staff claimed that the Liberation Party was active throughout Jordan, particularly in the Hebron area. The party leadership had singled out Hebron as one of its major centers of activity, along with Nablus and Tulkarm, and called on its Hebron members to help strengthen the party in Jerusalem, where it had made little headway.[5]

During the following decade, party activities were relatively unobtrusive, for a number of reasons. The 1955 Preaching and [Religious] Instruction Law, which controlled the use of the pulpit for political propaganda, greatly reduced the party's effectiveness in the mosques. Internal dissension also weakened the party in the mid-1950s, when Taqi al-Din (who had moved to Beirut) clashed with several leading party activists in the West Bank. This led to the resignation of several members in Samaria in 1956, which virtually reduced the party in that area to the branch in the town of Qalqilya. Two years later, Taqi al-Din expelled several other leaders who disagreed with him. And orders for expulsion from the country issued by the authorities against several of the party's most prominent members in mid-1959 brought about a self-imposed temporary moratorium on its activities in Jerusalem.

For all that, the party did engage in considerable relatively inconspicuous activity during the years 1956–66. Leaflets continued to be distributed, study groups were held regularly (mostly in the homes of members), and indoctrination in the villages even increased. The more isolated villages, which were not subject to the same strict surveillance by the security services as were the towns, were conducive to political activity, and several new branches were established. (The rural areas failed to produce any prominent leaders, however.)

Both in villages and in cities, special stress was put on the month of Ramadan, when emotional and religious fervor were at their height. A concerted effort was made to rouse public reaction on other special occasions as well, such as the visit of the Pope to the Holy Land in 1964; demonstrations were organized during that visit despite widespread arrests and detentions that preceded it.

Principal Types of Activity

One of the most characteristic forms of activity of the Liberation Party, and the one that distinguished it from all other parties in the area, was its practice of organizing study groups (*halaqa*). The term itself, derived from traditional Islamic education,[6] clearly reflects the party's fundamental political outlook. While its aim, like that of any political party, was to influence the government by political means, the Liberation Party believed that this could best be achieved by inculcating the masses with the correct concepts (*mafahim siyasiya*).

The party's approach was not to discuss or analyze events in attempting to arrive at ultimate political truth, but to teach this truth to those ignorant of it. There were two ways of doing this, both sanctioned by traditional religious practice: the religious lecture, or sermon, and the *halaqa* (which had traditionally been conducted in the courtyard of the mosque, but in more recent times had been transposed to private homes). The *halaqa* was seen from the very start as more effective than the sermon, and was accordingly given considerable attention by the party, though in later years the relative importance of the two underwent a major change. The *halaqa* approach characterized the Liberation Party at every level; even instructions passed down by the party leadership (whether issued personally by Taqi al-Din or in printed pamphlets and circulars disseminated from Beirut) were suggestive of the one-directional flow of ideas that took place within the traditional Islamic study group.

Most study groups were organized in individual neighborhoods or villages. There were, however, a few groups based on profession rather than on locality, comprising teachers and students, or occasionally artisans and shopkeepers. Level of education was often an important factor in the formation of study groups; certain groups were formed for the more educated party members, others for the less educated, and still others for those without any formal education at all.

The study groups usually met in the evenings, more for reasons of convenience than of secrecy. They were usually conducted by a religious functionary or a teacher, but because teachers were subject to the close attentions of the security services, less qualified members sometimes had to lead groups. (On one occasion, a study group was conducted by an illiterate who interpreted a text that had to be read for him by another member of the group.) The local leadership appointed group leaders and organized the study groups in its area: it determined their composition and the times and places of meetings, and made literature available. And it determined matters of substance, deciding what subjects were to be studied and how these should be presented, on occasion even providing model lessons. Supervisors were appointed in each town to oversee the study groups,[7] and they sometimes paid visits to the neighboring villages to supervise the activities of groups there; where this was not possible, group leaders from the villages had to come to the towns for guidance and instructions.

Each meeting was centered around a lecture on a religious or political topic, sometimes based on a pamphlet or some other publication put out by the party. These publications were not distributed at the meetings, but were read beforehand by the group leader, who memorized their contents and then destroyed them. The early practice of distributing literature to the members was soon abandoned, as it was regarded a criminal offense to possess such literature. Thus the rank-and-file were acquainted with the party literature only at second hand, as transmitted verbally by the group leader at their meetings. Each study group comprised between five and ten members, although one-man "groups" were formed for government officials or army personnel, for security reasons.

Rank-and-file members did not join a study group until they had belonged to the party for a short trial period, usually a month, occasionally several months. During that time they met with a veteran member once a week and received instruction in the party's ideas and aims. They were required to read one of the basic tracts put out by the party, usually Nabhani's *Nizam al-hukm fi'l-Islam*. Only after candidates had mastered and accepted the basic tenets of the party's philosophy were they sworn in, given a code name, and attached to a study group.

The study groups attempted to hide their activities from the security services, trying to keep secret the places and times of the meetings and the identity of those attending. But these efforts were not very serious or effective, and the authorities were generally well informed about the groups.

The party's second major vehicle for teaching was the sermon, delivered in the mosque. The mosque was ideally suited to the party's purposes, since it brought together a large assembly of believers to whom the party could convey its message in the course of the Friday sermon (many of the party's leading figures were religious functionaries, and thus well versed in the traditional sermon form). This method of teaching was first used at al-Aqsa in Jerusalem and the Cave of the Patriarchs in Hebron; it spread rapidly to the town and village mosques throughout the West Bank, with the party preachers becoming less and less inhibited about the political nature of their sermons. Propaganda from the pulpit gradually became one of the party's most potent weapons, gaining ground rapidly in 1953–54. Not only did preaching provide the party with a regular, broadly based audience; it also made the party's influence appear to extend well beyond its actual membership, and the authorities viewed this apparent influence with growing concern.

As its self-confidence increased, the party began to ignore the repeated warnings issued by the authorities, and even began openly to incite the congregation against the regime. The government's reaction came somewhat belatedly, but when it did, it was forthright and effective. Late in 1954, the government introduced a bill making it illegal to preach or teach in a mosque without the written permission of the chief qadi or his representative, such permission to be revocable at any time. The bill was passed into law in January 1955, and anyone found violating it was subject to a fine or even imprisonment.[8]

This put an effective end to the party's political sermonizing in the mosques. Many of its preachers were not granted licenses, and those that did obtain them were obliged to purge their sermons of all political content and even renounce publicly all ties with the Liberation Party (which step they were authorized to take by the party leadership in Syria). There were isolated attempts to continue using the mosques for propaganda purposes: party members occasionally interrupted sermons with questions in the spirit of the party's philosophy, or repeated the speeches of Ahmad al-Daur, the party's representative in parliament, after services, or entered into political discussion with other worshipers when leaving the mosques. But these attempts had little significant effect, and the fact remained that the party had been deprived of its mass audience in the mosques,—that is, of a group advantage it had in the past enjoyed over its political rivals. Henceforth, the party would have to rely almost exclusively on the study groups to spread its message and gain new adherants. But the study groups were far more difficult to organize, required an entirely different mode of operation, and could reach only a relatively small audience, the already committed. Thus the party could no longer aspire to an immediate mass following, but instead had to try to develop a compact organizational framework that would serve the mass following it hoped to acquire in the future. In this, however, the Liberation Party was far less successful than its political rivals, a fact that became increasingly apparent as its influence dwindled in subsequent years.

Like the other political parties in the West Bank, the Liberation Party took part in the general elections in Jordan. Taqi al-Din al-Nabhani had run unsuccessfully for parliament in 1951, before the party was formally established (he had been defeated by the Baath candidate, Nawas, who had received 5,000 votes to al-Nabhani's 2,300). After the party was founded, it contested two general elections, in 1954 and 1956. Its candidates in 1954, who ran as independents (their political affiliation was, however, clear to all) were: Daud Hamdan (Jerusalem), Abd al-Qadim Zallum (Hebron), Asad Bayyud al-Tamimi (Hebron), Abd al-Ghafar Katiba (Hebron), Ahmad al-Daur (Tulkarm), and Muhammad Musa Abd al-Hadi (Jenin). Of these, only al-Daur of Tulkarm was elected; he had cooperated with the Moslem Brothers and conducted a lively campaign in the villages and refugee camps in the area.

When al-Daur took his oath, he swore his allegiance to king and country, as required, but also to God. He played an active role in the parliamentary opposition, fighting vigorously for the abrogation of the treaty with Britain; at the same time, he maintained close ties with his electorate in the villages and camps of western Samaria. In the 1956 elections, the Liberation Party again contested seats in Jerusalem, Hebron, Jenin, and Tulkarm; again, al-Daur was the only Liberation candidate elected. Faris Idris failed in Jerusalem, receiving half as many votes as the Baath candidate, and less than a quarter as many as the JCP candidate. All three candidates failed in Hebron: Abd al-Qadir Zallum received 2,700 votes, Asad Bayyud about 2,000, and Yusuf al-Sughayr about 1,500; the victorious Moslem Brotherhood candidate received more than 5,000. Muhammad Musa Abd al-Hadi failed once again in Jenin (and this time was warned to prevent his supporters from carrying out violent demonstrations, as they had done after he lost in the 1954 elections). Al-Daur's self-confidence increased considerably after his second successive election, and he continued to pursue an uncompromising opposition line. But he was expelled from the House of Representatives in 1958, charged with carrying out activities hostile to the regime, and sentenced to two years in prison. The party did not contest any subsequent elections.

For all its stress on indoctrinating the Muslim masses, the Liberation Party also engaged in considerable conventional political activity in those areas where it exerted the greatest influence. In the larger, more Westernized cities with large Christian populations,

Ramallah and Bethlehem, its influence was negligible; even in Jerusalem and Nablus, it was no match for the secular nationalist and left-wing parties. The party enjoyed its greatest strength in the more conservative areas of the West Bank, Hebron, in the south, and the Jenin-Tulkarm area in the north. That its candidates were not elected in Hebron, despite the conservative religious nature of the people in the area, can be attributed to the superior strength of the Moslem Brothers there; in Tulkarm, on the other hand, the personal appeal of al-Daur, combined with the conservative nature of the population in that area, gave the party its only election success.

As a member of parliament, al-Daur strongly opposed the government's policy of forbidding political activity in the schools. This policy heightened the party's interest (and that of the other parties also) in the students of the West Bank, whom it saw as potential recruits. Even though the Liberation Party was somewhat less successful among students than its rivals, it persisted in its attempts to establish itself among them. Like Taqi al-Din himself, who taught at the al-Ibrahimiya Secondary School in Jerusalem, many of the party's other leading members were schoolteachers (in Jerusalem, Nablus, Tulkarm, and Hebron), and from the beginning used their positions to convey the party's ideas to their pupils. In the early years, they even used some of the party's texts (most frequently, al-Nabhani's) in class. As of mid-1955, however, teachers were explicitly forbidden to include political material in their lessons. From 1956 on, the party ceased the practice, and its activities among the students were henceforth conducted secretly and not in the schools themselves. The students were organized into study groups of five, with the group leaders receiving instructions from a schoolteacher who belonged to the party. Thus the cessation of open activity in schools by no means meant that the party had lost interest in the students, but rather that it had had to adopt different methods to reach them.

Of particular interest was the Liberation Party's attempt to recruit members from the army and the police force. Letters were sent directly to army officers; members of the National Guard were harangued in the mosques (particularly in the Friday sermons); and from the beginning, party members were asked to influence their friends and relatives in the armed forces. In the mid-1950s, the party in Jerusalem appointed a special official to maintain contact with army personnel. Because of the extreme sensitivity of political activity in the army, study groups were not established within it, and army members received individual instruction. It is difficult to establish the extent of the party's success in the army, but from the available information, its success here appears to have been relatively modest. According to party documents, somewhat greater success was achieved among the paramilitary National Guard.[9]

The Liberation Party competed with the other parties in the West Bank for the support of the local population. Its chief rival was the Moslem Brotherhood, from which the Liberation Party had itself broken away and which sought its principal support among the same conservative religious groups. Accordingly, some of the Liberation Party's fiercest barbs were aimed at the Moslem Brothers. The Brothers were denigrated as lackeys of the king and of British imperialism, and accused of presenting an incomplete and inaccurate picture of Islam. But on occasion, because of the obvious common ground existing between the two parties, the Liberation Party would try to forge an alliance with the Moslem Brothers. The legitimacy the Brotherhood was accorded by the authorities, and the prestige it enjoyed in certain parts of the West Bank (Hebron, for example), undoubtedly influenced the Liberation Party to overlook some of the "deficiencies" in the Brothers' approach to Islam. There were several attempts at cooperation between the two parties between 1953 and 1955 (Arif al-Arif, the historian, played a leading role in these attempts), but none of them proved successful.

While fundamental ideological differences may have hindered meaningful cooperation between the two parties, there seem also to have beem pragmatic organizational reasons for their failure to make common cause. Negotiations broke down at the end of 1953 because, among other reasons, the Moslem Brothers insisted on keeping any alliance secret; but the Liberation Party, which sought the legitimacy such an alliance would accord it, wished to make any rapprochement as public as possible. The following year, however, the Brothers did help Ahmad al-Daur, the Liberation Party's candidate in Tulkarm, win election to the Jordanian parliament, although no actual agreement on principles had been reached.

Talks on unification opened again at the beginning of 1955 and reached advanced stage, dealing with such issues as the name of the proposed combined party and changes that might be necessary in the regulations of the present parties. But the West Bank Liberation Party leadership was not prepared to take responsibility for such important decisions, and referred the Moslem Brothers to the party's central leadership in Syria.[10]

It appears from the available material that, of the two parties, the Moslem Brothers were actually the more interested in effecting a union; they felt that union would end the unnecessary competition between the two parties and would also eliminate some of the very destructive criticism to which they were being subjected by the Liberation Party. The Liberation Party was somewhat apprehensive of any far-reaching form of union with the Brothers, fearing that this would cost it its distinct identity and submerge it in the party from which it had once broken away, without enabling it to realize its principles or exert even the limited influence it enjoyed as a separate party.

Thus the Liberation Party attempted to acquire a mass following by preaching its message in the mosques of the West Bank; it attempted to achieve its political goals within the constitutional framework of the Hashemite kingdom by contesting the elections to the parliament in Amman; and it attempted to inculcate its political-religious ideas by organizing secret study groups among the Muslim faithful,—and all without ever receiving the legal sanction of the authorities. It was, from the outset, an *illegal* organization, dedicated to the overthrow of the Jordanian regime and its replacement by one based on fundamentalist Islamic principles. At first, the party believed that all that was required to achieve this objective was to establish a suitable underground apparatus, made up of committed idealists who would be prepared when the time came to seize power. Naiveté and baseless optimism, reinforced by the successes of the Moslem Brothers in Egypt, generated quite unrealistic expectations in the early founders of the party. It was not long before this hard truth became apparent, and the party revised its strategy. Its first year was seen as a period of secret organization and preparation. The next phase was to be one of takeoff and of enlightenment of the masses. Once this was completed, the Islamic state would be a fact. Some of the party's planners estimated that this second phase would take about fifteen years to complete, while others counseled patience and refused to set a time limit. All agreed, however, that it would not be necessary to resort to physical violence to achieve the final goal: rather, it would come by controlling the state from within. Accordingly, great stress was placed on the need for intensive underground activity. Dramatic and quick successes were not anticipated. Apart from one or two isolated instances, the Liberation Party did not preach violence, whether in the form of demonstrations or more serious activities. The objective of seizing control of the government was not abandoned, but was postponed indefinitely. It was to be achieved slowly and systematically, by gaining positions of influence in the community, by preparing the population to accept the type of regime the party aspired to, and by taking part in the parliamentary life of the country. The authorities, however, were not misled by this gradualist approach; they viewed the Liberation Party's secret activities and uncompromising criticisms as constituting a serious potential threat to the regime, and took vigorous steps to prevent the party from establishing or consolidating itself. Its leading personalities were forced to leave the country, either because they found it impossible to operate in the hostile atmosphere or because they were expelled by the authorities (Taqi al-Din himself left voluntarily at the end of 1953, but was later prevented from returning; Daud Hamdan left in 1956). Other leading activists were arrested and imprisoned for extended periods (at the beginning of 1955 and of 1958, and in 1964). The expulsions, arrests, and various restrictions were applied to most of the party's activists at one time or another. The party attempted to escape harassment by improving its internal security and following a stricter code of secrecy, but with little success. The security services were very well informed of the party's activities and the party's internal security tended to be lax. The group was given a certain amount of latitude by the authorities as long as it did not pose any serious threat to the regime; but whenever it stepped out of line, voicing its criticism of the regime too shrilly or in any way disrupting the political life of the country, the security services clamped down, further reducing the party's chances of ever realizing its ultimate goal.[11]

STRUCTURE AND MEMBERSHIP

When the founders of the Liberation Party applied to the Jordanian Interior Ministry for a permit in 1952, they submitted a description of the party's proposed organizational structure. It was to be based on democratic principles: members were to elect by secret ballot an executive council which would in turn appoint a president. The decisions of the council were to be approved by majority vote, and were to be binding on all the party branches.

In addition, a general assembly was to be convened once a year. In actual fact, however, the organization of the party was far from democratic. After its request for an official permit was turned down, the party set about organizing itself as an underground movement. In the process, it abandoned the democratic principles it had outlined in its application, and evolved on distinctly autocratic lines. Shaykh Taqi al-Din al-Nabhani was the undisputed leader of the party, and he exerted his control through a centralized leadership committee which was known by a number of different names— *qiyadat al-hizb al amma* ("the general command of the party"), *al-qiyada al-ulya* ("the supreme command"), *al-lajna al-markaziya* ("the central committee"), or *lajnat al-qiyada* ("the leadership committee"). Occasionally, another body was referred to—the "advisory council" (*majlis al-shura*), which maintained some form of contact with the branches but whose responsibilities were never clearly defined.[12] This body first operated from Jerusalem, but after Taqi al-Din moved to Damascus in November 1953, it was transferred to the Syrian capital. In the years 1956 and 1959, when when the party's leadership was moved to Beirut, the advisory council followed suit. The leadership laid down the guidelines for all the party's activities, and monitored these through the reports it received from time to time and through supervisors when it sent out to the various branches. Taqi al-Din's authority was absolute, regarding decisions of both the party's ideology and its day-to-day management. Those who disagreed with him were liable to expulsion, and a number of the party's leaders were in fact expelled.

Below the centralized leadership were the national leadership bodies in each of the Arab countries. These, however, had little freedom of action, and had to follow the instructions issued by the central committee in Damascus or Beirut. The party's headquarters in Jordan were situated in Jerusalem throughout the 1950s. A proposal to shift these to Amman in 1958 was overruled by the central leadership. In the early 1960s, however, it appears that the headquarters were, in fact, moved to Amman. The national leadership bodies were also known by a number of different names —*lajna fariya* ("subcommittee"), *lajna mahalliya* ("local committee"), *lajnat al-urdun* ("jordanian committee"), *majlis wilaya* ("ruling council"), *majlis al-umana* ("council of deputies").[13] The central leadership kept a tight rein on the local committees through its special supervisors (*mushrif*) or roving envoys (*masul mutajawwil*). The local committees also regularly requested, and received, instructions from the central committee. In the larger towns of the West Bank (Jerusalem, Hebron, Nablus, Qalqilya) there were regional committees. These comprised between five and eight members, and were responsible for the routine activities of the party in their respective areas—indoctrination, recruitment, and liaison with the local (national) committee. In Jerusalem, for example, where there was considerable party activity, individual members were charged with the responsibility for certain specific tasks (raising funds, gathering information, distributing pamphlets, running the study groups, and so on). Occasionally a subcommittee would be set up under the regional committee to deal with a specific project—the writing and production of leaflets, for example, or propaganda and indoctrination. The local committee itself would receive regular instructions from the party leadership in Syria or Lebanon, studying them carefully before passing them on to the study groups. Activities were better organized in Jerusalem (the seat of the local committee) than elsewhere in the West Bank, but the same general procedure was followed throughout the area. In Jerusalem as well as in the other towns (Jericho, Tulkarm, and so on), efforts were made to gain followers in the surrounding villages and refugee camps and to set up branches subordinate to the urban center. The party was most successful in its attempts to penetrate the rural areas in northern and western Samaria (Arraba, Yabad, Azzun, Anabta). There were even attempts to establish branches in other Arab countries (Iraq, Kuwait, and Egypt), but this was the work of the central committee, not of the leadership in Jordan.

The party in Jordan was linked to the central committee not only organizationally but also financially. Considerable sums of money were received from the central leadership to pay the salaries of party functionaries, support the families of imprisoned members, and cover the cost of printing and distributing pamphlets. The financial link was important, and whenever funds were slow in coming from Damascus or Beirut, the party's leaders there were reminded by their subordinates in Jordan that "without money, it is not possible for us to disseminate the (party's) message among the people."[14] Money would usually reach the West Bank via Amman, arriving in Jerusalem from where it was distributed to the other centers. The sums varied, and were sometimes as high as several hundred dinars. There is no clear indication of where the money originated, but at least two foreign sources were rumored: Hajj Amin al-Husayni (the former Grand Mufti of Palestine and Taqi al-Din's early mentor) and, rather more persistently, the United States. While the Americans were vigorously attacked by the Liberation Party, it was suggested that this very attack provided the Americans with just the cover they needed for their subversive activities in the area. The party's fanatically religious nature suited the United State's anti-Communist stance, while its attacks on the Moslem Brothers and the British were also welcomed by the Americans at a time the United States was trying to weaken the position of the British in Egypt. To what extent an American connection actually existed will not be known until more American archival material becomes available. There was, however, apart from stories told or anecdotes reported, at least one more direct reference to American aid to the party. In the spring of 1956, the Lebanese government officially informed the Jordanians that it had confiscated a check for $150,000—issued by the U.S. Embassy in Beirut and deposited in Taqi al-Din's account.[15] If such huge sums were being made available by the Americans, the party clearly did not need any other source of income. Nevertheless, there is no evidence that such large sums ever reached the party in Jordan. The nature of its activities in the West Bank certainly did not point to the availability of large amounts of money. To all appearances, the branches in the West Bank relied on money from private sources, in the form of donations, to finance its day-to-day running costs. Unlike the other parties in Jordan, the Liberation Party did not collect dues from its members (it was opposed to this in principle, and criticized the Moslem Brothers for the practice). It preferred to receive donations from its members, and each branch appointed an officer whose job it was to coordinate the branch's fund-raising activities. The regularity with which donations were made, however, casts some doubt on the "voluntary" nature of the system: these donations appeared to differ in little more than name from the dues members of the other parties had to pay. Another source of income was the sale of party literature to members—another form of indirect taxation.

While the structure of the Liberation Party and many of its activities bore some resemblance to the other parties in the West Bank, it was much more amorphous and considerably less effective than its rivals. The party clearly lacked strong local leaders, its code of secrecy was only sporadically and half-heartedly enforced, and there was a wide gulf between its theoretical and actual form. These weaknesses, and the fact that the group deliberately placed greater stress on indoctrination than on organizing itself for any operations against the regime, did not prevent the Jordanian authorities from viewing the Liberation Party as a hostile organization that had to be closely watched. Every effort was made to prevent it from establishing itself in the area or evolving an effective leadership. In other words, the Liberation Party received the same treatment as any other illegal opposition party in Jordan. But because of the party's relative weakness and its reliance on conservative sectors of the population, the security services found it easier to penetrate and to a large extent neutralize what little danger it posed to the regime. In retrospect, it would seem that many of the harsh measures the Jordanian authorities took against the party were somewhat unnecessary. It should be remembered, however, that the Liberation Party, and especially its leader, Taqi al-Din al-Nabhani, had close ideological ties with Hajj Amin al-Husayni, one of the most inveterate foes of the Hashemite regime. The party was also the most serious potential rival to the Moslem Brothers, whom the Jordanians had recognized and were prepared to tolerate. Above all, the Liberation Party's central leadership was not locally based, and the Jordanian Security Services were inherently suspicious of any hostile group that received its instructions from outside the country.

Publications

As we have seen, the Liberation Party addressed itself to two groups: the community of Muslim believers at large, through the mosques, and its own initiates, through study groups. The party's activites among the first group were forced to stop after its first two years, when it became illegal to use the mosques for political purposes. Thereafter, indoctrination was carried out in the framework of the secret study groups. The nature of the party's publications reflect this shift in emphasis.

Unlike the other parties in the West Bank, the Liberation Party made little effort to put out regular publications, either for the public or for its own members. There were, however, two attempts to publish a newspaper: *Al-Sarih* ("The Truth Teller"), which the party put out soon after its inception in an attempt to win a mass following, but which was banned by the authorities in March 1953; and *Al-Raya* ("The Flag"), edited by Abd al-Qadim Zallum (with the exiled Taqi al-Din as nominal editor-in-chief), which replaced *Al-Sarih*, only to be banned as well at the end of 1954. After the second attempt to publish a newspaper of its own failed, the party advised its members to read existing papers that were sympathetic to its aims (the Beirut daily, *Al-Hayat*, for example).[16] Internal publications, intended for party members only, also appeared only sporadically. The party tried a few times to put out regular internal newsletters (*Al-Halaqat*, "The Groups," for example, in 1957), but they were short-lived. The void left by the absence of periodical publications was filled by a number of textbooks outlining the party's philosophy, which were used in the study groups. They were usually printed in Damascus or Beirut and distributed to members in Jordan. Harassment by the security services made it increasingly difficult to distribute the textbooks in the West Bank, and from the mid-1950s on, they were given only to study group leaders, who would memorize them and then brief the members of the group on what they had read.

The Liberation Party relied primarily on leaflets to bring its message to the public at large. These leaflets were generally no more than a single page, although when the subject required it, they were occasionally expanded into pamphlets of between four and six pages. The leaflets were initially printed outside the West Bank, in Syria or Lebanon, but as it became increasingly difficult to smuggle material into the area, more leaflets were produced locally. As most of the leaflets were rolled off on duplicating machines, in 1958 it was decided simply to smuggle the wax stencils into the West Bank, and use these to produce the actual leaflets on the spot; occasionally, smuggled leaflets were painstakingly copied out by hand.

A number of methods were used to distribute the leaflets: they were sent through the mail to senior government officials and other important functionaries; they were distributed to the public either by placing piles of them in central locations or by leaving them on the doorsteps of private homes; they were also sometimes pasted on walls, or even read out aloud in public meeting places, such as coffeehouses or mosques. From the mid-1950s on, to prevent the seizure of the leaflets and, more important, the arrest of those distributing them, more clandestine methods had to be developed. The leaflets were transferred from place to place hidden among "innocent" items (fruit, vegetables, and so on) and carefully concealed in a hidden cache until distribution. Then the leaflets were given, secretly, only to known sympathizers of the party, and the recipient sometimes had to utter a special password. Jerusalem was the main distribution center in the West Bank, and a number of local members were charged with transmitting the leaflets to other centers in the area, usually at night to cut down the chances of detection. While in the early 1950s the leaflets (which included the speeches of Ahmad al-Daur in parliament) were distributed to the public at large, in the 1960s, for security reasons, they were limited to actual members of the study groups. Only on very special occasions (for example: the eve of the Pope's visit to Jordan in late 1963 and the creation of the Palestine Liberation Organization in 1964) were attempts made to distribute protest leaflets to the general public.[17]

The central leadership almost invariably prepared the content of the leaflets, unlike the practice of most other parties, which composed many of their leaflets at the local level. This centralization of information was not complete, however. From time to time, the local branches, whether in Amman or in Jerusalem, would compose and distribute their own leaflets on a certain subject, even before the "official" version arrived from Lebanon. The content of the leaflets varied, but usually related to some important political event. Of the more than two hundred different leaflets preserved in the files of the Jordanian Security Services, about 40 percent were critical of the various Arab countries (including Jordan) and their leaders, and the same percentage dealt specifically with imperialism and its activities in the area. About 25 percent dealt with the Palestine problem, with Israel and the Jews. The issues cannot always be separated, however, and the need to fight imperialism—and particularly Israel—is implicit in almost every context. Social issues received little attention, as did, somewhat surprisingly, the major religious topics. Nevertheless, religious motifs and terminology (and excerpts from the Koran and the Hadith) abound in the leaflets.

IDEOLOGY[18]

Despite their separate development, the Liberation Party and the Moslem Brothers shared historical roots that were evident even in later years. One particularly clear manifestation of this common heritage is found in the parties' ideologies. Terminology, important ideas and concepts, method of argumentation, and many of their conclusions were similar—indeed, at times identical. Nevertheless, over the years some ideas peculiar to the Liberation Party emerged and were further developed.

Imperialism, both Western and Eastern, is very often bitterly attacked in writings of the Liberation Party. The stereotypal arch-enemy, though, is Western imperialism, the cunning hands of which are to be seen behind many political events in the Arab world: there is no single Arab regime that has not been infiltrated by Western agents. But in the eyes of the Liberation Party it is not a single, monolithic force: rather, there is an ongoing rivalry between Britain and the United States, who are vying for influence and power in the Arab world. The Liberation Party also viewed the Soviet Union with hostility, and often accused it of using the Arabs in its conflicts with the West; but the degree of criticism leveled against the Soviets is much smaller. In the eyes of the party, their being Communists is reason enough to regard them with contempt, but the display of a relatively mild attitude toward them is explained by their "lack of presence" in the Middle East: their danger is less acute than that of the West.

It is the conspiracy fomented by the U.S. (sometimes even with the active support of the Soviets in order to oust the British) which should be feared most in the Middle East.[19] The West, to promote its aims in the Middle East, tries to lure the Arab countries into military and economic alliances with it. The military pacts are depicted by the Liberation Party as outright attempts to subjugate the semi-independent Middle Eastern states. And various projects of economic aid are presented as a somewhat more astute form of imperialism, intended to bring about political hegemony through financial infiltration. All these alliances are seen as aspects of one overwhelming strategy: the attempt to involve Muslim countries in the struggle for power of the imperialist infidels. Be they overt or more often subversive and hideous, these attempts are being exposed by the party, and their potential victims are being given a detailed, proper warning.[20]

The imperialist powers were viewed as the major culprits for the decline of Islam. But unlike the Moslem Brothers, the Liberation Party did not see any sinister ideological motive behind their conspiracy, but rather more prosaic considerations—the control of natural resources, military strategy, and so forth. Economic dependence on the West and political division of the Muslim world into some twenty separate states were the direct outcome of the severe religious and ideological identity crisis of that world. Total liberation from the cultural, economic, and political control of the West was the means to resuscitate the Muslim world: but the ultimate

227

goal should be the creation of a single Islamic state. In its internal affairs this state would govern every facet of the lives of its inhabitants according to the tenets of Islam, and in its external affairs it would embark upon a holy war in a concerted effort to impose Islam on the entire non-Muslim world. Only the West's technological achievements were to be preserved in this future state, and most particularly in order to develop a massive armaments industry.[21]

The ultimate objective proposed by the Liberation Party was the conversion of the entire world to Islam. This should be reached through activity on three successive levels: that of the conscious individual, that of the "chosen group," and that of the ideal state. This final stage, in which all Muslim peoples would be united in one omnipotent state, was not merely an apocalyptic dream. The embryo of it was in the Arab countries, and therefore most attention should be directed at them. One should thus avoid any reference to the existence of various Arab peoples: "the Jordanian People" or a "Palestinian People" were all parts of an encompassing identity—Islam. The concept of Arab nationalism was an imperialist creation, an innovation antithetical to the very spirit of Islam. (Even the well-known catch-phrase "the sister countries"—*al-duwal al-shaqiqa*—was regarded as offensive to Liberation Party ideologues.) Only Islamic nationalism could serve as the basis for the existence of a nation whose ultimate realization would be that of a unified Muslim state. In actuality, however, little attention was given to other countries of the Islamic world. The major political focus of the party was not even on the Arab world as a whole, but on the problem of Palestine.[22]

Palestine was no ordinary Muslim country; it occupied a special place in Islam. The very existence of a foreign rule there (and most particularly in Jerusalem) was considered a disgrace. The proper solution would be a holy war; the resettling of the refugees elsewhere or restoring them to their homes under Israeli rule was not to be countenanced. The emergence of a Palestinian "entity" was likewise unsupportable: on this issue (unlike others) the party showed a highly consistent position and did not hesitate to attack openly the Palestinian Liberation Organization (PLO) for its support of the concept of a separate Palestinian state. Creation of a separate Palestinian state not only was antithetical to the party's most fundamental belief in pan-Islamic unity, but also might put an end to the Palestine problem. And that end was the objective of the imperialist West, Israel, and some of the Arab leaders who wished to rid themselves of the entire problematic situation. Hence, for the Liberation Party, "the creation of a Palestinian entity and a state in the West Bank is a great crime, and is absolutely forbidden."[23]

While the Qawmiyun did in fact adopt a similar position until 1964, following Egypt's support for the PLO that year the Brothers began to back the idea of a Palestinian entity in the West Bank. The Moslem Brothers had supported from the very start the idea of the Palestinians organizing themselves, and made frequent appeals to the residents of the West Bank to take their destiny into their own hands. The Liberation Party, however, was the only party in the West Bank (and perhaps in the Arab world) which consistently opposed the PLO and any other organization that shared the PLO's aims. It is interesting that it was on this question of a separate Palestinian entity—a question that was to become so predominant in the political thinking of the inhabitants in the West Bank—that the Liberation Party refused to bend its principles to curry popular favor. The party consistently resisted any attempt to degrade the problem of Palestine to the level of a refugee problem, but just as consistently it refused to recognize it as a particularistic national problem. Anything that fell short of the reconstitution of the Muslim world as a single, united state was, in the party's opinion, not worthy of serious consideration. But its insistence on remaining loyal to its fundamental principles on this of all issues is evidence of the Liberation Party's extreme political shortsightedness.

6. Conclusion

Munib al-Madi and Sulayman Musa, in their book on the history of Jordan in the twentieth century, describe in the following terms the period of the Nabulsi government (1956–57) that preceded the dissolution of all political parties:

> In the Nabulsi period general activity in the country took on a party color. If only people would engage in party activity in sportsmanlike and noble manner, guided by that sense of responsibility binding upon each and every citizen! Party activity among us has become a source of haughtiness and arrogance and the business of sloths and parasites....
>
> Urban society began to function as though it were stricken with a sickness, a fever, and the clashes between the various parties began to multiply....The fault lies in the mistaken notion that party activity is heroic, and that a man ought to be identified with a party [*hizbi*] rather than possess positive moral qualities.[1]

The attitude expressed in this passage may best be summarized by three statements: (1) the Nabulsi period was one in which political activity in Jordan acquired an organized party character for the first time; (2) this political activity was beset by a lack of sporting spirit and was motivated instead by negative moral qualities, irresponsible feelings, and dishonorable conduct; and (3) the parties' operations even at their peak were restricted to urban society only. I will examine the validity of these three contentions within a wider historical perspective and in the light of evidence suggested by my research, as well as offer my own interpretation and general conclusions.

To the first statement one can counter that organized and established party activity was in fact prevalent in Palestine and Transjordan long before Abdallah annexed the West Bank to his kingdom. There had been branches of Ottoman and post-Ottoman parties among the Palestinian Arabs and new parties were established in the first years of the Mandate. The Husayni-Nashashibi rivalry acquired a party character in the mid-1930s when the Arab Palestinian Party (al-Hizb al Arabi al-Filastini) and the National Defense Party (Hizb al-Difa al-Watani) were established. Other parties were also founded during this period,[2] six were established in Transjordan in the late 1920s and early 1930s. Despite their different names, all were intended to accomplish one task—support the king and his regime. All these parties tended to rely on certain families or groups, the members of which belonged to the same traditional, conservative social circles. The 1930s also saw the first beginnings of political organization on a nonfamily basis with the formation of the Istiqlal and Communist parties, which gained their greatest impetus in the 1940s. In addition to the "classical" type of political party, new groups began to appear on the political map of Palestine and Transjordan.[3] They attempted to base themselves on religious principles (for example, the Moslem Brothers, from the mid-1940s), or, like the Communist Party, on social ideas.

The Moslem Brothers set up branches in Nablus (1945), Jerusalem (1946), and Hebron (1949). While their activities in these early years were limited, they were not fundamentally different from those the Brothers engaged in on a broader scale from the 1950s on. The same is true of the Communist Party. The Palestinian Communist Party of the 1930s emerged in the following decade as the National Liberation League, only to be renamed the Jordanian Communist Party in the early 1950s. The name and sometimes even certain political positions changed but the essential framework of activity remained intact and the same basic political line was maintained.[4]

The main period of party formation in the West Bank followed the promulgation of the new Jordanian constitution on January 3, 1952.[5] It provided for party activity with certain stipulations, among which were that political activity must be peaceful and nonviolent; it must be directed toward lawful ends; and the internal regulations of the parties must conform to Jordanian law. In other words, while the constitution permitted political organization in principle, it required every prospective party to submit to investigation in order to determine the extent of its conformity to these conditions. Only after such scrutiny would the decision to grant or deny an official permit be taken.

Conclusion

In this regard the major parties that emerged in Jordan after 1950 fell into three categories. In the first were those parties that became active in 1950–52 but did not request a permit for organization according to the new constitution. The Moslem Brothers was one of these. Following its practice in other parts of the Arab world, it carefully avoided the name "party." Instead it called itself an "association" and registered as such under the Ottoman Law of Associations (still valid in Transjordan). This was confirmed in an official order published in January 1953. Although it was well known that the Brothers' aims were political as well as social, the regime preferred to accept the contention that the Brothers was an association. This tolerant relationship was the result of the government's conviction that it could look to the Brothers for support in internal and inter-Arab political matters, and that it was expedient to permit it to function. The same basic reasoning had led the royalist regime in Egypt to recognize the Brothers as an association, but while in Jordan the ties with the regime were firm and growing, in Egypt they were steadily degenerating. That the Moslem Brothers did, in fact, support the Hashemite king became apparent during the 1957 riots. Nevertheless, the authorities found it prudent to keep a wary eye on the association, and later, during periods of tension between it and the regime (1959, 1963, and 1965), members were left under strict surveillance and several were even arrested.

Other groups that did not request a permit were the Arab Nationalists Party (al-Qawmiyun al-Arab) and the Communist Party. The latter had been outlawed by the so-called War on Communism Law of May 2, 1948, and its 1953 revision. Both the original and the revised versions made membership in the Communist Party or activity within any sort of Communist framework, in the service of Communist ideas, illegal. The 1953 law imposed severe punishments of long-term imprisonment with hard labor on those who belonged to the Communist Party or propagated Communist ideas, and three years' imprisonment on anyone even found in possession of Communist leaflets.[6] These severe measures were intended to intimidate and defer potential party recruits. It is therefore not surprising that the Communist Party did not even attempt to obtain a permit for political activity as required by law.

The second category comprised those parties that requested and received a permit to organize and function. One of these was the National Socialist Party, founded in 1954 in Amman. Its main aims were liberation of the Arab homeland from foreign rule, Arab unity based on a close link with Iraq, preservation of the royalist regime by offering a clear alternative to the left-wing parties, and very moderate social reforms. The leading members of the party were, for the most part, members of the large traditional families—Anwar and Rashad al-Khatib, Hikmat al-Masri, and Haza al-Majali, the party's general secretary. Despite their apparent swing to the left in 1956–57, the National Socialists had basically been a conservative group, both in social composition and political position. For example, the group's call for closer links with Iraq as a first step toward Arab unity meant uniting with the Hashemite state of Nuri al-Said, the protégé of the West. It is not surprising that such a party gained official approval, as did another, the National Party (Hizb al-Umma), also founded in 1954. Its leaders too were members of large conservative families and supporters of the regime. They included Kamil Arikat, who later became chairman of the Jordanian parliament, Samir al-Rifai, and Abd al-Rauf al-Faris from Talluza. A third organization, the Arab Constitutional Party, founded in April 1956, was also explicitly intended to present an alternative to the left-wing groups. Some of its leaders were considered, by leftists and others, socially and economically conservative, even reactionary. They included East Bankers such as Riad al-Muflih and Ahmad al-Tarawina, and West Bank dignitaries like Anwar Nusaiba of Jerusalem and Tawfiq Qattan of Bethlehem, who eventually emerged as staunch supporters of the Hashemite regime.[7]

The third category was made up of parties that received a permit for their activities but only with great difficulty. The most prominent of these was the Baath, whose existence in the West Bank can be traced to 1949 and the establishment of two separate groups in Jerusalem and Ramallah.[8] In February 1952, shortly after the promulgation of the constitution, leading members of these circles, such as Abdallah Rimawi, Abdallah Nawas, Bahjat Abu Gharbiyya, and Munif al-Razaz, requested permission to establish the Arab Renaissance Party (Hizb al-Baath al-Arabi). The application was rejected on the grounds that the proposed party would be a branch of the Syrian Baath and that its aims contravened paragraph 16 of the constitution, which stated that political parties must have "a peaceful purpose and internal regulations that do not run counter to the constitution." The Baathists persisted and in 1953 they slightly revised the party regulations (which they were required by law to submit) and renewed their request for a permit. Once again their request was turned down by the authorities. They made a third attempt in 1954. They changed not only their regulations, but in view of developments in the parent party in Syria, requested permission to establish a Socialist Arab Renaissance Party (Hizb al-Baath al-Arabi al-Ishtiraki). Their application was refused again, this time on the grounds that their intention was actually to overthrow the regime in Jordan. Several of the applicants were men who, in view of their legal training, were unwilling to operate without official permission. They therefore took their case to the Jordanian High Court of Appeal. On August 28, 1955, the court ruled that the government's refusal to grant the party a permit was illegal. With the government's decision overturned, the party was allowed to operate on the basis of the regulations and internal procedures they previously had adopted and announced, but the Jordanian government continued to consider it illegal and the Minister of Defense instructed the Minister of Interior, and through him the district governors and others, that the party was still illegal despite the ruling of the High Court. Its active members were arrested and brought to trial. Early 1956 saw the last phase in the struggle of the Baath to establish itself as a legitimate party. Two members from the Bethlehem area were arrested for distributing leaflets, tried, and acquitted. This marked a turning point, and from then on the Baath was considered legal by the government. Thus the party whose requests for a permit from 1952 on had been consistently blocked enjoyed one year of legality, from 1956 to 1957. In 1957 the Baath was banned together with all other parties.

The Liberation Party (Hizb al-Tahrir) was another group that received a permit with great difficulty. Like the Baath, it requested an official permit in 1952, shortly after the publication of the constitution, and like the Baath its request was refused. The authorities charged that the party's ideology ran counter to the constitution in two respects. First, in stressing religion as the decisive element in national life: this struck at one of the foundations of the state by dividing its residents along religious lines. Second, in declaring as one of its basic precepts that the type of regime should be a matter of choice; this directly contradicted the constitution, which declared quite specifically that Jordan was a kingdom, precluding any possibility of choice in the matter. The party was thus seen as harboring intentions to overthrow the regime, and consequently its activities were not authorized. After its request was turned down, the Liberation Party discovered that it did not in fact need to request authorization as a party; instead it could register as an Ottoman association, as the Moslem Brothers had done. In March 1953 party leaders sent a letter to the Minister of the Interior and asked to be so registered. The request was also published in the party newspaper. From that time, although it was not authorized as a party, the Liberation Party was recognized as an association. In the elections of 1954 and of 1956 it campaigned openly, and on both occasions its representative, Ahmad al-Daur, was elected to parliament.

A renewed and different type of party activity, it seems then, began in Jordan around 1950 and gained its main momentum after 1952. Many of the parties that emerged were supporters of the government. All of those included in the second category mentioned above either were established directly at the initiative of the authorities or, by virtue of their structure and the social status of their leaders, could be expected to support the regime.

The main most "meaningful" parties were in fact the opposition parties. Some, such as the Moslem Brothers and the Liberation Party, had a right-wing, religious orientation; others, such as the Communists, the Baath, and Arab Nationalists, displayed varying degrees of left-wing ideology. These opposition parties not only were Jordan's largest but also possessed a comprehensive and relatively well-crystalized ideology. That is why the study of their composition and ideology as well as their relations with ths government is significant for any attempt to understand and evaluate political life in Jordan.

The second point raised by al-Madi and Musa—that party activity was unsportsmanlike and lacking in responsibility and honor—is more substantial. The opposition parties made extreme demands on the regime and in fact worked against it: their objective was to overthrow the existing authority. The right-wing parties wanted a regime with a more religious tone; the Communists and to a certain extent the Baath favored a leftist orientation; the Arab Nationalists and the Baath demanded a pan-Arab regime. Yet on closer examination, it appears that neither in practice nor in theory did these parties explicitly demand or work for the overthrow of the regime or the ouster of the existing government in Jordan.

We will look at three parties with respect to their attitude toward the regime—the Baath, the Liberation Party, and the Communists. The Baath, from its beginnings in the early 1950s, made the increased democratization of political life one of its chief demands. This meant giving greater representation to the people, granting additional rights and more weight to parliament, and decentralizing authority through the delegation of power by the central government to its representatives in the various districts. All these reforms were to be made within the general framework of the constitution and the existing political structure; there was no demand for fundamental political or constitutional changes. There was room for improvement—the Emergency Laws should be annulled, for example —but the regime need not necessarily undergo any fundamental change and it certainly need not be abolished. The party's major criticism of the Hashemite regime's political line stemmed from the basic goal of the Baath—Arab unity. They demanded that the king sever his personal and political ties with imperialism and draw closer to the rest of the Arab world, but these demands lay well within the framework of the current political setup.

The Liberation Party, on the other hand, definitely rejected, both conceptually and ideologically, a separate Jordanian entity. This rejection, which extended also to the concept of a separate Palestinian entity, derived from a basic and fundamental belief that Islam as a concept as well as a system should be decisive in determining political direction in the Arab and Islamic worlds. The party held that the common ground for a political community is religion—Islam—and not the narrowly based political state. But the Liberation Party was also explicitly opposed to the use of violence in achieving its goals. It preached action through cooperation with the regime, and presented many examples from Islamic history and tradition showing that the Prophet acted in this way when he spread Islam at the outset of his mission. Just as Muhammad had acted by means of persuasion, first winning over those closest to him and then ever widening circles without resorting to violence, so too should the Liberation Party achieve its goals through non-violent means.

The Communists took the most negative attitude toward the king. Abdallah was frequently called the "dog of the imperialists" in Communist leaflets distributed in Jordan. In the middle of 1950 the party even explicitly called for his assassination (it may be assumed that after he was in fact assassinated, the Communists had cause to regret this appeal since they had in no way been involved). Talal and Husayn also received sharp censure from time to time, but even the Communists never actually called for the overthrow of the Jordanian regime. In 1956, when Husayn adopted a policy favored by the Communists, they praised and supported him.

The Baath, the Liberation Party, and the Communists all followed a policy of attacking the political line of the various Jordanian governments and demanding its modification; but my sources record no call for a fundamental change in the political structure of the country or the overthrow of the state. Nevertheless, it should be pointed out that the strict adherence of the Communists to the 1947 partition plan, even in the 1950s and 60s, and their continued demand for a separate Arab state in part of Palestine as provided for in the plan, contained an element of implied subversion. Had the partition plan been fully implemented—the logical if not explicit conclusion of their stand on this issue— it would perforce have impinged on the territorial integrity of the Jordanian entity. For this reason rather than any incompatibility of the social outlook, the Hashemite regime opposed the Communist Party and singled it out for special persecution.

On the practical level, it is clear that these parties did not engage in any violent activities which endangered, actually or apparently, the regime in Jordan. They all followed the rules of the accepted political game: they nominated candidates for election, conducted election propaganda, and sometimes changed the name of the party (it was expedient for the Communist Party, for example, to call itself the National Front in the election campaigns of 1954 and 1956, although it was perfectly clear to everyone that this was essentially the Communist Party). Some parties even managed to achieve considerable political success within the system, electing members of parliament, some of whom later became ministers in the government. The nearest the parties in Jordan came to actual violence was in the staging of demonstrations, and even these were irregular and sporadic outbursts of limited duration in response to specific events. Celal Bayar's visit in the 1950s was such an event, as were the nationalization of the Suez Canal, when demonstrations were organized by the Baath, the Communists, and the Arab Nationalists, and the Pope's visit in 1964, when the Liberation Party organized demonstrations. Antigovernment agitation was generally restricted to the distribution of leaflets or other publications critical of specific actions or positions, and violence was never espoused. The degree of danger to either side during the sporadic outbursts of violence was thus negligible.

Nevertheless there is reliable information that in the years 1957–58 the government was aware that at least three parties were planning to resort to force against the regime. There is information indicating that members and supporters of the Qawmiyun al-Arab in Syria were undergoing military training with a view to returning to Jordan to seize power. In the archives of the Jordanian Security Services there is detailed evidence given by Communist activists who admitted smuggling weapons from the Gaza Strip through Israeli territory and storing them in the Hebron area, with smaller caches in Ramallah. These weapons, smuggled during 1957–58, were to have been used to seize power by force. Finally, there were clear indications in Baathist circles from 1957 on that the party intended to infiltrate and base its future activity on the army (*Askartariyya*, that is, army-oriented, instead of *proletariyya*, proletariat-oriented), and to prepare a military coup scheduled for a year or two later. The Baath actively sought out West Bank men and sent them to Syria for military training, with the explicit intention of using their cadres to seize power. This activity was intensified by the formation of the United Arab Republic, following which the party showed ever-increasing signs of becoming a pawn of the new union which was basically interested in subverting Jordan's regime and annexing it. The actual preparations had gone quite far and constituted a very real threat to the Jordanian regime.

The authorities were quite tolerant of the parties, and in the 1950s and 1960s the Jordanian regime seemed prepared to play a cat-and-mouse game with them: they followed the activities of the parties very closely while allowing them to continue to operate. The Jordanian Security Services maintained an extensive apparatus, trailing and reporting all the activities of party members, however insignificant. Security service informers were planted in the cells of the various parties. Intelligence penetration of the Liberation Party was especially extensive (for which the researcher can be most thankful), but precise reports concerning the activities of the left-wing parties also exist. The security services kept comprehensive lists of the members of all the parties and their main branches. These were periodically updated and were detailed enough to grade each member according to his importance in the party. From time to time the regime would inflict a small blow of one sort or another on the parties, but generally they were allowed to operate and organize, even when enough was known about their activities to justify punishment. The Communist Party was the most striking in this respect: even though the authorities knew that it was operating illegally, they allowed it to continue.[9] This cat-and-mouse struggle was most intense around the secret publication of the party leaflets and pamphlets. The regime tried to prevent their publication or at least their distribution to the public. The effort met with only limited success, and foreign publications and pamphlets (mainly from Syria and Lebanon) were distributed throughout the kingdom.

The same may be said of the sporadic party demonstrations that broke out periodically. It is clear that the regime knew of the various activities and deliberately allowed them to continue so long as they did not constitute a substantial threat. When the situation was re-evaluated in mid-1957 and a new approach was adopted, the parties came under direct attack. But even then, after the parties had suffered a decisive blow and gone underground, the authorities chose to ignore their outlawed subterranean activities. The cat-and-mouse game continued until 1967, it being clearly understood that the regime was to play the cat and the parties the mouse, and not the reverse.

The third conclusion drawn from the passage by al-Madi and Musa—that the parties' operations were restricted to urban society —is broader than the previous two and pertains to the structure and composition of the parties. It well deserves a detailed examination of the main tenets of the parties as seen from this perspective. The first characteristic of the structure of all the parties under discussion is that they were highly centralized.

The Communist Party had a single national central committee of seven or eight members whose core, the politburo, was composed of three or four members. The latter was the party's de facto executive body, but it derived its authority from the central committee. Under the central committee, in each of the main towns, were regional committees composed of five members, including the heads of the various branches and centers around that town. Under them there sometimes were local committees which united the party branches in the smaller towns and villages. The basic unit was the cell of five members. Every such cell had a secretary, an ideologue, and a treasurer—every member was delegated some responsibility. The cell was the active unit, generally holding one meeting weekly or fortnightly. At these meetings instructions were received from the central committee by way of the regional committees. These included plans of action and, more important, the political line concerning current events and upcoming developments. The cell held discussions and deliberations on the basis of these instructions and engaged in criticism of political and social events, mainly self-criticism (in keeping with the traditional Communist dogma). Reports, questions, requests for instructions, and various suggestions regarding future activity, recruitment, and so forth filtered upward from the cells by way of the same intermediary bodies. The money collected from each member, either as dues or as contributions, also flowed upward. The general secretary of the party during the entire period was Fuad Nassar who, judging by all available evidence, in power and charisma towered above the other members of the politburo and the central committee. He laid down the political line to be followed and the instructions for its implementation. He and over half the central committee were from the West Bank. Some, but not all, members served on the central committee during the entire period. At the highest level of the party there were no democratic election procedures. Membership in the central committee and the politburo was determined by internal power struggles, and not as a result of elections in the lower ranks of the party.

A similar structure (using slightly different terminology) is characteristic both of the Baath and the Qawmiyun al-Arab. At its apex the Baath also had a central committee, called the "National Leadership." Its seat was in Amman and was composed of eight members, half of them from the West Bank. Under this committee there were a number of intermediate bodies; the central branches (*far*), which were set up only in Jerusalem and Nablus; under these the *shuba*, in each of the big towns: each *shuba* was, in turn, composed of three *firaq*; and at the bottom of the organizational hierarchy was the cell (*halqa*). Party activity was also similar to that of the Communists—the lines of communication were arranged vertically, never horizontally between branches and cells, and all instructions came from above. Here, too, there were no internal elections for central institutions, and leadership passed from person to person according to the internal balance of forces. The structure of the Qawmiyun al-Arab was similar in terminology, methods of communication and reporting, and the imposed appointment of leadership.

In the Liberation Party an attempt was made to maintain a similar pyramidal structure with the main power concentrated at the apex and the various subordinate bodies ranged below; but in this case, the structure was less clearly defined. An attempt was made to create such a structure in theory, but there were, in fact, only two units—the cell and the leadership. The intermediate levels existed only on paper, except for regional committees in Nablus and Jerusalem. The leadership body, called the general command or the central committee, was first located in Jerusalem, then moved to neighboring Arab capitals. An intermediary body may have been acting in Amman, but the main link was from the center directly to the cells, which were essentially small units for the study of Taki al-Din al-Nabhani's thoughts and the party ideology. Since the party felt that this structure was not rigid enough to guarantee an acceptable degree of central control, a "roving inspector" was appointed whose task it was to supervise the activities of the various branches. This practice, while it may well have resulted in greater central control, was highly detrimental to party secrecy.

Another distinctive characteristic of these parties is that they drew their main support and membership from the educated middle class, with farmers and urban workers playing a decidedly secondary role. The parties did not center around the traditional leading families although members of such families, selected on their merits, were sometimes found in party ranks in Nablus and other places. Similarly, property played little part in determining success or influence in the party hierarchy, although there were cases of large property owners reaching the highest ranks of leadership, even in the Communist Party. Generally, however, the party leadership and the decisive majority of members came from the educated urban elite and owned little or no property.

Teachers and students comprised the most active element of the urban elite within all these parties and much party action was based on this circumstance, with its obvious advantages. High school students constituted a very high percentage of the total population and were the main reservoir from which the parties could draw in their efforts to create a mass base. These students had a greater political awareness and youthful susceptibility to political agitation and incitement which made them an important object of interest. Moreover, since many educated Jordanians emigrated to other Arab countries, they became the means for spreading party doctrine and ideas throughout the neighboring states. Inside Jordan itself the practice of transferring teachers from place to place every few years, coupled with their natural influence on their pupils, made them the ideal vehicle for the propagation of party ideology. Furthermore, as urban intellectuals, teachers tended to have a strong desire to change the regime. In the Baath, for example, statistics show that teachers constituted more than a quarter of the total active membership. This party, which also attempted to establish student organizations, based much of its activity in schools such as the Teacher's Seminary in Bayt Hanina, from 1956 to 1960, and the al-Ibrahimiya High School in Jerusalem.

A similar situation existed in the Communist Party, which set up special student organizations in Jerusalem and Ramallah.[10] The party tried to activate the leftist sympathies of teachers and students by drawing them into party activities through the allocation of specific tasks—teachers served as coordinators of the student networks, while the students themselves regularly distributed leaflets. Al-Qawmiyun al-Arab also put a strong emphasis on organizing students, and attempted to set up various student bodies throughout the West Bank. Teachers were used as coordinators of student cells. One of their centers of power was Kuliyat al-Najjah in Nablus, a hothouse of political activism in which al-Qawmiyun al-Arab was especially successful. One of the spiritual leaders of the party in the West Bank, Muhammed al-Amad, served as a teacher there and exerted a great influence on his students. The Liberation Party also stressed the role of teachers and students in its various activities. A significant proportion of its activists were teachers of religion. Not only had Taki al-Din al-Nabhani been an instructor at the al-Ibrahimiya school in Jerusalem in 1952, but the party also had many supporters at the al-Salahiya and al-Khalidiya schools in Nablus, and Tulkarm High School (1953–54). Because of the great attention given to imparting the party's "basic concepts" to its members, teachers were employed in a coordinating and guidance capacity in their study circles; and from 1957 on there were even explicit instructions from the leadership to establish study circles of students outside the schools and, as far as possible, to place teachers in charge of them.

The great interest shown by all the parties in the student and teacher sector was derived from the place of education in their scale of priorities. This also accounted for the minimal attention they paid the villagers and workers, a phenomenon that was not the accidental result of their general perspective. In the 1940s the Communist Party, in its previous form as the National Liberation League, had been largely based on workers. In the early 1950s the party decided not to base itself on the urban proletariat, but rather to turn mainly to educational circles. This decision was taken following a power struggle between Fuad Nassar and Ridwan al-Hilu. Nassar's view was accepted, namely that the party's chances of success and expansion in Jordan, and especially in the West Bank, would be far greater if efforts were directed toward the educated elite rather than the urban proletariat.[11] Even so, the workers were not entirely neglected and occasionally there were some cells, such as those of the Ramallah metal workers in the 1950s, in which the majority of members were workers. There was, however, even less interest in the peasants. It is therefore not surprising that the leadership and membership of the party was for the most part made up of village magnates such as Rushdi Shahin or Abd al-Qadir al-Salih and a large number of white-collar workers and professionals, many of whom were physicians (Dr. Abu Khajla, Dr. Yaqub Ziyadin). Much the same is true of the Baath, although there was not the type of reasoned argument encountered in the case of the Communist Party. In addition to the high percentage of teachers among the party members, there was a striking number of lawyers and, to a lesser extent, doctors among the founders of the party and first-rank activists. On the other hand, worker representation in the Baath was very limited; a prominent example such as Husni al-Khuffash (secretary of the Trade Union Federation in Nablus) or Sadiq Sunuqrut (secretary of the Cobbler's Union in Hebron) are exceptions. The statistical data used show that the percentage of refugees among the members was low (less than 15 percent) and that the status of urbanites in the party was much the same as that of rural dwellers. But from personal interviews as well as the first-hand impressions of different local leaders, it seems that the urban dwellers were, in fact, more prominent and that there was greater party interest in this sector of the population. While al-Qawmiyun al-Arab gave the impression of having an educated leadership (including several prominent physicians such as Dr. Subhi Ghosha of Jerusalem, Dr. Salah al-Anabtawi, and Dr. Walid Qamhawi of Nablus), behind this facade the party was far more heterogeneous than the others, and among its members were many drivers, craftsmen, and laborers. The Liberation Party also had relatively fewer educated members, and particularly prominent among them were religious functionaries and those educated in religion. Large and small-scale merchants also had a larger representation than in other parties. Although it too was most active in the cities, the Liberation Party, unlike the Communists, decided to make a systematic and concentrated appeal to the village and uneducated sectors. By 1953 the party decided to establish a broad popular base by appealing to villagers, and many village representatives were in fact invited to Tulkarm or Jerusalem for guidance and direction. In the cities themselves, several attempts were made to establish special cells and study groups for the uneducated which would be led by students. However, these plans were never fully realized, and despite its penetration of the villages, the party continued to receive its main support in the urban centers. The Moslem Brothers too had a noteworthy number of uneducated urban members, especially in Hebron, Nablus, and Jerusalem.

The increased politicization of public life in Jordan in general and of the Arab Legion in particular, especially the integration of the mostly Palestinian National Guard into the army in 1956, facilitated the penetration of oppositionist ideas into this sensitive military sector. The political parties had long displayed an interest in the offices of the Legion as possibly sympathizers (there is clear evidence of this in the case of the Baath and the Liberation Party, and some indication in the other parties) and exploited the opportunity to step up their efforts among them. But they met with only limited success, and although the Legion was to some degree affected by party factionalism, the effect was minimized by the vigilance of security services and the preventive measures taken by the regime.[12]

From the material at my disposal it appears that all parties were predominantly Muslim. This is true not only of those parties which were Muslim by definition (the Moslem Brothers and the Liberation Party), but of all the others as well. While Christians such as Fuad Nassar were prominent among the leadership of certain parties, particularly the Communists and Baath, this was of very little significance and neither party members nor their opponents called attention to it.

At this point, three general conclusions may be drawn, to be further elaborated below. First, the parties enjoyed considerable popularity (though varying in degree) not only in the large towns of the West Bank, but also in many of the smaller towns and villages. Second, their active membership was rather limited in size, though substantially wider in terms of general support and sympathy. Finally, although the parties operated on both banks of the Jordan, and some of them even had their headquarters in Amman, the West Bank formed the territorial center of their political activity and its residents their mainstay, both quantitatively and qualitatively.

The Liberation Party was most successful in the northern and northwestern towns of the West Bank—in the Tulkarm, Qalqilya, and Jenin area, where they had their greatest successes in the parliamentary elections. In the south, the main centers of activity were Jerusalem and Hebron. While it was most active in the towns, the party also made many substantial gains in surrounding villages and refugee camps. As a religious party with a conservative outlook, it drew its main strength from the traditional centers (Hebron, Tulkarm, and Qalqilya) where the social structure was less affected by modern developments. The Moslem Brothers also concentrated their main activities in the larger towns of Hebron, Nablus, Jerusalem and its vicinity, Tulkarm, and Jericho and its neighboring villages. The Baath was most successful in the Ramallah-Jerusalem area throughout most of the period, although in the mid-1950s it also made substantial gains in Nablus, where its membership came to equal or perhaps even exceed that in the Ramallah-Jerusalem area. Even then, however, its outstanding personalities and leaders, and later its parliamentary representatives, were from the latter area. Although branches were set up in all the major West Bank towns, there were far fewer in the area south of Jerusalem, and the Baath was weakest in Hebron. West Bankers were predominant in the party leadership, constituting fully two-thirds of those elected at its first official convention in 1955. The Communist Party developed in the opposite territorial direction. It gained its first major success in the Nablus area, and only later did it manage to gain a foothold in and around Ramallah. In the more traditional areas, where the old social structure was better preserved (such as Jenin and, even more so, Hebron), the party began its activities much later (in Hebron, for example, only in 1953), and its gains were far smaller. In the final analysis, the Communist Party too operated in all the major and many of the minor towns and villages of the West Bank. Al-Qawmiyun al-Arab centered its activities and had its greatest success in the two main urban centers of the West Bank, Nablus and Jerusalem. During the 1950s, however, its activities extended to the Tulkarm and Ramallah areas as well.

From Jordanian press reports of 1955–57 and the reminiscences of local residents, one might infer that several large and powerful parties were active in the 1950s and 1960s. A careful reading of the files of the Jordanian Security Services and interviews with leading party figures of the time, however, cast doubt on this impression. The security services kept meticulous lists of everything pertaining to party members, and even in doubtful cases in which the person concerned might have ceased his party activities years before, they tended to view him as an active member. It clearly emerges from these lists that even during the peak period of party activity in 1956–57, the membership of the Communist Party in the West Bank never exceeded one thousand,[13] and never even reached that number in the East Bank. The most generous estimate of membership in the Baath does not exceed seven hundred, about the same as that of the Moslem Brothers. Membership in the Liberation Party was placed at somewhat less than this, while the Qawmiyun al-Arab was believed to have had no more than a few hundred members. The distinction between party activists and party members is arbitrary and is made almost impossible by the tendency of the written sources to rank every member as an activist to some degree or another. Nevertheless, it is possible that these estimates may have been inflated by the existence of relatively new and tentative cells, inactive members, and certain (probably very few) cases for which the security services may not have known all the facts. Since the Communist Party had a clearly defined and rigid structure and members were accepted only after a certain period of candidacy, one may assume that the figure of eight hundred to one thousand in the West Bank accurately reflects the size of the party at its peak. On the other hand, the Baath, which was more lenient in accepting members and defining its supporters, may have been larger though less stable. As for the Muslim religious parties, the above figures should be taken as the upper limit, for their less rigid structure enabled them to include in their ranks people who would be better described as supporters than as bona fide members.

One of the reasons that the parties often seemed larger than they actually were was the high percentage of high school students among their supporters. They were not usually considered to be members, but wherever the parties took to the streets in demonstrations, the students played a major role. An interesting feature of the political history of the West Bank is that when these students matured and reached the age of party membership they tended, in many cases, to grow away from the parties; and as a result the parties did not grow in size as one might have expected, but remained relatively small. The parties in Jordan were based on a relatively small number of staunch supporters, and though "mass parties" by definition, none of them was massive in volume. This was a major source of their weakness vis-à-vis the regime, and the main reason why they were tolerated to such an unusual degree.

The parties' influence on the general public stemmed from two main factors. The first was their identification with major political trends developing in the region. As one or another trend became popular, the influence of the party that identified with it increased accordingly. This was the case, for example, with al-Qawmiyun al-Arab party, which gained considerable importance during the Nasserite heyday of the 1950s. The second factor was the efficiency of party organizations—the degree to which it was able to bring its message to a broad audience; to assert influence and public pressure greater than its numerical strength; and to withstand the periodic crises caused by the regime's attacks on the parties. In both these areas the left-wing groups had a clear advantage over the Moslem Brothers and the Liberation Party. The rise of Nasserite pan-Arabism, the growing appeal of socialism, and the Soviet Union's friendship with some of the Arab countries all served to enhance the left wing's strength far beyond that registered in the files of the Jordanian Security Services. Moreover, in times of stress, particularly when they were being hounded by the authorities, it was rigid and ordered organization that enabled the parties to survive the crises intact. The Communist Party, which had perhaps fewer supporters than the Baath or al-Qawmiyun al-Arab during certain periods, was the best equipped in this respect, and therefore proved to be the most resilient throughout the political vicissitudes of the decade 1957–67.

The most spectacular party activities in Jordan, particularly in the West Bank, were those that brought about a collision with the government—mass demonstrations, arrests, and political trials. But in retrospect, during the two decades of Jordanian rule in the West Bank, the most prominent and sustained party activity was propaganda. Actual indoctrination was restricted to party members, the natural object for such activity; but propaganda efforts were aimed at a much broader audience, and calculated to win new supporters and bring the party message to the masses. Internal ideological guidance and indoctrination were common in the left-wing parties, which distributed leaflets to their members and held regular meetings to discuss and sometimes even to criticize the party line (the principle of criticism and self-criticism was especially honored in the Communist Party, but the Baath and al-Qawmiyun al-Arab resorted to it as well). The principle of ideological guidance was a basic tenet of the Moslem Brothers and was applied in the West Bank where cell meetings were referred to as "religious lessons." Ideological indoctrination was even more emphatically practiced in the Liberation Party.

A steady stream of publications demonstrated all the parties' constant awareness of the major political developments of the period, and a wide range of nonpolitical topics as well. During the 1950s, although pan-Arab problems facing Jordan still took precedence, these problems were coupled with a rather limited interest in socioeconomic problems. The religious parties were primarily concerned with political matters and so too were the left-wing groups, despite their protestations of concern. The Baath's constitution contains many references to socioeconomic problems, but they were given very little attention in the party's regular publications or in the many speeches of Baath leaders which have been preserved. Even the Communist Party which as the First of May approached would annually raise the banner of "Bread and Work" in the West Bank, did not devote more than 10 to 15 percent of the space in its various leaflets, pamphlets, and publications to socioeconomic matters.

"Imperialism," and Israel in particular, occupied a very important place in the propaganda of these parties and in their general outlook. The Baath saw the establishment of the State of Israel as the first stage in an imperialist plot to strike at the Arab nation. Therefore, the fight against Zionism, the destruction of the Jewish state, and the return of the usurped lands were all seen as different aspects of a single goal no less important than those of the party slogan—"Unity, Freedom, and Socialism." This was not always the basic outlook of the Baath. In 1950 Abdallah Nawas still foresaw a moderate solution to the problem. He believed that the mistaken notion of the Jewish state would become universally clear within ten years and that the State of Israel would then disintegrate and its Jews abandon their intention and blend into the social fabric of the Middle East. However, when it became obvious that this prediction would not be realized, the State of Israel began to appear as "the historic challenge to the entire Arab nation" which, having once failed, would continue to struggle more successfully for the final destruction of the Jewish state. Israel's Jewish population would continue to reside in the successor state that would form part of the greater Arab nation. Al-Qawmiyun al-Arab saw the 1948 war as a turning point in history, and held that the entire Arab nation must work to avenge the humiliation it had brought on itself. Responsibility for the defeat belonged not only to imperialism and the UN and the military superiority or the enemy, but to the internal weakness of the Arabs themselves, which was thus revealed in all its acuteness. The Arab nation had to reform itself both politically and socially and take revenge; it was not to be satisfied with compromise solutions but had to uproot the Jewish entity entirely. "No peace, No negotiations, No partition, No compromise" was the basic stand taken by the party in the 1950s. The idea of Arab unity which became central to its ideology during the 1950s and the very early 1960s had to give way, temporarily, to the concept of a Palestinian entity. Still, in this context too, the party did not modify its attitude about the Jewish state or the Jewish nation, whose assimilation into the sociopolitical processes overtaking the Arab world it foresaw. Thus the main pillar and raison d'être of the State of Israel would cease to exist. The Moslem Brothers, like the Baath, held imperialism responsible for the establishment, the continued existence, and the success of the State of Israel. They conceded that the Jewish people also played an important part, but held the most decisive reason for Israel's success was the weakness of the Arab world, and this, in turn, was derived from the neglect of Islam. The final and complete solution to the problem would be achieved only when the states of the region returned to tradition. Meanwhile the Brothers claimed that holy war was a proven way to advance to the final solution even before the Arab world had fully accomplished its religious revival. The Liberation Party saw the establishment of the State of Israel as the result of collusion between imperialism and certain traitorous Arab rulers. It rejected attempts to solve the problem by internationalizing Jerusalem or by creating a separate Palestinian entity; the former would result in the total removal of the Muslim-Arab presence in Jerusalem, while the latter would perpetuate the State of Israel. The ultimate solution was seen as the establishment of an Islamic state which would, at the appropriate time, take its revenge on imperialism. But the State of Israel was to be dealt with more immediately, by much swifter and more radical means—the *jihad:* the Liberation Party advocated war to the death against the Jews in Israel, citing various religious authorizations.[14] The position of the Communist Party was the most moderate of all, even though it too underwent a certain process of radicalization. The Communists also saw the 1948 war as a plot of imperialism, international oil interests, and the Arab League. But the victims of aggression were Israel and the partition plan, the latter of which they viewed favorably. The Arab armies that invaded Palestine were seen as "armies of conquest," challenging Israel's right to political existence inside the partition borders. Israel, of course, also suffered criticism, but it was directed against the country's reactionary ruling circles and not against the entire nation; nor was the fact of Israel's existence disputed. In the mid-1950s the Communist position began to shift. Greater attention was paid to general Arab problems, references to Israeli aggression increased, and the Arab aggression was forgotten. Nevertheless, there was no direct call for the destruction of the State of Israel and the party continued to view both nations—Jewish and Arab—in a positive light.

The high percentage of Palestinians in the various parties gave the Palestine problem an essential and decisive place in the ideologies and statements of the parties. The more right-wing the party, the more extreme its stand on the roots of the conflict and the means of its solution. With the passing years, despite the receding historical distance of the 1948 trauma, the positions of all the parties became more and more extreme. The different shades of opinion which had at first been distinguishable now began to disappear, giving way to a more or less uniform negativism.

The opposition parties were not merely small groups of men sharing common political views and interests, but organized bodies which despite a relatively small active membership had ties to certain sectors of the general public. These parties, whose views ranged across the political spectrum, had hardly any traditional leaders, but rather members of the educated elite and the free professions. Only when they tried to extend their influence to the villages that all of them, including the Communists and the Baath, relied almost totally on the old traditional rural leadership—the *mukhtars.* This, together with the very limited attention these two parties gave to economic and social problems in their publications, and their minimal dependence on the working class, leads to the conclusion that they were far less left wing in the accepted sense than might generally have been supposed. Like their right-wing counterparts they were primarily political parties in the narrow sense of the term— their main concern was with political events and developments in the region and in Jordan itself.

The parties under examination were all relatively young Jordanian branches of their parent parties in other Arab countries, with which they had strong financial ties often dictated by insufficient independent resources. Organizationally and ideologically, the Liberation Party and the Baath and to a lesser extent the Communist Party were closely linked with the parent parties in other states.

But fundamentally these were all local parties with a local leadership and a primary interest in local problems; and because of difficulties in communicating with other branches, based mostly in Lebanon and Syria, they became more and more independent.

Because the parties enjoyed considerable popularity among the more educated sectors of the general public, particularly students, they served as useful indicators of political inclinations and trends, and as accurate barometers of public opinion. The authorities appear to have appreciated this, which may be the reason why they allowed the parties to operate with considerable freedom, despite their illegality. That the parties did not cease to function but reorganized themselves whenever the regime did strike at their leaders bears witness to their considerable vigor and vitality.

Although all the parties under discussion operated on both banks of the Jordan, and some of them had their headquarters in Amman, the majority of their leaders and members throughout Jordan (generally the most prominent) were from the West Bank. It is hardly surprising, then, that most of their parliamentary representatives were West Bankers. Their numerical strength (and perhaps even the resultant emphasis on the Palestinian problem) make it possible to view the parties as primarily belonging to the West Bank. As free voluntary organizations they served as a legitimate, or at any rate safely tolerable, outlet for the Palestinians' feelings of frustration, desire for social change, and search for a political solution to their predicament. As such, they manifest the increasing political awareness in the West Bank and the political traditions of the area. Paradoxically, they can also be seen as an expression of the West Bankers' growing acquiesence to the political framework and concept of the Jordanian state that had been forced upon them. These parties did not have their roots in traditional Transjordanian politics, but rather in the growing political awareness of the Palestinians under the British Mandate. Their subsequent growth, largely dictated by the political realities of the Hashemite era, indicated an increasing degree of identification with major trends in the Arab world. It is this ever-present tension between their emerging particularist consciousness of their being Palestinians, and their basic loyalty to the wider, well-established and all-embracing concept of the Jordanian state, which was the most conspicuous feature of Palestinian political thinking and activity during the years leading to 1967, and after.

Epilogue

The history of the last fourteen years in the Israeli-held West Bank bears out the truth of the saying that old parties never die. The validity of the Jordanian ban on any organized political activity has never been questioned by either the Israelis or the local population. Still, as had been the case under the Jordanians until 1967, its effect is rather limited. Political activity found somewhat different channels, largely dictated by the new reality both in the West Bank and in the Arab world. Political aims and tactics took an altogether different configuration: the Palestinian Liberation Organization (PLO) challenged the very concept of the Hashemite state—a challenge that developed into a very substantial threat. Although the group was a seemingly new phenomenon, one could trace the old structures, positions, and many of the veteran activists of the political parties underneath the new guise.

The Moslem Brothers (and to a certain extent even the remnants of the Liberation party) have been keeping a very low profile ever since 1967. An upsurge of Islamic sentiment occurred with the eruption of the Islamic revolution in Iran. It brought about a re-activaton of the old formations of the party as well as the introduction of new elements within the same political framework. Thus, for example, in conformity with the general tendency in most Egyptian universities, and in sharp contrast to the left-wing supremacy in the largest West Bank university of Bir Zeyt, the pro-Moslem Brothers students seem recently to have gained the upper hand in al-Najjah university in Nablus.

The Qawmiyun al-Arab underwent a metamorphosis and became the Popular Front for the Liberation of Palestine, opting for more militant involvement in public life. On a few occasions they tried to deepen the political dimension of their organization by introducing underground indoctrination to some of their cells. But these ventures (and similar attempts by the Baathists) proved futile and short-lived. The supporters of George Habash preferred to direct their relatively limited energy in the West Bank to the planting of explosives rather than the distribution of leaflets.

The only party that did not cease its highly motivated and well-organized political activity was the Communist party. Some of its leaders had to leave the West Bank and pursue their political life in the Hashemite East Bank. The party compensated itself for the loss of its hinterland in the East by turning to new horizons opened in the opposite direction. There it could resume its links with its Israeli counterpart which had been cut off in 1948. The Communist party's support for Jordanian unity implied an opposition not only to the Israeli occupation but also to the notion of a Palestinian identity. They preferred clandestine indoctrination to the PLO's concept of an "armed struggle." The abortive attempt in 1969 to launch their own fighting body called "The Partisans" (Quwwat al-Ansar) was a milestone on the new road of rapprochment with the PLO. A further step was taken late in 1972 when an umbrella organization, the Palestinian National Front (PNF) was set up between the two groups in Beirut. In January 1973 Fuad Nassar, the Communist party's secretary general, joined the Tenth Palestinian National Council as an active member. After the Yom Kippur War it was officially declared that the PNF would represent the PLO in the West Bank. But this time the Communist party had drawn the right lessons from its mid-fifties experience: they carefully separated the cells aimed at military activity from the main body of the party. Thus when the Israeli Security services dealt the PNF a mortal blow the party itself came out only partially harmed. Up to this writing, the Communist party is still active in the West Bank, albeit surreptitiously, preparing their cadres, ignoring the built-in ideological differences between them and the various factions of the PLO, openly criticizing both the Israeli occupation and, to a lesser extent, the Hashemites (only this time instead of *Al-Muqawama al-Shaabiya* they have a new organ, *al-Watan*). As long as the Soviet Union officially supports the PLO the Communists prefer political expediency to any other consideration.

Still, a growing internal tension between the radicals and the more moderate elements has developed recently within the PLO and indicates that further changes may lie ahead. The old strains and stresses between pro-Hashemite elements and the critical opposition parties which had its ups and downs for more than three decades has not yet been resolved.

Notes

Preface

1. A facsimile of a circular sent out by the director general of the security services on January 13, 1957, is reproduced in *The West Bank: Ferment, Resistance, Suppression* (Jerusalem: Israeli Ministry for Foreign Affairs, Information Division, n.d.), p. 25.

1. Some Empirical and Conceptual Considerations

1. "Hizb," by D.B. MacDonald, in *Encyclopaedia of Islam*, new ed., vol. 3; henceforth cited as *EI*.

2. "Hizb," by E. Kedourie, in *EI*, vol. 3.

3. S. Neumann, "Toward a Comparative Study of Political Parties," in S. Neumann, ed., *Modern Political Parties* (Chicago, 1967), p. 396.

4. S.D. Johnston, "The Role of Parties in Political Development in the Arab Middle East," *Social Science* (April 1968), p. 85.

5. M. Duverger, *Political Parties, Their Organization and Activity in the Modern State* (London, 1954), p. 3.

6. Ibid., p. 427.

7. Ibid., p. 58.

8. For a description of the composition and the performance of these parties in Europe see Duverger, pp. 2, 31, 48, 64, 79, et passim. The element of membership cards is naturally missing in our case.

9. Ibid., pp. 2, 23.

2. The Communist Party

1. The details of the ideological difference as well as the personal rivalry were hardly mentioned at all in the archives. They were made available to me by various ex-party activists, among them the late Ridwan al-Hilu. See also below, pp. 68–70.

2. *Al-Muqawama al-Shaabiya* 4/13 (July 1952); hereafter cited as *Muqawama.*

3. Most members of the preparatory committee (including Hamza al-Zirr, Musa Qwaydir, and Fuad Qassis) were arrested in spring 1952.

4. *Muqawama*, 4/5 (March 1952); *HaMizrah Hehadash* ("The New East," in Hebrew), vol. 3 (1951-52), p. 262 (hereafter cited as *HaMizrah*).

5. For a detailed description see *Muqawama*, 4/13 (July 1952); *HaMizrah*, vol. 3 (1951-52), pp. 367-68.

6. The central figure was Sami Ghadban.

7. MKM/2/24, pp. 59-69.

8. For many details see 2703-36.

9. Nabih Irshidat, Mahmud al-Mutliq, and Fayz Rusan.

10. The Jordanian delegation consisted of ten members, and all their expenses were covered by their hosts.

11. Dr. Yaaqub Ziyadin and Dr. Abd al-Rahim Badr. For more details see *HaMizrah*, vol. 5 (1953-54), p. 45.

12. As early as spring 1952 there were indications of this in Nablus, where members of the Moslem Brothers reported Communist activities to the police, as well as openly preached against them in mosques.

13. *HaMizrah*, vol. 5 (1953-54), p. 115.

14. Ibid., p. 294.

15. Ibid., vol. 6 (1955), pp. 142-45.

16. Most active were Naim al-Ashhab, Yusuf al-Baytuni, Abd al-Rahim Badr, and Umar Dana.

17. Abd al-Hayy Arafa on August 10, 1955 (MKM/4/1, p. 95).

18. MN/17/1, pp. 25, 28, 54, 59.

19. MN/21/288-86, p. 129 of August 9, 1956.

20. MKM/4/9, p. 281.

21. Fuad Qassis, Sulayman Najjab, Amin al-As in Bayt Ilu, Qibia, and Dayr Qaddis, among others.

22. For example, "We want peace, Gamal" (Abd al-Nasser) in Bethlehem (MLS/18/50, p. 21).

23. In Jerusalem, for example, these were Tariq and Munir al-Asali who led the demonstration after the nationalization of the Suez Canal (MLS/18/50, pp. 11, 13, 44).

24. Messages were also sent in protest of Nuri al-Said's policies on December 3, 1956 (MN/7/1, p. 298).

25. MKM/4/9, p. 347.

26. For a description of these meetings see *al-Difa*, October 18, 1956.

27. *HaMizrah*, vol. 8 (1957), p. 146.

28. *Filastin*, November 17, 1956.

29. *Al-Difa*, November 22, 23, 30, 1956.

30. An article in *al-Hayat* of May 28, 1957, described the growing importance of the Communists as contrasted with the clumsiness, lack of experience, and unsystematic activity of their major rivals.

31. *HaMizrah*, vol. 8 (1957), p. 221, citing *al-Jihad*, January 27, 1957. This initiative proved to be inconclusive, and further steps had to be taken a month later (*al-Ahram*, February 22, 1957).

32. *Al-Hayat*, January 1, 1957.

33. MKM/4/9, pp. 5-6.

34. Ibid., p. 59-63, 86, 89.

35. Ibid., p. 9 of January 16, 1957.

36. For many details, including locations and members in charge of arms caches see 2703-36; *al-Difa*, December 17, 1956; *HaMizrah*, vol. 9 (1958), p. 196.

37. Baghdad Radio, May 3, 1957.

38. Cf. below, pp. 85-86.

39. Amman Radio (February 2, 1957) pointed out the major arguments used by the king: the danger of Communist penetration to the Arab world in general and to Jordan in particular; his intention to avoid any involvement of his kingdom in the Cold War; Soviet support for the creation of the State of Israel.

40. Amman Radio, April 30, 1957; *al-Difa*, February 25, 1957.

41. Amman Radio broadcasting from Ramallah, April 25, 1957. By that time these references were already outdated, see below, pp. 71-72.

42. *HaMizrah*, vol. 9 (1958), p. 85; vol. 10, p. 79.

43. In most cases issued in Hebron or Jericho (348-15, p. 317).

44. *Filastin*, August 6, 1957.

45. *Al-Difa*, May 8, 1957; *al-Jihad*, April 27, 1957; *Filastin*, December 7, 1957.

46. MKM20/1/Z, p. 105; 695-5, p. 66; *al-Jihad*, October 9, 1957; *al-Difa*, October 31, 1957, February 18, 1958; *Filastin*, July 16, 1958.

47. 737-12, p. 129 of April 25, 1959; *al-Difa*, July 26, 1959.

48. MKM/20/1, pp. 47, 271.

49. MKM/20/1/Z, p. 178.

50. Abd al-Munim al-Asali and Fuad al-Salfiti (MKM/20/1/Z, p. 51).

51. MKM/20/1/Z, pp. 19, 80; 707-8, pp. 973, 976, 1009, 1062.

52. Dr. Adli Dallal.

53. For many details about activity and membership toward the end of 1959 see 707-8, pp. 893, 945, 960, 973, 976, 1009, 1062, 1168.

54. 366-8, p. 48; *al-Hayat*, July 25, 1959; *Filastin*, July 26, 1959.

55. For details see MKM/20/1/Z, pp. 1-10.

56. 279-14, p. 114 of March 23, 1964.

57. 695-1, p. 52 of January 29, 1963.

58. Other members mentioned at the beginning of 1952 included Daud al-Turjuman, Fuad Qasis, and Musa Quwaydir; in 1957, Fuad Nassar, Fahmi al-Salfiti, Isa al-Madanat, Dr. Yaqub Ziyadin, Fayiz al-Rusan, Ahmad Maruf, Fakhri Maraqa, Talat Harb, and Fayiq Warrad.

59. Abd al-Majid, and Shakir Abu Hijla, Khaldun Abd al-Haqq, Said Abu Fatima, Ibrahim al-Husri, Fathi Sad al-Din, Jafar Hashim, Rushdi Shahin.

60. The central committee for Jerusalem (1954): Daud Antun al-Turjuman (secretary), Naim al-Ashhab (indoctrination), Yaqub Ziyadin (treasurer), Ibrahim Ali al-Maghribi (leaflets distribution); in 1956–57 Al-Ashhab became secretary, Munir al-Asali (students), Tariq al-Asali (workers and peasants), Sadiq Turjuman (treasurer).

61. 707–8, pp. 960, 973, 976, 1062.

62. Ibid., p. 824 of October 28, 1959.

63. The 2/6 (June 1950) issue was quite exceptional in this respect.

64. Very similarly *al-Wathba* appeared around the same time in Irbid.

65. MKM/13, pp. 81, 245.

66. For a detailed report dating May 1956 see MN/17/1, p. 255.

67. MN/17/1, pp. 179–80.

68. MKM/4/9, p. 291.

69. The security services openly admitted that they failed in all their attempts to trace the printing press and its modus operandi in a report of January 29, 1963 (695–1, p. 52).

70. In 1953–54 about 200 copies of *al-Muqawama al-Shaabiya* were regularly sent to Hebron; 250–500 copies were sent to Nablus. This may serve as an indication of the party's estimate of its potential readers, which must have been higher than the actual membership. W. Laqueur's estimate of 700 members as early as 1951 seems, therefore, highly inflated (W.Z. Laqueur, *Communism and Nationalism in the Middle East* [New York, 1956], pp. 129, 131).

71. A pamphlet "What Is Next?" dated 1949.

72. *Muqawama* 1/8 (August 1949); 8/5 (May 1956).

73. Ibid., 1/10 (September 1949).

74. Ibid., 4/13 (July 1952).

75. A leafet dated May 1957.

76. *Muqawama*, 2/5 (May 1950).

77. Ibid., 1/14 (December 1949), 8/5 (May 1956); a leaflet of February 1957.

78. Platform of the National Front, Jerusalem 1956; leaflet of 1954; *Muqawama* 6/1 (January 1954).

79. *Muqawama* 1/6 (June 1949).

80. Ibid., 4/5 (March 1952).

81. Ibid., 6/7 (May 1954).

82. Leaflets dated September 3, 1948, December 1952; *Muqawama*, 6/7 (May 1954).

83. Leaflet dated July 1950.

84. Leaflet dated February 1957.

85. *Muqawama*, 2/6 (June 1950).

86. Leaflet for May Day, 1950.

87. Leaflet for May Day, 1956.

88. Leaflet dated 1949.

89. *Muqawama*, 1/8 (August 1949).

90. Ibid., 1/4 (June 1949), 1/10 (September 1949).

91. Leaflet dated September 3, 1948.

92. *Muqawama*, 3/10 (October 1951), 4/13 (July 1952), 5/4 (March 1953), 5/6 (April 1953), 5/15 (December 1953), 8/5 (May 1956).

93. Leaflet dated April 14, 1956; *Muqawama*, 7/2 (February 1955).

94. See Laqueur, pp. 42–43.

95. See above, n. 1.

96. For the Iraqi CP see Laqueur, pp. 179–80; for the Egyptian CP see ibid., p. 37.

97. Cf. Laqueur, pp. 39–41.

98. Leaflet for May Day, 1953; *Muqawama*, 7/12 (November 1955).

99. Leaflet dated March 1956.

100. *Muqawama*, 5/4 (March 1953); leaflet for May Day, 1956.

101. *Muqawama*, 1/14 (December 1949); 5/4 (March 1953); 6/7 (May 1954); 7/2 (February 1955).

102. Ibid., 5/6 (April 1953); leaflet dated 1949.

103. Ibid., 1/4.

104. Instructions sent to local branches by the district committee of Nablus, April 1959.

105. *Muqawama*, 6/7 (May 1954).

106. Ibid., 7/2 (February 1955).

107. *Nidal al-Shab*, 1/6 (October 1955).

108. Leaflet of April 14, 1956.

109. Leaflet of early March 1956.

110. *Muqawama*, 1/3 (November 1949), 2/4 (April 1950), 3/10 (October 1951).

111. Leaflet of March 24, 1952.

112. *Muqawama*, 1/12 (November 1949).

113. Ibid., 2/4 (April 1950). However, when Abdallah was later killed they accused American imperialism of it.

114. Ibid., 2/4 (April 1950), 3/10 (October 1951).

115. Ibid., 8/1 (February 1956), 9/2 (August 1957).

116. Ibid., 1/6 (June 1949), 1/13 (November 1949), 3/10 (October 1951), 4/5 (March 1952), 4/13 (July 1952).

117. Ibid., 2/5 (May 1950).

118. Leaflet of August 1948; *Muqawama*, 1/6 (June 1949).

119. *Muqawama*, 1/4 (June 1949); leaflets of late 1949.

120. *Muqawama*, 4/14 (August 1952), 5/4 (March 1953).

121. Ibid., 6/1 (January 1954).

122. Ibid., 9/2 (August 1957), 11/1 (January 1959).

123. Ibid., 8/5 (May 1956).

124. Leaflets of August–September 1948.

125. *Muqawama*, 1/4 (June 1949), 3/10 (October 1951); *Nidal al-Shab* 1/6 (October 1955).

126. *Muqawama*, 1/10 (September 1949); leaflet for May Day, 1950.

127. *Muqawama*, 4/13 (July 1952).

128. Ibid., 1/10 (September 1949), 4/13 (July 1952); 1/8 (August 1949).

129. Ibid., 1/6 (June 1949), 3/10 (October 1951); leaflets for May Day, 1951, 1953.

130. *Muqawama*, 3/10 (October 1951); leaflet of early May 1953.

131. *Muqawama*, 5/6 (April 1953); leaflets of May 1953.

132. *Muqawama*, 7/11 (November 1955), 10/3 (April 1958); *Kifah al-Shab* 2/6 (March 1956); *Nidal al-Shab* 3/4 (December 1957).

133. *Muqawama*, 10/3; *Nidal al-Shab* 4/1 (May 1958); leaflet of March 1957.

134. Leaflets of August–September, 1948; *Muqawama* 1/9 (August 1949).

135. Leaflet of July 1950; *Muqawama*, 1/4, 1/6 (June 1949).

136. *Muqawama*, 3/10 (October 1951); pamphlet "What Is Next?"

137. *Muqawama*, 1/4 (June 1949), 1/8 (August 1949), 2/2 (February 1950), 3/10 (October 1951).

138. Ibid., 5/5 (April 1953).

139. Ibid., 5/6 (April 1953); leaflets of May 1953, December 1955.

140. *Muqawama*, 2/2 (February 1950), 3/10 (October 1951), 5/6 (April 1953), 6/7 (May 1954); leaflets of April–May 1951.

141. Leaflets of early May 1953.

142. *Muqawama*, 10/3 (April 1958), 7/11 (November 1955); leaflets of March–July 1956.

143. *Sawt Jabal al-Nar*, 1/2 (April 1956); leaflet for May Day, 1956.

144. *Al-Wathba*, 1/3 (April 1956).

145. Leaflets of November 1956, March 1957; *Muqawama*, 10/8 (September 1958).

146. Leaflet of October 1957; *Kifah al-Shab*, 2/6 (March 1956); *al-Wathba*, 1/3.

147. *Muqawama*, 10/3 (April 1958); *Nidal al-Shab*, 3/4 (December 1957), 4/1 (May 1958).

148. *Muqawama*, 10/8 (September 1958), 8/6 (June 1956); leaflets of November 1956, March 1957.

149. *Muqawama*, 1/9 (August 1949), 2/5 (May 1950), 7/11 (November 1955).

150. Leaflets of August 1948, 1949; *Muqawama*, 1/4 (June 1949).

151. *Muqawama*, 3/10 (October 1951), 5/5 (April 1953), 1/4 (June 1949).

152. Ibid., 7/11 (November 1955), 10/7 (July 1958).

153. Ibid., 4/3 (February 1952).

154. Leaflet of late July 1952.

155. Leaflet of December 1952; *Muqawama*, 5/5 (April 1953), 7/3 (February 1955).

156. *Muqawama*, 7/2 (February 1955).

157. *Muqawama*, 7/11 (November 1955); *Nidal al-Shab*, 1/6 (October 1955).

158. *Muqawama*, 8/5 (May 1956), 8/7 (August 1956), 9/2 (August 1957), 15/5 (May 1963).

159. In his book *Tariq al-Istiqlal* (1939) as cited in Mustafa Ghalib, *al-Hizb al-Shuyui al-Suri* (1954), pp. 92–94. See also E. Murqus, *Tarikh al-ahzab al-Shuyuiya fi'l-Watan al-Arabi* (Beirut, 1964), pp. 149–50.

160. Cf. Ghalib, pp. 64, 96–97, 101–6; Murqus, pp. 221–24. 232;

161. Leaflets of May 1954, June 1955, December 1955.

162. *Muqawama*, 7/12 (November 1955); leaflets of May–April 1951, May 1954.

163. Murqus, pp. 237, 244–46, 249–54.

164. Ibid., pp. 256–62, 266.

165. Leaflets of March 1956; *Kifah al-Shab*, 2/6 (March 1956); *al-Wathba*, 1/3 (April 1956).

166. *Nidal al-Shab*, 2/1.

167. "Statement of the Central Committee" of mid-November 1956.

168. Leaflets of February–March 1957, October 1957; *Nidal al-Shab* 3/4 (December 1957); *Muqawama*, 10/7 (July 1958).

169. Murqus, pp. 109–11, 266; U. Dann, *Iraq under Qassem* (Jerusalem, 1969), pp. 101, 157–58, 163; A. Abdel Malek, *Egypt, Military Society* (New York, 1968), pp. 272–73; M.S. Agwani, *Communism in the Arab World* (Calcutta, 1969), pp. 170–73.

170. *Muqawama*, 10/8 (September 1958).

171. *Nidal al-Shab*, 4/8 (January 1959).

172. Circulars of the district committee of April 1959.

173. Murqus, pp. 110–11, 266; Dann, pp. 157–58.

174. Cf. Y. Harkavy, "The Problem of the Palestinians," in his *Arabs, Palestinians and Israel* (Jerusalem, 1975, in Hebrew), p. 34.

3. Al-Qawmiyun al-Arab

1. W.W. Qazziha, *Revolutionary Transformation in the Arab World: Habash and His Comrades from Nationalism to Marxism* (London, 1975), pp. 25–27.

2. B.R. Qubaisi, "The Arab Nationalist Movement, 1951–1971: From Pressure Groups to Socialist Party" (American University, Washington, D.C., 1972), pp. 70–71. A central member in the movement in later years told us that this version is basically incorrect.

3. Qazziha, however, regards their activity even at this stage as much more meaningful: indoctrination among members of the Arab Cultural Club, publication of the movement's newspaper as early as 1954, propagandizing among the Palestinian refugees in their camps, and so on (pp. 25–27). There is no reason to doubt the authenticity of these facts, but hardly any reference to them is to be found either in Jordanian press of the day, or the security services' files. It seems, therefore, that although they were already active, this activity was relevant only for a very limited number of people.

4. W. Qamhawi, *Al-Nakba wa'l Bina fi'l Watan al-Arabi* (Beirut, 1962), vol. 2, pp. 427–28. Though not an official publication of the movement, Dr. Qamhawi's book was a fair presentation of the ideology shared by the Qawmiyun in Nablus and the West Bank during the fifties.

5. Qazziha's description (p. 29) of the Qawmiyun, as the only political leadership left over to organize opposition to the government while all others allegedly deserted, is highly exaggerated.

6. This in turn triggered off an internal controversy among the leaders as to the advisability of keeping at least some aspect of their structure of activity secret even from the Egyptians. See below, p. 130.

7. MN/20/1, p. 306 of September 11, 1963.

8. One report describes a high school teacher in Qalqilya late in 1963 telling his students that they may listen to any broadcasting station—BBC, Egypt, or even Israel—but never to Amman Radio (MN/20/1, pp. 296, 318).

9. MKK/20/1, p. 54 of May 12, 1963.

10. *HaMizrah Hehadash*, vol. 6 (1955), p. 43.

11. MN/20/1, p. 413 of October 8, 1961.

12. Qubaisi, pp. 100–103.

13. Ibid., pp. 103, 107; interviews with party leaders. This procedure was also followed by the Baath.

14. Qubaisi, pp. 110–14.

15. Ibid., pp. 107–10. A well-informed member of the party argued in an interview with us that this was mainly Habash's view.

16. In Jerusalem (mid-June 1963) there were Abd al-Ghani Abu'l Khalaf, Khalil Sufian, Kamal Suhayl.

17. Qamhawi, vol. 2, p. 185.

18. B. Shwadran, *Jordan—A State of Tension* (New York, 1959), p. 341.

19. Qamhawi, vol. 1, p. 50.

20. Ibid. See also an internal circular (in Arabic) "On the present stage and its aims" in Qazziha, pp. 50–51.

21. Cf. *al-Wahda*, May 1963.

22. Qamhawi, vol. 2, pp. 429–30. The war of 1948, Qamhawi argues, is the best historical proof to it: through unity, initiative, and self-sacrifice a small group of Jews managed to defeat the Arabs and commit its crimes unpunished.

23. H. al-Hindi and M. Ibrahim, *Israil: fikra, haraka, dawla* (Beirut, 1958) as cited in M. Suleiman, *Political Parties in Lebanon* (Ithaca, 1967), p. 169.

24. *Al-Wahda*, August 1962, May 1963, June 1964; leaflets of May 15, 1956, titled "Revenge is the only solution" (681–9).

25. Qazziha, p. 52.

26. *Al-Shab Aqwa*, December 1957.

27. *Al-Wahda*, May 1963 (379–4); "The disaster of May 15," a leaflet dated May 15, 1956 (681–9). Cf. Qazziha, p. 51, for similar views of H. Darwaza, who entertained close links with the Egyptian government.

28. Qamhawi, vol. 1, pp. 50, 175.
29. *Al-Shab Aqwa,* December 1957.
30. Leaflet "Revenge."
31. Qamhawi, vol. 2, pp. 429-30.
32. *Al-Wahda,* May 1963; 758-70, p. 540.
33. Qamhawi, vol. 1, p. 188.
34. Leaflet "Revenge."
35. Most Qawmiyun leaflets either open or end with this slogan.
36. Interview with a party activist. See also Qazziha, p. 54.
37. Qazziha, p. 54.
38. Though these slogans recur more often and more intensely in the sixties, they were used by the party in earlier publications too. For the fifties see leaflets "Defense of the [Suez] Canal—a holy duty," (August 1956), "France the enemy of the Arabs" (July 1956); for the sixties: *Al-Wahda,* July 1962; leaflets against the Baath (mid-1963); "Communiqué on the Palestinian entity" (April 1964).
39. For a full and detailed communiqué of the Iraqi branch see *Al-Wahda,* July 1964. One may also assume that the writings of the party's prominent members (e.g., Al-Hindi, Ibrahim) reached the West Bank in spite of the government's ban.
40. Qamhawi, a respectable and respected physician in Nablus, had to publish his book in Beirut in 1962, and in it he made many explicit references to "revenge." By that time party publications in Beirut were already replacing these motifs with new and different ones.
41. Leaflet "Arab [financial] support—victory for the people," January 1957.
42. Leaflet "Sons of the Arab people," February 1958.
43. *Al-Wahda,* July 1962; leaflets of February 3, 1958 ("A day of great happiness'), May 15, 1958 ("Do not forget this day"), May 15, 1961 ("Fellow Arab citizen").
44. Leaflets "No borders, no divided entities," July 16, 1956, "Defense of the [Suez] Canal."
45. See below, pp. 130-31.
46. "Circular on collusion against [Arab] unity," October 1961.
47. The intrinsic link between the tragedy of Palestine and unity is best pointed out when lessons of 1948 and of 1961 are being drawn, usually on the eve of the commemoration days. See below, pp. 122-28.
48. *Al-Wahda,* May 1963, July 1964. See below, pp. 128-30.
49. Ibid., December 1963, June 1964.
50. Leaflet "The will of the Arab nation," June 1956.
51. S. al-Husari, *Ahadith wa Ara fi'l Wataniya wa'l Qawmiya* (Cairo, 1944), pp. 97-98.
52. Leaflet "No borders."
53. Leaflet of February 3, 1958; Qamhawi, vol. 1, p. 246.

54. Husari, pp. 88-98.

55. On the importance of history see leaflets "No borders," "The will of the Arab nation."

56. *Al-Wahda*, July 1962.

57. Their social criticism is largely imbued with the concepts of Aflaq (cf. his *Fi sabil al-Baath* (Beirut, 1963), pp. 159-63.

58. Leaflet "The disaster of May 15."

59. *Al-Shab Aqwa*, December 1957.

60. Leaflet "The will of the Arab nation."

61. Leaflet "No borders."

62. Leaflet "Arab [financial] support."

63. Leaflet "Do not forget."

64. Leaflet "The will of the Arab nation."

65. Qamhawi, vol. 2, p. 49.

66. Leaflet of February 3, 1958.

67. As was the case with the Baath. Cf. Aflaq, *Fi sabil al-Baath*, pp. 52, 159-63, 170-73.

68. Leaflets "The will of the Arab nation," "No borders."

69. Leaflet of October 1961 expressing the party's view of the breakup of the UAR.

70. Leaflet "Fellow Arab citizen." See also Qamhawi, vol. 2, pp. 181-82; Aflaq, pp. 55, 160, 173.

71. *Al-Wahda*, May 15, 1963.

72. Ibid., August 1962; Qamhawi, vol. 2, pp. 181-82.

73. Leaflet "Martyr," October 1963.

74. "Circular on collusion."

75. *Al-Wahda*, August 1962. Basically adopting Abd al-Nasser's concept on the destructive role of feudalism, they do not refrain from criticizing harshly some of the ways undertaken to implement his principles.

76. Communiqué to discuss the merger, n.d., published about March-May 1963; *Al-Wahda*, May 1963.

77. *Al-Wahda*, December 1963, May 1963.

78. Leaflet of October 1963.

79. N. Rejwan, *Nasserist Ideology* (Jerusalem, 1964), pp. 256-59.

80. *Al-Wahda*, July 1964, on which the following three paragraphs draw quite extensively.

81. Cf. Rejwan, p. 257.

82. Leaflet "Avant-garde," October 1963.

83. Qamhawi, vol. 2, pp. 196-97.

84. Leaflets of October 22, 28, 1963.

85. *Al-Wahda*, July 1964.

86. Interview with a central member of the party.

87. Pamphlet "The fourth lecture: the concept of democracy in Arab nationalism," September 1962.

88. Here the party is being carried away by its own concepts, which at the beginning of the century, naturally, were still dormant, to say the least.

89. Qubaisi, pp. 34–35.

90. The only leaflet in which this term is specifically used is "Sons of the Arab nation in Jordan" of 1959.

91. "Circular on collusion."

92. Qazziha, pp. 66–67, 80–81. This approach was adopted by Abd al-Nasser in 1959 (cf. al-Nasser's *Nahnu, al- Iraq wa'l Shuyuiya* (Beirut, n.d., pp. 23, 28).

93. Qazziha, p. 65.

94. *Al-Wahda*, May 1962.

95. Ibid. Cf. Haykal in *al-Ahram*, June 22, 1962; K. Maqsud in *al-Ahram*, June 8, 1961; Rejwan, p. 218.

96. *Al-Wahda*, May 1962.

97. *Al-Hurriya*, January 1964, cited in Qazziha, pp. 72–73.

98. Qazziha, pp. 74–81.

99. Communiqué to discuss the merger, published about March–May 1963. Cf. Rejwan, pp. 222–25.

100. As expressed in articles of Kamal al-Din Rifat in *al-Katib* (Egypt) in the mid-sixties.

101. *Al-Wahda*, December 1963.

102. The Nasserite line was openly and directly criticized by *al-Hurriya* in 1966–67.

103. Qamhawi, vol. 2, p. 421.

104. Ibid., p. 423. The implied "legitimacy" of the Jordanian entity was given up altogether by the party in later years.

105. *Al-Wahda*, May, July 1962.

106. Ibid., May 1962.

107. Ibid., July 1962.

108. Ibid., July, August 1962.

109. Ibid., May 1963.

110. "Communiqué...on Palestinian entity," April 1964.

111. This term was introduced here into the publications of the party as a further indication of their new concepts.

112. "Communiqué...on Palestinian entity."

113. Leaflet for May 15, 1964.

114. "Communiqué...on Palestinian entity."

115. Implying Ahmad Shuqayri et al.

116. *Al-Wahda*, June 1964; "Communiqué...on Palestinian entity."

117. *Al-Wahda*, June 1964.

118. Though the ambiance described here seems authentic, Shukayri was neither at the service of King Husayn nor did he enjoy any "free hand."

119. *Al-Wahda*, June 1964.

4. The Moslem Brothers

1. There are, however, some vague references to earlier activity in Nablus in 1945 but these are inconclusive (718-40, p. 69 of July 27, 1954; 718-40, pp. 1-2 of March 2, 1946).

2. Ishaq Musa al-Husaini, *The Moslem Brothers* (Beirut, 1956), pp. 80-81.

3. Ibid.; 982-16, pp. 24-27 of July 8, 1953; 831-7, p. 8 of December 4, 1949; 1274-3 of November 22, 1949.

4. 718-40, p. 35 of January 16, 1953; 982-16 of November 16, 1953.

5. "The General Guide" (*al-Murshid al-Amm*) was the official title of the head of the movement in Egypt. In Syria, too, the movement was headed by a "supervisor" (al-Husaini, p. 76).

6. He was elected by the "Administrative Office" (*al-Maktab al-Idari*), which was a different pattern from that set by the movement in Egypt. See P.M. Mitchell, *The Society of the Muslim Brothers* (London, 1969), p. 165.

7. *Al-Difa*, August 13, 1951, January 15, 1953; *Filastin*, December 17, 1952; 1274-53 of April 14, 1954.

8. 55-5 of September 8, 1955; 718-40, p. 63 of May 17, 1954; 489-4 of September 22, 1965; 718-40, p. 206 of March 17, 1956; *Al-Difa*, October 28, 1956; MN/30, p. 1 of January 3, 1963; M-3, pp. 38-39 of May 19, 1963.

9. 431-3, p. 270 of June 26, 1950.

10. *Filastin* and *al-Difa*, July 25, 1952.

11. *Filastin*, May 8, October 16, 1952; 631-3, p. 47 of July 30, 1950; 718-40, p. 35 of January 16, 1953.

12. *Filastin*, November 20, 1953; *al-Difa*, June 1, 1953; 718-10, pp. 11-12, 19 of December 4, 1951, January 7, 1952, respectively; 718-40, p. 464 of June 21, 1959.

13. *Al-Difa*, August 13, 1951; 718-40, p. 94 of September 9, 1954; 718-40, pp. 99-100, 104 of September 27, October 3, 1954, respectively; 2872-14, p. 7 of September 27, 1956; 407-7, p. 164 of November 6, 1962.

14. 831-37, p. 8 of December 4, 1949; 982-16, p. 27 of July 18, 1953.

15. 2872-14, p. 40 of May 2, 1957; 718-2, p. 980 of September 15-16, 1957; 718-40, pp. 33, 66, 243, of January 8, 1953, August 21, 1954, December 15, 1955, respectively.

16. *Al-Difa*, August 13, 1951; 1274-30 of July 29, 1951; 641-13 of November 25, 1963. For their oscillating positions vis-à-vis the Egyptian regime see below, pp. 150-51.

17. 718-40, p. 69 of July 27, 1954.

18. *Filastin* and *al-Difa* of late 1955, cited in *HaMizrah Hedadash*, vol. 7 (1956), p. 131, cited hereafter at *HaMizrah*; 8168/315-13 of April 21, 1955; MNW-61, pp. 11, 15, 51-52 of February 19, March 30, October 20, 1955, respectively.

19. 2872-14, pp. 1, 15 of August 23, November 22, 1956, respectively.

20. 2872-14, p. 37 of April 18, 1957.

21. 2874-14, p. 55 of June 27, 1957; 102-9, p. 110 of May 5, 1957.

22. 718-40, p. 327 of October 8, 1957; 718-40, pp. 334-38 of June 1958.

23. 439-6 of June 22, 1959; 1621-3 of September 1, 1959; MN/20/1, p. 744 (1958), of July 15, 1959.

24. *Al-Hayat*, October 25, 1957, cited in *HaMizrah*, vol. 9 (1958), p. 86; *Filastin*, May 6, 1959, cited in *HaMizrah*, vol. 10 (1959), p. 367; 426-7 of June 2, 1959; MN/1/MM, p. 8 of January 6, 1963; MN/30/1/MM, pp. 38-39 of May 19, 1963.

25. 489-4 of September 22, 1965. See also Mitchell, p. 7.

26. Mitchell, pp. 8, 16-17, 42-43, 90-91, 94, 96-104.

27. Ibid., p. 7.

28. See below, p. 156.

29. Mitchell, pp. 9-10, 330-31.

30. See below, p. 166.

31. Mitchell, pp. 176-78, 197-200.

32. 718-40, pp. 324, 510 of August 27, 1957, p. 582 of January 14, 1962.

33. Mitchell, pp. 177-78.

34. 431-3, p. 27 of June 26, 1950.

35. *Filastin* and *al-Difa*, July 25, 1952; 718-40, pp. 135, 532 of November 3, 1954, March 9, 1961, respectively; Mitchell, pp. 164-65, 168-69.

36. 2872-14, p. 30 of February 28, 1957; MN/30/1/MM, p. 33 of August 2, 1954; Mitchell, pp. 18, 200-205.

37. 718-40, pp. 25-28, 57, 58, of March 27, 1952, March 23, 1954, May 3, 1962, respectively.

38. Mitchell, pp. 164-69.

39. Ibid., pp. 171-75.

40. *Al-Difa*, April 26, 1954; MN/30/1/MM, p. 3 of January 3, 1963; 370-24 of May 24, 1964.

41. Mitchell, p. 9.

42. *Al-Jihad*, June 9, July 3, 1960, cited in Y. Oron (ed.), *Middle East Record* (Tel-Aviv, 1960), vol. 1, p. 321.

43. Mitchell, pp. 30, 32, 174, 195-208.

44. Ibid., pp. 165, 183.

45. Members of the Irbid branch paid 10 kurush per month in the early 1950s, whereas in Burqa 25 kurush were paid a decade later.

46. October 20, 1953.

47. Mitchell, pp. 193-95.

48. 3369-2 of May 4, 1955.

49. 718-40, p. 7 of July 28, 1950.

50. 775-16, p. 17 of July 25, 1954; 718-40, pp. 92-94 of September 29, 1954; MNW/61, p. 33 of July 2, 1955; 370-33 of November 9, 1954.

51. 1274-30 of July 29, 1951.

52. The latter was also mentioned as a leading member of the Liberation Party.

53. 718–40, p. 532 of March 9, 1961.

54. MKM/H/5, p. 120 of February 2, 1955.

55. 718–40, pp. 25–27, 582, 598 of March 3–27, 1952, May 3, 21, 1962, respectively.

56. October 20, 1953.

57. Mitchell, pp. 12–13, 329–31.

58. 718–40, p. 347 of March 25, 1959.

59. In Hebron they met regularly on Tuesday evenings (1274–3 of February 4, 1958), and this seems to have been the case in other branches also. Cf. Mitchell, p. 330.

60. 718–40, pp. 33–36 of January 7–8, 1953 (Nablus); 1274–30 of July 29, 1951 (Hebron).

61. 718–40, pp. 9, 246, 302, May 3, 1951, August 11, 1957, March 31, 1959, respectively; 695–9 of June 13, 1959; *Akhbar al-Usbu*, September 2, 1966; *Al-Difa*, June 1, 1953; 370–24 of August 19–20, 1964.

62. 380–6, p. 222 of August 21, 1954; 718–40, p. 87 of August 10–11, 1954.

63. 718–40, pp. 25–28 of March 3–27, 1952; 370–33 of December 22, 1954; 718–40, p. 140 of November 22, 1954; MNW/61/30 of July 3–9, 1955; 1274, pp. 1, 3 of February 4, 1958; 2872–14, p. 17 of November 29, 1956.

64. Mitchell, pp. 188–92, 208.

65. 380–6, p. 319 of November 30, 1954; *Filastin*, October 2, 1953.

66. MNW/61/25 of May 21, 1955.

67. For example, a gathering in Nablus on November 3, 1961, in support of the Algerian revolution.

68. 718–40, pp. 9, 142, May 3, 1951, November 27, 1954, respectively, 1274, pp. 33–39, 42 of November 30, 1951, February 13, 1952, respectively.

69. *Al-Difa*, August 9, 1954, January 1, 1957, *Filastin*, May 24–26, 1954, August 25, 1954, cited in *HaMizrah*, vol. 6 (1955), p. 46, vol. 8, p. 147, vol. 9, p. 86, respectively; 718–40, p. 327 of October 8, 1957.

70. In many leaflets the entire verse is quoted: "some of them have fulfilled their vow of death, and some are still awaiting, and they have not changed in the least" ("The Confederates," Sura 33, verse 23, trans. A.J. Arberry.)

71. *HaMizrah*, vol. 11 (1960), pp. 285, 321; 718–40, pp. 280–82, 285, 295, 478, August 18, November 11, December 29, 1956, July 22, 1959, respectively; 489–4 of September 25, 1965.

72. 370–33 of November 3, 1954; 718–40, p. 312 of June 30, 1957.

73. 718–40, p. 10, 206 of May 3, 1951, March 17, 1956, respectively; 392–16 of February 28, 1957; 385–10, p. 212 of December 14, 1957.

74. 3369, p. 23 of January 8, 1952; 982–16 of November 22, 1953.

75. Cf. Husaini, p. 80.

76. 718–40, pp. 51, 78, 85, 128, 277 of September 23, 1953, August 23, 25, November 1, 1954, June 30, 1956, respectively; 2872–14 of March 28, 1957.

77. 718–40, pp. 225, 278, 542 of October 10, 1955, August 7, 1956, August 21, 1961, respectively; 2872-14 of August 9, 1956; 2872 of August 27, 1957; 370-24 of August 4-6, 1966.

78. *Al-Difa*, April 11-12, 1953, *Filastin*, April 12, 1953, May 10, 1953, cited in *HaMizrah*, vol. 4 (1952-53), p. 272.

79. *Al-Difa*, December 10, 1953, *Filastin*, December 4-12, 1953, *al-Jihad*, December 12, 1953, cited in *HaMizrah*, vol. 5, pp. 115-16 and *Middle East Record*, 1960, p. 320.

80. *Filastin*, July 7, 1955, cited in *HaMizrah*, vol. 7 (1956), p. 42; MKM/ H/5, pp. 55, 114 of September 8, 1954, January 13, 1955, respectively.

81. *Filastin*, November 24, 1954, cited in *HaMizrah*, vol. 6, p. 145; MKM/ H/5, pp. 18, 30, 55-57 of June 29, July 18, September 8-16, 1954, respectively.

82. MKM/H/5, pp. 28-29, 37, 39, 45, 51, 124 of June 21, July 10, 11, 31, August 5, 31, 1954, February 28, 1955, respectively.

83. MKM/H/5, pp. 139–40 of July 2-3, 1956; 446-48, p. 28, February 8, 1959.

84. *Al-Jihad*, January 26-31, 1960, cited in *Middle East Record*, 1960, p. 321; *Middle East Record*, 1961, p. 360; *HaMizrah*, vol. 12 (1961), pp. 254-55; MKM/H/5, pp. 91-92, 103-4, 107, 113-16, of December 4, 15, 30, 1954, January 13, 1955, respectively.

85. 718-40, pp. 170-72, January 21, 1955; *al-Jihad*, December 21, 1954.

86. Mitchell, pp. 223-24, 235-36.

87. 1-370-24 of May 23, 1964.

88. 718-40, p. 253 of March 21, 1956; 718-52 of March 31, 1956.

89. Mitchell, pp. 231-32, 249.

90. 407-7 of June 19, 1962.

91. 718-40, p. 148 of December 19, 1954; 1274-14 of September 19, 1956; 982-17 of November 15, 1957; 1274-3 of March 20, 1960. Cf. Mitchell, pp. 224-27, 233-36.

92. 718-40, p. 603 of June 9, 1962; 370-24 of December 2, 1964. Cf. Mitchell, p. 250ff.

93. 718-40, p. 183 of April 20, 1955; MN/30/1/MM, pp. 21-22 of February 13, 1963.

94. 718-40, pp. 106-7.

95. MNW/61, p. 10 of February 19, 1955; 982-13, p. 33 of January 28, 1953.

96. 718-40, p. 66 of August 21, 1954; 2872-14, p. 1 of August 30, 1956; 370-24 of January 24, 1965. Cf. Mitchell, pp. 223, 254-59, 292.

97. *Filastin*, April 12, 1953, cited in *HaMizrah*, vol. 4 (1952-53), p. 272; MN/30/1/MM, p. 23 of February 13, 1963.

98. 718-40, p. 543 of August 28, 1961; MN/30/1/MM, p. 8 of January 16, 1963.

99. 718-40, p. 598 of May 21, 1962; 370-24, December 2, 1964. Cf. Mitchell, pp. 230-31.

100. *Al-Hayat*, January 5, 1960; 280-6, p. 123 of May 26, 1954.

101. MNW/61, pp. 38-42 of July 26-28, 1955.

102. *Al-Difa*, November 12, 1954, cited in *HaMizrah*, vol. 6 (1955), p. 145; 2705-4, pp. 303, 486 of August 7, November 18, 1954, respectively; 718-40, pp. 99-100 of October 3, 10, 1954.

103. For further details see below, p. 223.

104. 982-16, p. 53 of October 25, 1953. For similar accusations in Egypt see Mitchell, pp. 112-113.

105. 380-6, 114, p. 2 of May 26, 1954; 2705-4, pp. 171, 182, 184, 188 of May 22, 24, 29, 12, 1954, respectively.

106. 2705-4, p. 211 of June 15, 1954; 2872-14, p. 15 of November 22, 1956. See below, p. 227.

107. 718-40, p. 214 of July 27, 1955; 2872-14, p. 40 of May 2, 1957.

108. 2872-14, p. 29 of February 21, 1957.

109. 718-40, p. 204 of July 24, 1955; MN/30/1/MM, pp. 57, 60 of July 29, August 4, 1963, respectively.

110. MN/30/1/MM, pp. 56-57, 70 of July 29, August 12, 1963, respectively. This assertion was factually wrong: the prime minister in 1963 was al-Baytar, a Syrian Muslim.

111. 718-40, p. 204 of July 24, 1955; 407-7, p. 118 of September 10, 1962.

112. Mitchell, p. 218-19, 225-27.

113. *Filastin*, January 7, 1953.

114. 982-16, November 16, 1953.

115. 718-40, p. 56.

116. 718-40, pp. 128, 138 of November 1, 3, 1954, respectively.

117. 718-40, pp. 136, 148, 163, 170-72, 180, 186, 233 of November 3, December 19, 1954, February 9, January 21, April 6, May 4, October 30, 1955, respectively; MKM/H/5, p. 69, November 5, 1954.

118. As was their initial highly reserved reaction in Hebron immediately after the nationalization (2872-14, p. 2 of August 2, 1956).

119. *Al-Difa*, August 15, 1956, cited in *HaMizrah*, vol. 8 (1957), pp. 54-55.

120. 509-39, p. 48 of August 18, 1956.

121. 2872-14, p. 13 of November 8, 1956; 780-40, p. 285 of November 11, 1956; *al-Jihad*, December 10, 1956, cited in *HaMizrah*, vol. 8 (1957), pp. 146-47.

122. 718-40, p. 310 of June 30, 1957; 679-1, p. 249 of July 15, 1957.

123. 407-7, pp. 61-69, 159 of July 16, October 29, 1962, respectively.

124. *Al-Muharrir*, March 29, 1965; 1274-21, p. 26 of August 14, 1965; B/71/240-1, p. 528 of November 9, 1965.

125. *Al-Manar*, December 25, 1955, cited in *HaMizrah*, vol. 7 (1956), p. 131; 718-40, p. 180 of April 6, 1955.

126. *Al-Difa*, June 21-22, 1954.

127. 407-7, pp. 61-69 of July 16-20, 1962.

128. 718–40, pp. 307, 475 of June 8, 1957, July 14, 1959, respectively; 982–16 of November 8, 1953; 370–24 of January 1, 1965.

129. 718–40, p. 175 of February 10, 1955; 982–16 of July 25, 1953; MKM/H/5, p. 124 of February 28, 1955.

130. Only Nuri al-Said and Nasserite Egypt were accused of outright treason (718–40, p. 285 of December 29, 1956).

131. 1274–12 of March 20, 1960; 982–16 of July 18, 1953; 982–17 of November 15, 1957.

132. 718–40, p. 303 of April 13, 1957, pp. 334–38 of June 1958; 982–16 of July 17–18, 1953; 584–5 of June 16, 1954; 109–39, p. 176.

133. 718–40, p. 222 of October 16, 1955; 392–16 of February 28, 1957.

134. 718–40, p. 263 of May 11, 1956.

135. 509–39, p. 118 of October 28, 1956; 718–40, pp. 40–46, 186, 263, 302 of August 27–29, 1953, May 4, 1955, May 11, 1956, March 31, 1959, respectively.

136. 1–370–24 of May 23, 1964.

137. 718–40, p. 13 of December 12, 1951.

138. 370–24 of August 6, 1966; 982–16 of July 25, 1953.

139. MN/30/1/MM, p. 40 of June 1, 1963.

140. There were, however, specific references about the Brothers' intrinsic antagonism to the secular concept of nationalism: "Islam is neither nationalism nor unity, nor Aflaqism" (MN/30/1/MM, p. 60 of August 4, 1963).

141. *Al-Jihad*, June 20, 1957, cited in *HaMizrah*, vol. 8 (1957), p. 309; 718–40, p. 475 of July 14, 1959.

142. 718–40, pp. 305, 475, 531 of May 27, 1957, July 14, 1959, March 8, 1961, respectively. Cf. Mitchell, pp. 264–65.

143. Mitchell, p. 266–67.

144. 718–40, pp. 305, 475 of May 27, 1957, July 14, 1959, respectively.

145. 718–40, pp. 332, 486 of February 20, 1958, September 16, 1959, respectively; 509–39, p. 177 of January 24, 1957.

146. 718–40, pp. 305, 332 of May 27, 1957, February 20, 1958, respectively; MN/30/1/MM, pp. 40–41 of June 1, 1963. Cf. Mitchell, p. 264–67.

147. 718–40, pp. 486, 617 of September 16, 1959, December 24, 1962, respectively; 2872–14, p. 15 of November 22, 1956.

148. 718–40, pp. 283, 617 of October 22, 1956, December 24, 1962; 1274–14, p. 46 of September 19, 1956.

149. *Al-Difa*, May 3, 1956, against French atrocities in North Africa.

150. See below, pp. 206–7, 228.

151. Mitchell, pp. 267–69.

152. 718–40, p. 301 of February 28, 1957.

153. Mitchell, pp. 267–68.

154. 718–40, p. 542 of August 21, 1961.

155. 718–40, p. 32 of March 31, 1959; MN/30/1/MM, p. 21–22 of February 13, 1963; 370–24 of August 6, 1966.

156. *Al-Jihad,* December 12, 1953, cited in *HaMizrah,* vol. 5 (1953-54), p. 115; MN/30/1/MM, p. 8 of January 16, 1963.

157. 718-40, p. 222 of October 16, 1955; *Al-Difa,* December 10, 1953, cited in *HaMizrah,* vol. 5 (1953-54), p. 115; *al-Jihad* and *al-Manar,* January 19, 1961, cited in *HaMizrah,* vol. 12 (1961), pp. 254-55.

158. 718-40, p. 543 of August 28, 1961; 982-16, p. 5 of March 28, 1953; MN/30/1/MM, pp. 21-23 of February 13, 1963; 982-16 of October 19, 1953.

159. 718-40, p. 617 of December 24, 1962.

160. 718-40, p. 8 of February 28, 1951; 407-7, p. 21 of March 27, 1962.

161. Mitchell, p. 264.

5. The Liberation Party

1. 699-14, p. 18 of November 19, 1952; 1451-17 of April 29, 1952. The Lebanese daily *al-Jarida* mentioned (October 7, 1969) Taqi al-Din and Nimr al-Masri as the founders of the party. Other sources also attest to the important role of the latter in the hierarchy of the party, however, he did not sign the formal application submitted to the government in request to establish the party.

2. *Filastin,* March 10, 22, 1953, cited in *HaMizrah Hehadash,* vol. 4 (1952-53), pp. 190-91, hereafter cited as *HaMizrah.*

3. *Filastin,* April 8-10, 1953, cited in *HaMizrah,* vol. 4 (1952-53), p. 272.

4. MKM/2/24 (982-16), p. 29 of June 7, 1953.

5. 1097-1, p. 105 of April 4, 1955; 443-2, p. 29 of August 21, 1955; 445-12, p. 332 of July 18, 1955.

6. J. Heyworth-Dunne, *An Introduction to the History of Education in Modern Egypt* (London, 1939), p. 40.

7. For example, in Jerusalem, 1959, these were Faris Idris, Faruq Muhammad Abd al-Al, Abd al-Azim Sharawi (439-8, p. 25 of April 23, 1959; 443-2, p. 50 of September 18, 1955; 402-8, p. 204 of November 9, 1958).

8. Jordanian official gazette, January 19, 1955; *Filastin,* January 12, 1955, cited in *HaMizrah,* vol. 6 (1955), p. 227; 2705-4, pp. 504, 536 of December 4, 18, 1954, respectively.

9. 445-12, p. 299 of June 25, 1955; 1097-1, p. 140 of July 3, 1955; 2705-4, p. 447 of October 26, 1954.

10. 323-336, p. 2 of November 10-21, 1953; 2705-4, p. 303 of August 7, 1954; 445-12, p. 78 of February 9, 1955.

11. 63-9, June 5-9, 1953; 2705-4, p. 506 of December 6, 1954; 2705-4, p. 129 of May 2, 1954.

12. 761-45, p. 329 of December 8, 1954; 445-12, pp. 92, 244 of February 16, May 28, 1955, respectively.

13. 385-10, p. 134 of August 20, 1955; 430-7, March 14, 1957; 317-8, April 13, 1961; 408-4, p. 260 of June 8, 1962.

14. 443-2, p. 175 of November 29, 1955.

15. 761-45, p. 76 of April 30, 1956; *Al-Sarih*, April 28, 1956.

16. *Al-Misri*, March 26, 1953; *Al-Hayat*, September 15, 1954; 445-12, p. 33 of January 22, 1955.

17. 414-4, pp. 39-51 of December, 1963; 761-46, 498-7, 1021-1, December 1964.

18. I am currently writing an extended account of the various ideological dimensions of the Liberation Party. A fuller version of the chapter appears in Hebrew in my *Miflagot Bagada Hamaaravit Bitqufat Hashilton Hayardeni* (Jerusalem, 1980), pp. 208-48.

19. 443-2, p. 144 of November 19, 1955; leaflets of May 25, 1964; December 1, 1956, February 16, 1963.

20. Leaflets of April 9, 1960, December 25, 1959; Al-Daur's statement in parliament, November 11, 1954.

21. Leaflets of October 15, 1955, January 9, 1960; "An open letter to Arif" (n.d.); "The ideas of the Liberation Party" (Jerusalem, 1953), pp. 9-11.

22. Al-Daur's statements in parliament, August 24, 1955, November 11, 1954.

23. Leaflets of December 7, 1963, August 19, 1959, October 9, 1961, December 19, 1964.

6. Conclusion

1. Munib al-Madi and Sulayman Musa, *Tarikh al-Urdunn fi'l-Qarn al-'Ishrin*, (Amman, 1959), p. 664.

2. Y. Shimoni, *The Arabs of Eretz Yisrael* (Tel Aviv, 1947; in Hebrew), pp. 289-95; Y. Porath, *The Emergence of the Palestinian National Movement, 1918-1929* (Jerusalem, 1971; in Hebrew), pp. 174, 180-84, 201-209.

3. On parties active in Jordan prior to 1948 see A. Abidi, *Jordan a Political Study 1948-1957* (London, 1965), pp. 191-99.

4. On the early stages in the development of this party see Y. Porath, "Revolution and Terrorism and the Palestinian Communist Party (P.K.P.) 1929-1939," *HaMizrah Hehadash* (in Hebrew), vol. 18 (1968), pp. 255-67, and Y. Porath, "The League for National Liberation—Its Establishment, Essence and Collapse (1943-1948)," vol. 14 (1964), pp. 354-66.

5. Vatikiotis' contention (P.J. Vatikiotis, *Politics and the Military in Jordan* [London, 1967], p. 110) that the appearance of the parties was the result of young King Husayn's liberal policies from mid-1953 on should be corrected. In fact the publication of the constitution should be noted as their starting point, later to be taken up by King Husayn as one aspect of his policy.

6. Abidi, pp. 203-4.

7. Al-Madi and Musa, pp. 597-603.

8. Abidi, pp. 203-4.

9. Abidi, pp. 206–7; al-Madi and Musa, p. 664.

10. In 1952 in Amman, Communist cells were uncovered even in a girls' school. (W.Z.L., "Communist in Jordan in *The World Today*, vol. 12, no. 3 (1956), p. 114.)

11. Abidi's contention, p. 202, that the Communist Party relied mainly on the proletariat should therefore be corrected. This, like several other generalizations (for example, the contention, p. 205, that the party adopted a method of struggle for power as opposed to persuasion in distinction to all other parties) should be revised in view of the newly acquired evidence.

12. Vatikiotis, pp. 110, 119.

13. See a lower estimate in M.S. Agwani, *Communism in the Arab East* (Bombay, 1969), p. 155.

14. "There will be war between you and the Jew until the stone says: Oh Muslim, there is a Jew behind me, Arise and kill him in God's verdict with regard to the acceptance of compensation and the return [to Palestine] under Jewish Rule," an undated pamphlet, c. 1959.

Index

Index

Library of Congress Cataloging in Publication Data

Cohen, Amnon, 1936–
    Political parties in the West Bank under the Jordanian regime, 1949–1967.

    Translated and emended version of Miflagot be-Gadah ha-ma'aravit bi-
tekufat ha-shilton ha-yardeni.
    Includes index.
    1. Political parties—Jordan.   2. Jordan—Politics and government.   I. Title.
JQ1825.J67C6313   325.25695   80-25666
ISBN 0-8014-1321-4